A TASTE OF HEAVEN

Light-headed from his nearness, Kathleen tried to focus on something—anything—other than Charlie's twinkling eyes. She had inhaled deeply when he hugged her, and the scent of him was filling her up. The feel of him against her was at once reassuring and dangerous.

He pulled back, his smile still in place, and then captured her lips with his own. Just the touch sent her reeling.

Her hands clung to his shoulders, holding on for dear life. But when he deepened the kiss, her fingers found their way to his neck. His mouth caressed hers and his hands pulled her even closer.

Suddenly she felt as if she'd been captured by his sweetness, his gentleness. And she was thrilled he pressured no more than this, for surely she would be forced to flee. But where? her muddled mind asked, and the question echoed through her without answer. She didn't need one. Kathleen O'Day had just found heaven and she wasn't about to lose it yet. Not yet . . .

BLISSFUL

Rita Clay Estrada

Zebra Books
Kensington Publishing Corp.

http://www.zebrabooks.com

ZEBRA BOOKS are published by

Kensington Publishing Corp.
850 Third Avenue
New York, NY 10022

Zebra and the Z logo Reg. U.S. Pat. & TM Off.

ISBN 0-7394-0959-X

Printed in the United States of America

This story belongs to some very important people

For Charlie Spenella, who forwarded to me the original story of a town like Blissful, only it was in Nevada. Our lunches and conversations have always been thought provoking and fun. You're a talent and I can't wait to see your stories in print, too, Charlie.

For Steve Goodwin, who gave me the opportunity and encouragement to write this one. Your special brand of humor, generosity, and heroic ways have spilled into all the strong male characters I write, you dear and giving man!

For Evan Marshall, my agent, who sold this premise along with many others. Your support and help over the years were always there when I needed them most.

And for Georgia Murrey, who gave me her wonderful recipe for carrot cake. So, at first bite, I knew what Kathleen was going to bake.

Thanks to you all!

One

August, 1889

"Let's kill the sheriff on Thursday." The man's deep voice held a west Texas twang, and Charlie Macon instinctively flattened against the outside kitchen wall, the curved clapboard siding pushing into his butt. He craned his neck closer to the open kitchen window.

"We can't kill him on Thursday. He just got his badge last Friday." The soft, feminine voice had a Southern accent, and if her tone was to be believed, the subject was closed.

"We killed the *last* sheriff the same day he got his badge."

"The timing was right. This sheriff will be killed the *next* time, but not this one."

"Then what about a nice bank robbery?"

"It's too soon. We did that last month."

"Hellfire! We gotta do somethin'! We cain't jest sit

around twiddlin' our thumbs. We got a reputation at stake!''

"Y'know . . ." The woman's voice softened. "Maybe that's just what we *should* do—lie low for at least a week."

Charlie heard a masculine grunt, a string of epithets, and a spurt of tobacco juice hitting what sounded like a brass spittoon.

"I told you not to spit in my house!" Her tone was indignant.

"You keepin' a spittoon in th' kitchen fer your own chaw?"

"You know better than that," the female voice said. "It's no secret how that spittoon got there. And it's no secret how I hate it. But I'm keeping it as a memento, anyway. And you're keeping it *clean.*"

The man grumbled, coming closer to the open kitchen window. Charlie tried to push himself right through the wood siding and make himself invisible. He was too close to catching Vic now to be found out. . . .

A well-aimed shot of tobacco juice barely missed the top of Charlie's head, splatting to the grass at his feet. If he hadn't had nerves of steel, he'd have ducked. Then those lousy murderers would have seen him. He wasn't ready for that yet. He needed to set up for the confrontation so he could have the advantage. Vic had killed over a dozen people already, and Charlie didn't want to be the next one. If it all went well, he'd have Vic in jail by sunup and ready to be transported to the nearest federal marshal or Texas Ranger by train. And the sheriff might be grateful— after all, Charlie was saving his life by stopping Vic on his next murderous spree.

"I don't see why you always have to have it your way, little missy," the dark voice drawled. Charlie

cocked his head so his ear was closer to the open
window. He could be mistaken, but the growl
sounded more like a whine.

"Because sometimes I have more common sense
than you do." The female laughed. "And you know
it. But we'll argue this another time. We're having a
nice dinner tonight before we start working on the
problem tomorrow. Amy's a great cook and it's our
second anniversary, so let's not argue now. We'll wait
and talk to the others first."

A rumble of wagon wheels echoed from the town
side of the road, alerting Charlie to more potential
danger. He pressed himself even closer to the house,
scrunched down, and worked his way around the
corner to the back of the house until he was sure
the wagon couldn't see him. Vic and his girlfriend's
conversation became muted; then he heard nothing.
When the wagon wheels stopped creaking, he heard
the front screen door slam.

They were leaving. *Damn!*

He wanted to follow, to beat the hell out of Vic
before he dragged him into the nearest federal marshal's office and saw him on trial and hanged. But it
wasn't time. No telling what Vic would do to remain
free, including hurting those around him. Better to
be patient and get what he wanted than to be in a
hurry and mess it up. . . .

The wagon started up again and he peered around
the corner just as it disappeared down the road. He
saw three couples seated in rows. One woman, the
one still settling into the seat, had red hair that resembled the color of an Oklahoma sunset. He hoped it
wasn't Vic's woman. It would be a shame to hide that
beautiful hair in a jail. And her waist was so tiny that
it . . .

Never mind.

He wasn't sure, but he thought the house was empty. Just to be on the safe side, he drew his gun and stealthily walked to the other side of the house and looked in the rear side window. It was an empty bedroom, neat and clean.

He moved on to the other window closer to the front of the house. It was a replica of the first bedroom, except maybe a little smaller. So was the bed.

Feeling safer for not having seen anyone, he walked around the back and carefully tried the door. It was open. He quietly stepped in and closed the door behind him. Dusk was fading into night, and one small window wasn't enough to allow him to see immediately. It took a few minutes for him to get used to the shadowy dark of the kitchen.

It was a warm place, kind of homey. A worn round oak table sat in the center of the room as though it had squatter's rights. A large sink with a pump sat by the window, and several shelves, neat as a pin, lined one wall from ceiling to floor. Over on the far end of the room was a baker's rack with a barrel of what most likely was flour, and lots of cake tins piled one on the other. The woman liked to cook. Charlie only hoped she found the time, what with murderers and rustlers coming and going. . . .

He moved quietly through to the large room into the smaller parlor. This room was just as cozy-feeling, and just as empty. Against one wall was a large fireplace, a sofa, and two stiff horsehair chairs that reminded him of his early life back east. Next to it was the front door. On the other side were two more doors. His gaze riveted to the opening leading into what had to be the main bedroom. Charlie turned to the door, then stopped in his tracks.

A squeak, similar to that of a chair under pressure, echoed through the quiet house. Charlie's trigger finger tightened, his breath halting. Tensed, he waited seconds, then minutes, but there wasn't another sound. With quiet stealth, he walked to the door and opened it up all the way, searching the corners of the room.

Framed on a patchwork quilt draped across a rocker arm, a fat, lazy calico cat was sprawled on its back, feet in the air, enjoying an early evening snooze. It didn't move.

Other than that, the room was empty.

The whole damn house was empty.

He walked the room, checking under the dresses hung on pegs, and in the small dresser, and under the bed. There was nothing that was the least bit masculine in the whole room.

So why was this woman talking about murder with another murderer? A male one? Why would that same young woman go out in broad daylight as if this were the safest place in the West?

Charlie looked around again.

Several dresses hung neatly on pegs driven into the wall next to the bedroom side of the fireplace. A dresser sat against one wall with a large cherrywood-framed mirror with a chipped corner hung just above it. In the corner was the cat's rocker, and across from it was a white iron bed—the same bed he'd seen when he looked into the room.

Funny. Those dresses didn't look like they belonged to a murderer. Nor to a lady of easy morals. They looked more like clothing belonging to a school-marm, except that he knew better. He'd heard her earlier, and although she had a charming voice, her words left a little to be desired from a teacher. That wasn't anything like the woman who'd taught him his ABCs. Neither was that golden copper hair.

Charlie walked back into the parlor and looked

through the lace-curtained windows across the road at the other two houses. Although there was a light in one, the other was dark as night.

He hesitated only a minute, then went through the kitchen and out the back door. Before he did anything else, he was going to take a night-time tour of the town. If it was safe enough for Vic's woman, it was safe enough for him. Especially if he hung in the shadows.

An hour later, Charlie bedded his horse Teaser in the barn, then entered the dark back door he'd left earlier. Now, however, he was even more confused than ever. It hadn't taken long to walk the mile-long road to the railroad track and train station. With the exception of a dim light in the closed telegraph office, there wasn't a creature stirring in the whole damn town. Several of the forty or so houses had lights burning, one or two had the windows open, and the spring night air drifted on a lazy breeze. He heard the laughter and occasional low voices of their occupants. But that was it. Peace was everwhere.

Standing in the center of the murderess's parlor, Charlie pushed his hat back on his head. "What in the hell kind of wild town is this?" he asked the silent room. He was confused. Until he reached the train station, he wasn't sure he was in the right place. But the sign hanging from a pole said BLISSFUL. It had been crossed out and HELLTOWN was clearly written below. Then it stated POPULATION 92, just as plain as day.

The calico cat awoke, mewed, and jumped down from the soft rocker cushion. After a big stretch, it sauntered into the living room.

Charlie looked around again. Everything seemed

the same. No clues were around that a man had been here. But he knew better. He heard him.

Charlie walked back into the parlor and looked through the lace-curtained windows across the street at the other two houses.

He couldn't be wrong. It was Vic's horse tracks leading to this town, it was Vic's horse in the barn just beyond the house, and it had to have been Vic who spoke to the woman in this very kitchen.

Charlie had watched this place all day. He'd kept himself wedged between the boulders that acted as a rear entrance to the small town laid out below. He'd made his watching spot at the far side of town, away from the commercial part over by the railroad station. This was the right town; he'd seen the sign. Its reputation was wicked and wild, even by Texas standards. More men had died in this small part of civilization than in any other place in the state.

It wasn't a safe place to be if you treasured your life. But Charlie was damned if his was going to be snuffed out by some no-account rustler—no matter who it was. He was going to be extra careful and walk away the winner with a hefty bounty in his pocket. And that meant that Vic Masters was alive and turned in to the law for judgment.

From his vantage point on the hill, he'd seen three houses sitting on the edge of town. Each was about two or three acres apart. All were whitewashed, one with bright yellow trim, one with blue, and one with green. Flowers blossomed in the front yards, while the backs were plowed and furrowed with growing vegetables of some kind peeping up in the sun. It looked as pretty as a peaceful picture could be. Charlie expected a Sunday school preacher to step out one of the doors and bless the day any moment.

But he knew better. This town had the wickedest

reputation in the country. Everyone with any sense knew to stay away from Helltown, formally known as Blissful. Gunfights, killings, and worse were a regular thing in the little town that clung to the edge of the West. Why, every train that paused long enough for coal and water saw someone get killed. That should have been a lesson right there. The place couldn't even keep a sheriff, let alone make it safe for the citizens of the town.

Charlie yawned. He needed a good night's sleep. He'd been on Vic Masters's trail for over a week now, and this was the closest he'd been to the scum-sucking bandit. Every time he'd found his trail, it was two or three days old. Until yesterday. Yesterday he'd hit the outskirts of Waco, just a day south of here. They'd bedded his horse for a while, until he'd made a visit to the sheriff's office. The old sheriff told him that only two hours before Charlie had arrived, Vic had picked up his horse and headed toward this town. The traveling farrier told him to stay clear of Helltown, that it was too wicked to go into. The sheriff swore that even big bad Vic Masters wasn't dumb enough to go to that town.

That made Charlie even more suspicious. What kind of citizenry would hide trash instead of expelling it? Especially Masters, who had a record as long as his trail.

So here he was, spending the day spying on a town that should have been dead by all accounts, yet looked more like something out of a painting of what settled family communities of the West should be.

But then he'd hit pay dirt. Raising his binoculars, he'd focused on the place where he saw a slight movement—either that or a bush was waving in the occasional breeze.

He stared hard at the view in his glasses, unable to believe his eyes. But it was true.

A young woman stood in the middle of the backyard of the yellow house. Unbound red-blond hair flowed down her back and nearly touched her firmly rounded bottom. She was wearing nothing more than a flimsy white chemise and full slip. The top of the chemise was undone, its golden ribbons hanging straight down as if it had never been tied this day. She held an armful of dripping-wet dresses, and hung one dress at a time on the sagging rope that served as a clothesline. She held an extra clothespin in her mouth as she finished draping the last gown over the line and slipped a pin over it as an anchor.

Then, without so much as a glance around to insure er safety, she lifted her hair off the nape of her neck to catch any breeze, then daintily picked her barefooted way down the path to the back of the house and slipped inside the screen door. The hot spring air was so quiet that even from this distance, Charlie heard the wood clap shut. He'd kept the binoculars trained on the ground where she'd stood earlier. Tracks—the same horse tracks he'd been looking for—headed toward her barn.

He grinned, but it wasn't a pleasant smile. He'd found his man.

Besides, there was no way a pretty little woman would walk out of a house dressed like that unless she felt safe because of what was inside the house to protect her. And, as dainty a picture as she made, she was dressed as if she'd just had a satisfying tumble in the hay moments before tripping into the backyard. That would be Masters's style. Charlie gave a grunt, meant to still the images those thoughts incurred. Disgusting Masters. He'd stop a woman in her work to make sure he was satisfied first.

He ignored the voice in his head that said, *So would you, and don't say you deny it.* Of course he would, especially if it was with a woman who didn't have the decency to belong to a regular town citizenry. But this wasn't a regular town. This was Helltown, the most wicked town in the West.

Kathleen watched the brilliant full moon peek through the oak trees as she headed home.

The McLendons had had a small gathering of just a few of the people on the Blissful committee to honor her time in their town. But the few there were close friends, and that made dinner special. When dessert time came, they all laughed over her choice: carrot cake. It was the very dessert that had led her to her outrageous plan to begin with. It was also the vegetable that changed the town.

She had to chuckle at that. Poor Mr. Milton was so paranoid about the newspapers or outsiders finding out their reputation was a farce and that Blissful hadn't seen a minute of crime since almost two years ago. His big concern was that someone would tell their secret and, once exposed, the town would go back to what it had been . . . a drying, dusty, shrinking Texas town.

But Kathleen knew better. Money had come to Blissful, giving everyone a chance to plant other crops, gain more head of cattle, open stores that shipped tools and goods to surrounding communities. They were on a different level of enterprise now.

Besides, who would tell?

She walked to the back of her house and opened the kitchen door. Fancy, her aunt's independent old cat, ran out the door, scooting between her legs and almost throwing her off balance.

"Fancy, can't you do anything the way other cats do? With just a little decorum?" she groused, closing the door behind her. It was all right that the cat had gone; she would have put her out for the night anyway. "At least you could have pretended that you were shy and demure," she muttered grumpily, but it was too late. The cat had disappeared into the darkness.

She closed the door behind her and stood in one place for a moment, letting her eyes get accustomed to the dark.

With only one small window left open, the house was stuffy. For the life of her, she couldn't imagine why she smelled tobacco. Or was it smoke from the stove fire earlier when she'd baked her carrot cake? McLendon had sucked on one of those cigars out on the porch. Perhaps the malodorous smell had clung to her clothing.

She opened the kitchen window and let the clean night breeze through, filling the interior with dew-scented earth and the sounds of leaves rustling gently.

It sounded so good, Kathleen did the same thing to the parlor window.

Still in the dark, she undid the ties on her bonnet, walked into her bedroom, and placed her bonnet and shawl on a peg, then turned to open the bedroom window wider. She was bone tired and ready for a good night's sleep.

Tomorrow they had a rehearsal for a new holdup scene. She'd better be on her toes and ready.

"Don't take another step," a male voice said softly, conversationally. "In fact, why don't you sit down on the edge of the bed so we can have a nice little chat?"

Her blood ran icy cold; her hands froze on the windowsill. She looked sideways, realizing the voice had come from the vicinity of her rocking chair. Then she saw the figure. It was definitely a man—a tall man if shadows didn't lie—sitting in her rocking chair. He held a gun aimed in her direction. She stared at his face but the brim of his hat hid his features.

Moving slowly, she straightened her back and stared at the stranger seated there. Although his gun wasn't aimed directly at her, his legs were crossed and he held it resting on his tree-trunk thigh. Heart beating so quickly Kathleen could hardly breathe, she did as she was told. The springs squeaked as she sat on the side of the bed and held on to the curliqued footboard as if she were drowning and it floated.

"There, isn't that better?" he said nicely.

In lieu of slapping his face, she clutched the bed even harder. Every escape she could think of came to mind and was discarded. There was nothing to do—yet—but go along with this until she could get help or get to her pistol in the side drawer in the parlor.

"What do you want from me?" she finally managed to ask.

"I want to know where Vic Masters is."

Surprised, she stared at him blankly. "Who?"

"You know. Vic Masters. He's a scum-sucking rustler who came to town early this morning. The same guy you discussed killing the sheriff with."

"You were eavesdropping?" she asked haughtily. Her mind scrambled around for a way out of this.

"Don't change the subject. Where's Vic?" His voice was impatient, cold.

"That wasn't . . . whoever you thought. It was a joke, discussed with one of the older men of the town. He was not really a killer. We're practicing for a play to be held here soon," she improvised, hoping he would buy her story. After all, in a sense, it really was true.

His smirk was large enough to be seen even in the dark. His white teeth flashed. "Even if I believed you, which I don't, the killer I've been tracking for two weeks still came to this town before dawn today. I found his tracks in your garden. So you can't hide the fact that he's here."

"Here? In *this* town?" Her voice squeaked.

He uncrossed his leg, letting his boot thud heavily to the floor. Kathleen jerked, thinking he was going to stand up and shoot her. Instead he rocked back and forth a little before answering. "Well, little lady, we can either do this easy or do this hard. It's your choice."

Irish stubbornness reared its head. Her mouth tightened in disapproval and she put on her logical schoolmarm attitude. "How is it my choice? I don't know a Vic whatever, and you're in my home invading my privacy looking for someone I don't know. The easy way would be for you to leave and go to the next town and look for him, because I seriously doubt if he's here. No rustler stays here. We don't even have a hotel, for heaven's sake."

There. That was logical and stated in a forthright manner. She only hoped he believed her and would leave without more questions.

"I don't believe you."

It wasn't going to be that easy to get rid of him. "I can't help that, Mr. . . ?" She waited for him to fill in the blank, but he didn't. "Whoever. Our hotel opens only in the spring, when the calfing season is on. So why don't you go knock on someone else's door? They might be more delighted to see you than I am. Right now I'm tired and want to go to sleep. Early tomorrow morning I have a garden to water and weed, cakes to bake, seeds to order, and a meeting to attend.

Perhaps you'll find your rustler somewhere else. But he certainly won't be here.''

"Are you a soiled dove?'' If his voice hadn't been so low and whiskey smooth and delightfully raspy, she might have snapped to the insult immediately. Instead she heard the friendly tone, then the words.

"No, I am not!'' She stood up. "And I'll thank you to leave now.''

"You're funny. You go outside and hang clothes dressed in practically nothing in a town that's known for its crime. Then you and Vic calmly talk about killing the sheriff before heading to the center of town.'' He smirked. "And then you wonder why I'd take you for Vic's woman of the evening.'' His laughter was soft, deep, and degrading.

"I'm not sitting here being insulted in my own home just because you can't find a friend of yours! I suggest you leave. Now.''

"Oh, I'm not going anywhere, and neither are you. And he's no friend, Miss. . . ?''

If he didn't have to answer her earlier, then she certainly wouldn't answer him now.

"And I suggest you sit back down before I decide not to be so friendly.'' He leaned forward. "Or maybe friendlier than I have been so far.''

Slowly, her eyes trained on him, she did as she was told. "My husband will be home soon,'' she whispered.

He grunted at her puny effort. "There hasn't been a man spending the night within miles of this place for a very long time, unless he was riding a fast horse on a road outside and stopping by for an hour or so,'' the man said smugly. "There isn't a piece of clothing here that could conceivably belong to a male. There wasn't even a hint of a whisker in the bowl, nor shaving equipment anywhere.'' She saw the fleeting trace of a smile on his full lips. "As a matter of fact, nothing in this house even smells like a man."

"He's traveling. He took his stuff with him."

"Liar," he said softly. "Unless you're talking about Vic. In which case I'll hear anything you have to say."

"You're a silly man if you think I'd admit to something I don't know about."

"Liar, again," Charlie said. "Experience has taught me that most women talk about something they don't know about. They talk about men, don't they?"

Kathleen crossed her arms, unwilling to say another word until she thought of the right words that might help her out of this mess.

"But keep it up. We've got as long as it takes."

"Takes for what?" she couldn't help asking.

"For you to tell me where to find Vic Masters."

She quelled her panic, knowing that she could lose this battle if she pushed too hard. Reason had to win the day. "I swear I don't know anyone by that name and doubt if my neighbors do either. But if it will make you happy, I'll take you to the town council tomorrow and they can tell you themselves."

"Town council?"

She nodded, relieved. Maybe he'd leave now. Although she guessed that sleep was going to be out of the question for tonight. It would take hours just for her muscles to unclench.

"Is this Blissful?"

She nodded.

"And you have a town council?"

She realized her mistake too late. "Yes. I mean, no. Well, kind of. You see, we're trying to clean up the town and we secretly meet to see what we can do."

"And when do you meet again?"

"Tomorrow at five o'clock, just this side of town."

"And when does the next train come through?"

"The next day. Thursday at four o'clock." They were supposed to be rehearsing for that next train. . . .

The man took his hat off and dropped it to the floor. "Well, ma'am, I suggest you make yourself comfortable on that bed and get some sleep. Because you and I are going to be fast buddies for the next day, so I can attend that meeting with you."

"Can't you go and come back when it's time?" she asked hopefully.

"And miss my opportunity? Or get shot in the back as I leave?" He smiled, his teeth gleaming in the moonlight again. At least he had teeth. "I'll just keep you company."

Unable to think of anything to do to turn the tide of this fiasco, Kathleen slid back and leaned against the pillows at her headboard. She had to clear her thoughts of all the other stuff that had been so pressing earlier, and think of a way out of this. But first she had to calm her own fears. If he was going to kill her, he would have done so already. Unless she made a wrong move, she doubted he would do anything right now. He could rape her, but he'd give warning of that, she was sure. If only through dialogue or at least getting up and coming toward her. If that was the case, she wasn't going to do anything to provoke him. Stiff as a board, she lay quietly and didn't move, pretending to sleep.

It was going to be a very long night. . . .

Two

The first light of dawn filtered through lace curtains and caressed Charlie Macon's stubbled cheek with its warmth. Opening his eyes, he stared directly at the sleeping woman on the bed. His mind was still fuzzy from the past week's tiredness, and he wondered who she was.

Then he remembered that she'd clammed up when he'd asked her name. And well she might. Though she neither looked nor dressed the part, she had to be a lady of the evening—or at the very least, a dance-hall girl. What decent woman would hang clothes outside in broad daylight dressed in her underwear and at the edge of a town as notorious as Helltown?

He shrugged and immediately regretted it. Uneasy with the thought of Vic returning anytime to claim his woman, Charlie had only dozed through the night. Trying to sleep in a less than comfortable chair was hard on thirty-three-year-old bones. He had a stiff neck and a hand benumbed from clutching the Winchester in a near death grip. His head ached and his mouth tasted as though he'd spent an evening in Fort Worth's Green Pig Saloon.

Maybe it was just from breathing the air in this god-awful hellhole of a place, he thought, ignoring the warm summer breeze wafting an aroma of honeysuckle through the open window. Once it was called Blissful, but Texans for miles around now referred to it as Helltown. Daily slaughter left no time to dig single graves, and the few decent citizens still there gouged long ditches on Cemetery Hill to bury the newly dead. Strangers viewed Helltown with revulsion, but that didn't stop them from riding the trains into its center, where invariably bloodshed and mayhem met their eager eyes. While the steam engine took on coal and water, fascinated passengers in the safety of their seats watched life-and-death dramas taking place just beyond the train windows.

Some people were just naturally bloodthirsty, Charlie decided.

However, he'd seen enough blood and gore to last two lifetimes. He wouldn't be here if he hadn't followed Vic Masters. And he wouldn't leave until he nabbed him—once this obstinate woman revealed the outlaw's whereabouts.

He went over the conversation he'd had with her last night. She'd flared with anger when he'd asked if she was a lady of the evening. And her eyes flashed fire as she denied knowing or ever hearing the name of Vic Masters. But her innocent expression faded when she mentioned the town council, and Charlie realized she had regretted her words. He intended to find out why.

He sat up and looked at her. One slender hand rested in the mass of thick red hair spread over her pillow. She had an ivory complexion, a light dusting of freckles sprinkled across a pert nose, and her sensuous, full mouth was slightly open, revealing pearly white teeth. Flaming hair matched her hot temper, and he'd bet his last dollar that she was Irish—or Scotch. And God knew she was stubborn—another Celtic trait, his German mama used to say. Except for her high-button shoes resting beside the bed, she was as fully dressed as she was last night when he'd ordered her to get some sleep.

He held his breath as the girl on the bed sighed and turned toward him. A moment later, the gentle, even rise and fall of her breast and long lashes resting without a flutter on high cheekbones told him she still slept. Last night he'd guessed her to be somewhere in her midtwenties. However, she looked much younger in sleep—and so innocent, though, considering her profession, she'd probably age fast. Watching her lovely face, Charlie felt his heart soften. What if she was telling the truth? What if she didn't know Vic Masters?

She was so young—and so completely desirable. That realization startled him, and he tore his eyes away. She was a shady lady—and because she certainly lied with confidence, she was also a practiced liar. He'd hoped she would tell him the truth last night, but she didn't, and it had been too late to challenge her. But when she awakened this morning he would prove she lied and rub her pretty little nose in the evidence.

What other story will she come up with, then? he wondered. No answer came to mind.

In the meantime . . . the chair creaked as he leaned back, pulled the hat over his eyes, and dozed again.

* * *

The morning sun had climbed the sky when Kathleen O'Day awakened. The tall, lanky man sleeping in the chair beside her bed had pulled his hat over his eyes and thrust long legs and booted feet toward the plant stand next to her window. The fact that he needed a shave failed to hide the lean, handsome face, the strong jaw and chin, and the full mouth she'd seen drawn into a thin, disapproving line when he'd called her a liar last night. Despite fear at discovering him in her home when she returned from the McLendons, she had noted his compelling dark eyes, thick lashes, and hair that matched his eyes—except where the sun had lightened it.

His voice, angry and demanding, was deep, striking a chord somewhere in her heart, and she wondered what he was like when he wasn't riled.

He'd said he was a bounty hunter after some outlaw named Vic Masters, but she'd been so upset at finding a stranger in her house that she'd failed to realize the import of his statement. Now, remembering his words, she wondered if she and the other citizens of Blissful had gone too far in trying to save the town.

More than two years ago, Kathleen O'Day had arrived in Blissful to visit her aunt. At that time, the town bloomed quiet and unappreciated on the vast central Texas prairie. Honest and orderly citizens, mostly small ranchers and farmers, worked hard and told themselves and each other that life would be much easier when the trains came through. Like Cinderella waiting for her prince, the residents of Blissful waited. They built their all-denomination church, repulsed outside efforts to bring in fancy women and gambling halls, and Sundays found their pleasant little saloon dutifully closed.

Unlike in many Western towns, there were no gun-riddled bodies buried on Cemetery Hill at the edge of town. There were only citizens who had died peacefully in their beds, Kathleen's aunt and uncle included. Violent deaths in Blissful were due to carriage accidents, food poisoning, the kicks of recalcitrant horses—or carelessness, like falling into hornets' nests, tumbling from roofs while shingling, or drowning in the town's only source of water—Bliss Creek.

By the mid 1880s train tracks stretched bright and shining through the center of the little town. However, railroad powers-that-be decided Blissful was too small, too insignificant for the train to stop on regular runs between Fort Worth in the north and the central town of San Antonio. At two o'clock every afternoon, the trains sped past disappointed Blissful citizens whose expressions matched those of brides left waiting at the altar. The steam engine's journeys north to Dallas and south to Houston had a choice of several burgeoning towns where water tanks and coal provided necessary fuel. Meanwhile, the citizens of Blissful were having to drive their cattle over a hundred miles to get them on cars to ship to the major feed markets. The railroad would not allow a stop in the little town for as long as it took to herd cattle on a car without substantial recompense. The town didn't have that much cattle . . . yet. But the surrounding area was truck farming, lots of vegetables grown in the sandy loam, and the produce had to reach the large markets quickly.

However, every Thursday the train headed west for the Texas and New Mexico border. It was a long stretch over desolate prairie, and Blissful was the last bastion for replenishment.

So Thursdays while the train took on water and

coal, hopeful citizens with friendly faces welcomed jaded passengers to their small depot restaurant. Then, plying them with coffee and sarsaparilla, they touted their wares. Farmers sold fresh fruits and vegetables for the journey; ranchers sold sausages and pickled pigs' feet; farm and city wives offered homemade breads, pies, and cakes, or proudly presented crocheted collars, knitted shawls, and intricately fashioned quilts and pillows.

But income from outsiders on that one day a week was not enough. And railroad shipping fees for cattle and farm produce was far beyond the range of town pocketbooks.

"We'd have to schedule separate trains," railroad representatives said. "We have enough resources for cattle and farm produce on our regular runs. If passengers came here on a steady basis, that might warrant adding cattle and produce cars."

Disillusioned and discouraged, the town fathers racked their brains to find some other means of survival. There was no doubt about it; the little town of Blissful was in danger of dying.

But Kathleen O'Day had her own ideas—and a very strong reason for wanting to save Blissful: she didn't want to go back to North Carolina.

An only daughter, she had been twelve when her mother died on the family farm. For almost six years after that, Kathleen was cook and housekeeper to a domineering father and an equally domineering brother. At eighteen, when her father died, she was considered a spinster. Her newly wedded brother decided it was time to marry her off to a rich old neighbor and combine their two farms. But hottempered Kathleen loudly and stubbornly refused. The house they shared became an icy cold war zone.

Soon after that, her mother's widowed sister had

sent a letter inviting her to visit the small Texas town called Blissful, and her life was changed forever.

In the year following her arrival, Kathleen helped nurse the little vegetable garden into providing additional income—and her aunt gave her the secret recipe to her famous carrot cake. Along with the townsfolk, farm and ranch wives came to buy the cakes and beg to no avail for the recipe.

When her aunt died in early November over two years ago, Kathleen inherited the small ranch and the carrot cake clients. She was elated, even though she knew of the hard work ahead. Earnings from garden produce had disappeared with winter winds blowing across the prairie. Eggs, chickens, and carrot cake income could barely sustain her, let alone provide feed for the livestock, so keeping only the chickens, two horses, and one cow, she sold the rest.

Six months after her aunt's death, Kathleen was still struggling to survive.

And so was the town called Blissful.

The town fathers held meeting after meeting but could find no solution. At last, hopeless and helpless, convinced that no one would buy their farms and ranches at the edge of civilization, they decided to take their losses and abandon Blissful.

But against all odds, the upstart, outspoken young redhead from North Carolina had an idea and was determined to make them listen.

On that final day when wise old heads were sadly deciding how to apportion the town's few remaining assets, Kathleen entered their inner sanctum and presented her alternative. At first her pleas fell upon deaf ears. After all, she was just a woman—and what did women know about trade and commerce with outsiders?

But Kathleen did know. And as a last resort, she convinced them to listen to her daring proposition.

"First and foremost," she told them, "it will require a vow of secrecy from every citizen: every man, woman and child not only in town, but on the surrounding farms and ranches. Then we'll see about getting railroad trains to ship our cattle and produce to other parts of the country."

When they protested that that had been tried and vetoed, she overrode their objections. "We'll make them want to ship our products," she said. "We'll put our town on the map by making it the most wicked town in the West."

The shocked town fathers piously shook their heads and said that, due to her aunt's death, the young lady from North Carolina had gone loco.

Ignoring their words, Kathleen told them loudly and with assurance how to begin saving the town.

"Next Thursday, and every Thursday after that," she said, "when the westward train stops to take on coal, wood, and water, we'll put on a blood show— but we'll make the travelers think it's the real thing. The first week, we'll have a gun battle between two gangs; the next week, a bank robbery, then a showdown between the sheriff and an outlaw."

"Travelers will never leave the train," was the objection.

"Not too many stepped off anyway. Let them stay in their seats. We'll take our wares to them and tell stories behind the shootings. They'll buy produce, meals, and souvenirs about the wild tales we tell them. When word gets around that Blissful is a two-fisted shoot-out town, people will come just for the thrill of seeing it. And I'll bet my garters those railroad owners will be only too happy to feather their pockets with frequent stops in our dangerous town."

And Kathleen was right. These past two years the pristine town of Blissful had become the notorious Helltown. And true to her prediction, railroad owners took advantage of this new source of revenue. Within a month after the first show, trains filled with eager, thrill-seeking passengers who came to gawk and buy expensive souvenirs from the most wicked town west of the Mississippi.

"The bullet that killed the third sheriff this month" went for the unheard-of sum of fifty dollars.

The bloody satin quilt where Blackjack Gus died in Mindy Mae's bawdy house on Main Street brought one hundred and fifty dollars after a knock-down-drag-out auction in the first-class passenger car.

And a fight broke out in the club car between a respectable Austin businessman and a Dallas entrepreneur over the purchase of the infamous pearl-handled six-gun of Gentleman Pat Garrity, whose silver tongue and smooth manners couldn't keep him from being hanged from the branch of a cottonwood tree at the edge of the river—a branch conveniently seen from the south windows of the train. Gentleman Pat, travelers were told, raped and killed respectable women throughout the West. But Blissful outlaws were enraged when the wife of a local gunman was raped, killed, and her body disposed of by burning down her house—leaving the gunman not only wifeless, but homeless.

And the torn lace chemise of Lottie Evans, famous woman gambler, mistress to "King" Ketchum, brought two hundred dollars to the town coffers. King had followed Lottie to the local hotel, found her in bed with a traveling drummer, and dispatched him with a well-placed bullet in the head. Then, with both hands around Lottie's slender white throat, he'd strangled her.

Enraptured by tales of murder and mayhem, thrill-seeking travelers failed to realize that not one of the wanted men's names sounded even vaguely familiar. No one had written articles back east about these men, nor had they read tales of their lives in the penny novels. They were stunned by bloody gunfights and three or four bullet-riddled bodies in coffins lining Main Street for all to view. Depending on how well the story was told, swatches of hair from dead outlaws went for ten to twenty dollars, and many a mustache cup inscribed with the name of a famous outlaw brought enough to pay town taxes for the year.

There was no doubt about it: souvenirs, bogus or not, meant money in the bank. Then last week came the news they were waiting for. The railroad commission promised that it would discuss stopping for shipment pickups with regularity, adding produce and cattle cars. Everything hinged on the next board meeting in one month.

Everyone was elated. Due to the amount of money brought in by individual sales of their wares, many families had larger crops and even larger herds. A percentage of the money that came from some of the souvenirs and plays went into the town coffers, and the small community now had a church to rival a big town, as well as a completely stocked schoolhouse and a small community center. It was also advertising in other larger cities for some sort of factory or commerce to come to the now-wealthy town. Everyone, including the town itself, had prospered over the past two years.

Now Kathleen was faced with another problem. Lying very still in her bed, she looked at the sleeping bounty hunter and frowned. He'd given her a new worry. His belief that the town really had attracted an outlaw had frightened her. How many real outlaws would feel the same way and decide this was a great place to visit?

Why hadn't the wise old town fathers thought of that? she wondered.

She'd given them the basic idea. Why hadn't they looked beyond their noses—and their pocket-books—and seen the very real possibility that the town's false reputation could place them all in danger? On the other hand, why didn't *she* think of the danger her idea might bring about?

With a quiet sigh, she decided to present that worry to the town council at their meeting tonight. Then she remembered her mistake. In a moment of fear she'd mentioned the town council, and this bounty hunter stated he would go with her to the meeting. What was she to do? She had to warn them somehow.

As if in answer to a prayer she heard the sound of a horse coming fast. Of course, it was old E. Z.! Ezra Zermatt was a man of indeterminable age somewhere between sixty and ninety. Spry, bald, and wiry, he was an intricate part of the town shows, not as an actor, but as a storytelling souvenir peddler. In the pace of a minute, he could spin a yarn that would stand visitors' hair on end, and they'd believe every word he said. E. Z.'s typical Western twang added authenticity to the fictional bad men, and he never failed to leave the train with a big grin on his face and pockets bulging with money.

The pounding hooves drew closer, and Kathleen shot a quick glance at the bounty hunter still sleeping in the bedside chair. He didn't move a muscle, but she suspected he might be playing possum. Quietly she swung her legs off the bed, grabbed her shoes, and tiptoed out of the room. After racing through the kitchen and out the back door, she ran toward the road, waving frantically at E. Z. to stop before he reached the house. But E. Z. only grinned, spurred his horse faster, and halted abruptly in a spate of dust within a few yards of her shoeless feet.

"Got news, missy," he said in his loud, gravelly voice. "A stranger hit town yistidday. Don't know why he come, and don't know where he went."

Kathleen placed a forefinger over her lips, signaling him to be quiet, but E. Z. either didn't get the message or didn't want to get it. In either case, Kathleen knew that if the stranger failed to hear the approaching horse, he certainly heard E. Z.'s raspy, blaring statement.

"Do we know who it is?"

"Nope. Dunno. I was just tol' to let you know," he said, as if that were the end of the matter. "An' Mort wants ta know who we gonna kill next?" he asked.

He frowned when her only answer was to drop her shoes, grab his horse's bridle, and, in her stocking feet, lead him back to the road.

Charlie awaked at the first sound of the approaching horse, but gave no indication of it when Kathleen slipped from the bed and quietly left the house. Telling himself that it was Vic Masters returning to her side, he stood up and peered through the lace-curtained window. But all he saw was the rear end and swishing black tail of a sleek roan mare. And four human legs.

When he heard the invisible visitor's whiskey voice, he was disappointed. That same voice was in the kitchen yesterday. It hadn't been Vic after all. An instant later, Charlie saw the girl, without her shoes, leading the horse back out to the road, talking a mile a minute.

Smart, he thought in grudging admiration. Whoever the old geezer was, she didn't want him saying anything Charlie could hear.

But he was puzzled by the old man's words regarding a stranger in town. Surely a town as notorious as this place had disreputable strangers wandering in and out all the time? And why had this innocent-looking girl been asked about who was to be killed tomorrow? There must be more deviousness behind that pretty face than he'd realized.

He watched the tableau at the roadside for five or six minutes; then, moving the chair closer to the window and balancing his gun on the sill, he sat down and watched the pair in deep, serious conversation. The man was old, wizened, but agile. He'd slipped off his horse and, obviously agitated, twirled the tips of his handlebar mustache while the girl spoke earnestly. Now and then he'd answer a question or fling both arms outward, palms open in a beseeching manner. Sometimes, with a puzzled look on his grizzled features, he removed his hat and stroked his bald head.

At last he mounted his horse again and, with a little salute to the girl, turned and galloped down the road toward town.

Kathleen stood watching E. Z. ride out of sight. A stranger in town, he'd said. Was it the Vic Masters outlaw the bounty hunter was seeking? Was it some other gunman scouting the town? Or was it the bounty hunter himself? The one sitting in her bedroom now? E. Z. said that the man was tall, dark, and looked menacing. While the bounty hunter had bullied her and tried to make her out to be a liar, she'd glimpsed chinks in his armor when he looked at her, and her fears had eased considerably. She really didn't see the bounty hunter—if that was what he really was—

as menacing, but she was still very wary. He very well might be when she went back inside and faced his questions. But his good quality was that he was hunting a bad guy, instead of being hunted.

The sun was warm on her shoulders. Butterflies fluttered amid the flowers in her garden, and a soft breeze carried the scents of honeysuckle, lavender, and mint. It was August, her favorite time of year. She longed to throw herself on the cool grass and find pictures in little puffs of clouds barely moving against the heavenly blue sky. But her mind raced to other problems. She had no idea what to say when the stranger in her house asked about E. Z.'s normal, everyday question: *Who we gonna kill next?*

She heard sounds coming from the barn and the chicken yard beyond. She had to milk the cow, feed the horses and chickens, then wrap Mrs. Ormsby's carrot cake for her church luncheon at noon today.

Her heart skipped a beat. *Mrs. Ormsby!* She was a sweet woman, and Kathleen usually looked forward to her visits, to their sitting down to coffee and light gossip. *But not today! Dear God, not today!* Not with an angry bounty hunter hiding in her bedroom—a dark, handsomely menacing man who insisted that she knew the whereabouts of a wanted gunman.

No matter what the bounty hunter heard, she was glad E. Z. came. At least the town council would be ready when he accompanied her to the meeting tonight.

With a sigh, she turned and resigned herself to facing the man waiting inside.

She had barely reached the kitchen door when Mrs. Ormsby's carriage appeared on the road. She must have passed E. Z., and Kathleen wondered if he'd had presence of mind enough to inform her of the visitor. Apparently he had not, for as the phaeton drew near, Mrs. Ormsby waved and smiled. Kathleen waved back, then sat down on the little bench beneath the tree and put on her shoes, hoping the bounty hunter would have the grace to hide until she rid herself of her visitor.

He did. And when Kathleen entered the house with Mrs. Ormsby, she was a nervous wreck wondering where he was.

"Are you going somewhere, Kathleen?" the woman asked. "You're dressed rather formally for a Wednesday morning."

Kathleen thought quickly. In the urgency of the past half hour, she'd forgotten she still wore last night's beribboned silk gown—her only dressy dress. "I planned to attend the church luncheon," she answered. "But E. Z. just brought a message from a ranch wife in Hockley. She's giving a birthday party for her husband tonight and has ordered six carrot cakes. I must change and begin baking."

"That gown is a little too formal even for a church luncheon, dear," Mrs. Ormsby stated calmly.

The woman was a flutterhead. Though given to gossip, she was sweet, kind, and couldn't hold a serious thought for more than a few minutes.

"Sorry," she said quietly to the older woman and received a gentle smile in return.

Kathleen tried to hide the fact that her hands were shaking as she took the carrot cake from its cloth wrapping, placed it in Mrs. Ormsby's narrow tin, and closed the tight-fitting cover. To Kathleen's dismay, the woman insisted on having her usual cup of coffee. With apologies for not having prepared it earlier, Kathleen pumped water into the blue enameled pot, added coffee, and lit the stove already stuffed with paper, wood, and coal, waiting for it to boil. And all the while she prayed that Mrs. Ormsby would say nothing that the bounty hunter shouldn't hear.

Her prayers were answered. The woman was so involved with her church work, her daughter's piano lessons, and the state of her husband's health, that the conversation went safely by during the longest, most anxiety-ridden forty-five minutes of Kathleen's life.

She was torn between wanting her guest to stay and wanting her to leave. On one hand, if the man in the next room tired of waiting, he just might appear and embarrass her beyond her wildest nightmares. If he failed to explain his reason for being there, this sweet, butterfly-brained woman would spread gossip for months. And if he *did* explain, it could be worse!

At last Mrs. Ormsby rose to leave. Picking up her cake, she moved toward the door, then stopped. "James and I both think these shoot-outs are getting out of hand," she said. "They're too bloody and not good for the children to see. Couldn't we somehow make them less brutal?"

Kathleen's mind raced again. How could she answer without raising more questions in the bounty hunter's mind? And how could she keep this woman from saying more? "I wish we could, Mrs. Ormsby," she said sadly. "But how do you control outlaws?"

Mrs. Ormsby's eyebrows rose in questioning surprise, but before she could say another word, Kathleen took her elbow and gently ushered her out the door. Following her outside, she helped her into the carriage. "I'll see what we can do about making the shows less bloody," she murmured.

With a relieved smile, the woman took up the reins, turned the carriage around, and headed slowly down the road toward town.

The bounty hunter was waiting for Kathleen when

she entered the kitchen. He'd helped himself to a cup of coffee and, seated in a high-backed kitchen chair, was nonchalantly nibbling on a piece of carrot cake from her cupboard—and he'd left the door wide open.

"You know your way about a kitchen," he said with a grin. "I smelled this cake when I came in yesterday."

"And apparently you found your way around my kitchen," she said sarcastically, noting that while she'd walked out to Mrs. Ormsby's carriage, he'd brought up bacon and eggs from her small underground cellar. "Were you hiding down there?"

He nodded, his grin widening. "I went down to find Vic Masters and found breakfast instead. I like my eggs sunny-side up."

"Then I suggest you fix them that way," she said cleaning up the dishes from Mrs. Ormsby's visit. She was furious, but she'd be darned if she'd let him know how much he was rattling her.

What nerve! The man not only accused her of lying; he raided her food pantry and expected her to cook for him as well!

Charlie stood up and gave her a courtly bow. "May I cook for you also, ma'am?"

Her green eyes narrowed. What was he up to? There was a smug look on his handsome face, and she clenched her fists to keep from flying at him and slapping it away. "I don't eat breakfast," she answered curtly.

His grin faded. "You'll need nourishment, ma'am. You're facing a pretty rough day."

She frowned. "Mr. What's-your-name," she began.

"Charlie, ma'am. Charlie Macon." A hard glint came into his dark eyes and he raised a thick black brow. "And your name, ma'am?"

"Kathleen," she answered with a proud lift to her chin. "Kathleen O'Day."

His lips formed a thin line as he studied her. "You're a good liar, Kathleen O'Day—and quick-witted. I heard you lie to your lady friend and I'll bet you lied to that old geezer who woke us up this morning, too."

"I don't know what you're talking about."

"You couldn't very well tell her that you slept in your go-to-meetin' dress last night."

She had nothing to say to that, so, getting a cup from the cupboard, she poured her second cup of coffee that morning. He sat down again and finished his cake. She waited. Heavy silence filled the room, and it was worse than the questions she'd dreaded, but which were obviously not forthcoming. More than anything in the world, she wanted him to leave and let her get on with her business.

At last he broke the silence. "You won't be out of my sight all day," he said in a voice heavy with implied menace.

"I *will* be out of your sight right now," she said, slamming her cup on the table and marching to the door of her bedroom. "I have chickens and livestock to feed and I certainly can't do it in my 'go-to-meetin' dress.' "

She'd already slammed the bedroom door, so she didn't see his face break into a broad grin.

There was a gun hidden in her mattress, but the chambers were empty. In fact, there were no bullets anywhere in the room. He'd made sure of that.

When Kathleen reentered the kitchen ten minutes later, she was ravenous with hunger. The delicious aroma of fried bacon and eggs had wafted into the bedroom while she changed into a light blue cotton dress and a pair of soft slippers. There were two plates of food on the table, and, unable to resist her growling stomach's demands, she sat down. He'd taken a lid off one of the stove burners and stood with a thick slice of bread on a fork, making toast.

He grinned when he saw her slippers. "You're not going to muck around in the barn with those on your feet, are you?" he asked.

His tone was derisive and her anger rose again. What was it about this man that could send her from slow, burning anger into outright rage in less than a minute? "I wear these slippers for comfort," she answered, biting off her words. "And when I get to the barn, I keep the slippers on and step into a large pair of boots to 'muck around,' as you say."

Again, that maddening grin.

In a silent gesture, he motioned her to join him. After her stomach growled on cue, she sat across from him and daintily ate in silence. He might have fixed the food, but she was darned if she was going to be a stimulating dining companion!

When they finished, he took their plates to the dish basin, pumped water from the sink pump, and let them soak.

Kathleen watched him warily.

He had something up his sleeve, she was sure. Whatever it was, she'd better be ready for it. Her insides were a bowl of jelly. Perhaps because, despite herself, she was attracted to this man and she feared him more than anyone she'd ever known. There was no doubt that he was a threat to her and to the town. He believed nothing she said—he stubbornly insisted that she knew the outlaw he hunted—and something in his eyes told her he held a trump card. And she hadn't the faintest idea what it could be.

"I'm going to the barn," she announced suddenly.
"I'm going with you."

She ignored him. As they crossed the field together,
he shortened his steps to match hers. He knew she
was nervous, and she had every right to be. All the
while they had eaten, he'd felt like he'd prepared a
last meal for a gal condemned to hang—and he was
the executioner. In a way, he felt sorry for her living
alone in the West. It was a hard life for a woman. But
it wasn't an excuse for her managing to get tangled
up with a poor excuse of a man like Vic Masters.

He watched her closely when they entered the barn.
As she'd told him, she placed her slippered feet into
a pair of large men's boots and went to scoop up
feed for the chickens. Though the horses whinnied
and stomped in their stalls, she didn't give them a
second glance.

Charlie leaned back against a hay bale and silently
took in her every move. She was stalling.

That was all right. He was a patient man. He could
wait.

But he couldn't. When Kathleen reached for the
pail to milk the cow, he lost all patience. He walked
over, took her hand, and led her to the farthest stall.

"Look at this dapple gray horse, Kathleen O'Day,"
he said, opening the stall door and walking in behind
her. "And tell me it doesn't belong to Vic Masters."

Lifting the animal's foreleg, he pointed with sub-
lime assurance at the malformed shoe on the horse's
hoof. He knew this horse hoof better than his own.
He'd been following it for over two weeks.

Then he watched a myriad of expressions flit across
Kathleen's face.

Three

Kathleen stared blankly at the horse's hoof, then up at him, then back down again. "I have no idea who it belongs to. It's not mine."

"Damn," he said. "I thought you'd try to lie, but I certainly didn't think you'd deny it down to your teeth. Not when you were bald-faced confronted with it."

Her eyes were wide, barely tamed copper hair framing her face and making her look almost fragile in the coolness of the shaded barn. "With what?"

"With Vic's horse."

"How do you know it's Vic's horse?"

"Because," he said through clenched teeth, wondering how long this conversation could continue before he lost control of his temper, "I've been following the damn thing for almost two weeks. I know this horse's tracks pretty well by now. It's Vic Masters's horse." He took a deep breath, letting go of her arm in case he decided to squeeze the daylights out of her. "Now, how do you think it got here?"

Instead of defending herself, Kathleen turned away, walking back to the pile of hay outside the stall. "I have no idea."

"And I'm a damned leprechaun, here to bring you a pot of gold," he said.

She glanced over her shoulder at him just as she reached for the pitchfork. "I doubt that. You're too bulky for the part."

That did it! Charlie put his hands on his hips and prayed he wouldn't reach for his gun to shoot the hell out of her. "Put that pitchfork down right now and answer me, or we'll both be in trouble. Me for killing you, and you for making me do it."

Kathleen didn't bat an eyelash. She continued to pitch hay into the trough for the cow. "You don't mean that. Just calm down and think a moment. If I'd known the horse was here, would I have bothered coming out here and letting you *see* it?"

Charlie stared at her, wondering why he could scare the hell out of any scum-sucking bandito, and couldn't seem to get this woman to bat one fearful eyelash in his direction.

Back at the ranch, his men believed him when he said he'd take action. His partners knew he wasn't kidding when he stated that his temper was on a short leash. Everyone who knew him took him seriously. But this woman didn't seem to pay the slightest attention. It could mean only one thing: she was more stupid than she looked.

"Drop . . . that . . . pitchfork," he finally gnashed out through gritted teeth.

Kathleen gave an exasperated sigh and placed the pitchfork against the wall, standing within inches of it. "Make it quick. I still have a cow to milk. That's

what I started out to do, remember? It was the reason
I came out here. I didn't know the horse was here
or I would have said something like, 'Why don't you
stay inside and I'll be right back?' But I didn't. I didn't
mind you coming with me because I didn't know
there was a strange horse in my barn that you believe
belongs to a real gunslinger.''

Charlie couldn't believe his ears. Was she saying
she didn't believe him? She really *was* stupid. "A *real*
gunslinger? What the hell does that mean?''

For the first time since they entered the barn, Kathleen looked guilty. "Nothing,'' she said. "I just meant
I didn't know where the horse came from.''

"Yeah. Right,'' he said disgustedly. "And you didn't
even look in its direction, even though you didn't
know it was there.''

Her tiny chin rose up in defiance. "That's right.''

"I don't believe you,'' he stated. He was gathering
his thoughts to tell her off, when she turned her back
on him once more and sat down on the three-legged
stool next to the old, swaybacked cow.

"Well, I can't help what you think, Mr. . . . But I
never saw that horse until now. I don't know a Mr.
Vic Masters. And I don't know what you might think,
but that's the truth.''

Except for the hollow squirt-squirt of milk hitting
the bottom of the tin pail, silence filled the barn. He
watched her hands, so tiny and frail-looking inside
the house, pull on teats with just the right touch to
deliver milk.

Charlie had never felt so frustrated. Well, almost
never. His wife had made him feel that way before
they married, but it certainly didn't count now. Right
now he had to keep his calm.

With slow, deliberate steps, Charlie stepped out of
the barn and did what he'd done when the horse was

discovered: he walked around the outside of the barn looking for tracks or some sign that he hadn't seen before. There was nothing. Several boot tracks were on the back side of the barn where Vic had led the horse inside, but Charlie couldn't tell what happened to them once they left the barn. It turned into mud, then prairie grass. The track was too old, or too many other barnyard animals had messed it up.

And Kathleen swore she didn't know a thing about it. Then why wasn't she even curious about a horse in her stall? He realized that there had to be another reason she wasn't surprised at finding another animal that wasn't hers. Anyone else would have noticed it immediately.

Charlie stomped back inside the barn; then, several feet from her, he stood and allowed his eyes to adjust to the dim light. Dust motes and hayseed still flurried and held in the air, creating a hazy screen between him and the redheaded woman. She had finished milking and had stood to whisper in the cow's ear.

"Good job. Thank you. You're such a wonderful cow," her voice crooned. "You've given great-tasting milk and I want you to know I appreciate it. Thank you, Hilde." The soft sound soothed his ragged nerves much like sweet honey tasted on his tongue. Dust motes and dim light hid the stains on her dress, and her silky, disheveled hair only added to the sensuous, tender picture.

Charlie knew he was in trouble. He knew when his immediate thought was that he wished he was a cow . . . .

He cleared his throat. "Why weren't you surprised to find a new horse in your barn?"

"I wasn't paying attention," she said coolly. "I had other things on my mind."

"Like what?" he demanded. "What could be so

pressing that you'd never bother to notice a strange horse in your barn?"

Kathleen looked at him as if he'd been stupid to ask the question. "Like a strange man breaking into my home and pointing a gun at me, ordering me around and demanding answers to questions I had no idea existed until he came on the scene."

He realized just how true that was. "Look, I—"

But she wasn't finished. "And all the while, this rude cowboy is telling me that someone I don't know and never met is mean and a liar and a bandit. So you see," she said quietly, "it's no wonder I'm not quite myself."

Charlie cursed softly under his breath. Somehow she'd just turned everything around, and he sounded more like the bad guy than that scum sucker he was after. "Look, you're making it sound worse than it really is," he began.

Kathleen never said a word. Instead, she raised a brow and looked as if she waited patiently for further explanation.

And Charlie Macon couldn't think of a thing to say in his defense.

He opened his mouth, then closed it again. Finally, feeling more like a jackass than the animal itself could have felt, he stomped out of the barn and into the house. For the first time in his life, he wished he knew the workings of the female mind. He was certain it wouldn't last long and soon he'd be back to himself. He felt like a coward for leaving the front of a battle royale, but right now, he was better off alone . . . .

Kathleen watched the big man storm out of the barn. For one wild, wonderful moment, she thought he was going to get his horse from the corral and ride out of Blissful. But the hope was fleeting, dying when she saw him angle toward her back door.

She sat on a bale of hay and sighed heavily, forcing tension to ease from her body. It was only momentary, she knew, but at least it was a respite. Feeling as if she'd been holding her breath for hours, Kathleen closed her eyes and leaned back against the barn wall.

What next?

How was she going to get rid of him? Anything she thought to do would probably cause more alarm in the community than his absence would cure.

The train was coming through in four days, and they were supposed to be ready for it. They had a whole scene sketched out where old Ed and his "gang" were going to rob the bank. But so far, no casting, no rehearsals, not even a loosely based script formed beyond the concept. Everything was stopped.

This was awful.

Tomorrow was usually Kathleen's baking day. She needed at least thirty cakes or more, and it would take all day and half the evening. Usually, with Josetta's help, that wasn't a problem. Josetta's husband helped some of the townspeople with their chores, and Josetta was wonderful with shredding the carrots for the cakes. It took all morning just to get that task done.

Even with the next play so close to her baking day, there normally wasn't a problem. At this time of the week, everyone knew their places and had an idea of how the new show would work. Usually.

She had to get away from Charlie Macon. She had to attend the afternoon meeting today and make sure everything was all right. After all, the town was so close to the prosperity they had all worked hard to achieve.

Along with that thought came Charlie's problem.

He could ruin everything, and all for the sake of some unknown gunslinger who didn't belong in their community.

Who and where was this Vic Masters anyway? Kathleen was truly as stunned as Charlie when she saw the horse in her stall. Having a strange horse in her barn was nothing new. The town had decided horses were more noticeable than people, so they switched out horses for the show. Often she found a new one in her stall that had been borrowed from another town or one of the ranchers outside of town but in on their secret.

But this time it was Vic whoever's horse, making Charlie even more determined to remain here.

So how did the horse get into her barn?

That was one question she'd ask when she reached rehearsal this afternoon. And somebody had better have an answer . . . .

Kathleen finished the rest of her chores and cooked the last of her potatoes and beans from last year's stock in the hayloft. Dinner was cooked and ready to serve before four-thirty that afternoon. Just before serving, she mixed in a little extra ingredient for Charlie—an herb that made one drowsy. In fact, she made sure that there was enough in the beans and potatoes to insure his sleeping through the night.

At dinnertime, just as in the early part of the day, Charlie was quiet, asking no questions and giving no opinions. His gaze followed her everywhere, but nothing was said, nor did he badger her about the horse. Kathleen wondered if this meant he would soon leave, but she certainly didn't count on it. So far, Charlie had been an unknown factor, never quite doing what she thought he would.

Her nerves sang with tension as she placed the stew pot on the table and sat two already filled bowls in their places. If her calculations were correct, one bowl of doctored soup should be all that was necessary for Charlie to sleep well all evening. She didn't want to overdo it because she wasn't sure of her dosage. It was her aunt who had let her know about the herb to begin with, but that didn't mean she was an expert.

As she cut off thick slices of bread and set it with a crock of fresh creamed butter, Charlie took his place at the table and waited for her, watching her movements like her cat watching an unaware lizard.

Finally, after serving two tall glasses of milk and the warm, soft bread, she sat down and began tasting. Charlie dug in right away, eating the soup as if satisfying a huge appetite for Kathleen's home cooking. Five minutes later he was on his second bowl of soup. By the time Kathleen finished her bowl, he'd eaten three along with several thick slices of fresh bread.

"Delicious," he pronounced. "You're a wonderful cook, Kathleen," he complimented generously.

"Thank you." She stood and reached for both bowls and silverware. "Would you like a piece of carrot cake?"

"You have some?"

"Yes. Tomorrow is my day to bake all day, but there's still a piece or two left."

Charlie gave a big yawn. "I'd love it."

Kathleen ignored the nervousness that seemed to make a nest in her stomach. She couldn't look at Charlie, didn't want to see the results of her action and feel the guilt that she knew would be there. She did what she did for the good of all of Blissful, and that was the end of it.

She reached in the pine pie pantry and pulled out the last of the carrot cake, slicing off a hunk and setting it in front of Charlie, still without looking at him.

"Coffee?" he asked hopefully.

"I don't have any made right now," she said quietly. "But the milk goes well with it."

"Thanks," Charlie stated dryly before taking a big bite of her cake.

Kathleen began the task of cleaning dishes in the small pail on the counter, setting each aside in the sink to rinse with a bucket of clear water that she'd already set on the floor.

With a mixture of both fear and anticipation, Kathleen heard Charlie yawn again. It was working faster than she thought, but then, she'd seen her aunt use it only once, on the long-winded traveling preacher who used to come through on occasion. The preacher had also imbibed a little of her muscadine wine, and who knew how it would react with alcohol? He had begun singing at the top of his lungs until, about fifteen minutes later, he looked startled, sat down, then closed his eyes and slept for over three hours.

Charlie gave another wide yawn.

"If you're tired, you're welcome to lie down for a while."

"Have I got food on my face?"

She didn't look over her shoulder at him. "Of course not. Why?"

"Are you anxious to get rid of me?"

"No." She hesitated. "Why?"

"Because you won't look at me."

She carefully placed a just-washed plate in the sink and reached for the towel before turning around. "What's the matter? Are you not getting enough attention? Am I not cooking well for you? Talking to you? Am I not being entertaining enough? Is there no end to what you demand out of your hostages?"

Charlie's answer was another big yawn. He stood up. "Never mind," he said. "I'm taking a nap." He looked at her strangely. "But don't try anything funny. My hearing is acute."

"Acute?" she asked. "*Acute?* Since when does a bounty hunter know the word?"

"You heard me," he said in a growl.

"I have to milk the cow."

He hesitated a moment for a small yawn. "Don't go any farther than the barn."

"Yes, sir!" she snapped out, turning once more to the soapy pail of water.

"Oh, and by the way, Miss O'Day . . . "

Kathleen faced him, allowing herself to show her anger and frustration.

"Great cake."

She smiled, both at his unexpected compliment and at his lopsided grin that was hard not to react to. "Thank you. It's my specialty."

"Thought so." Without another word, he stumbled out of the kitchen and through the parlor to the bedroom. Kathleen heard the squeak of bedsprings, then nothing.

She continued cleaning the kitchen, then placed her towel over the tin counter to dry. With calm steps that belied the turmoil churning inside her, she walked into the bedroom and watched the sleeping cowboy. Relaxed, his face was less threatening, less intimidating. Kathleen tilted her head and stared at the sleeping man. Telling herself he wasn't any good for her or this town, she turned away. But her eye was caught by the red and white crocheted afghan folded over the back of the rocking chair. Carefully unfolding it, she draped the covering over Charlie's long legs and lean hips. It wasn't cool yet, but once the sun went down, a chill would touch the spring night air. She certainly didn't want him waking up unexpectedly, before she was home. Charlie gave a soft snore and she slowly backed away.

It was time to get going while the going was good. Grabbing her own shawl, she tiptoed from the room and out the back door. Then she took a deep breath, telling herself it was all right to relax. She picked up the hem of her dress and ran as fast as the wind down the dirt road that led to the town meeting.

By the time she made it to Jacob's General Store, she was out of breath and angry at herself for worrying so much. Fourteen or fifteen men and women stood around, talking in groups like old friends enjoying a social evening.

Ed, the second in command for their scenes, wore a frown. He was always nervous, and it showed in a hundred different habits that reflected his true feelings. When he saw Kathleen enter the building, his frown was replaced with an expression of relief. He came toward her, his bald head nodding as he walked. "I was worried you wouldn't make it, but then I knew you'd do your part."

That was Ed—never quite sure which side of the fence to come down on.

She hid a yawn, chalking it up to having run so long and hard. "Well, I'm here now, but I've got to hurry home soon, so let's get started."

"Why the hurry, Kathleen?" Mildred came up and placed her hand on Kathleen's where she clutched her shawl.

"I have company," she stated. "A bounty hunter who refuses to leave until he finds a cattle rustler."

"A cattle rustler? *Here?*" Ed's pale face turned more paler. "In Blissful? Why here?"

Kathleen thought she'd heard enough whys to last a lifetime. Including her own. She gave a heavy sigh.

"Because that same cattle rustler exchanged horses here. He left his good stallion in my barn with one horseshoe missing, and took the little nag I bought from Silas last year."

"The swayback?" Ed's voice squeaked on the last word.

"I know it sounds ridiculous, Ed, but yes, the swayback I got taken on."

Ed began to wring his hands. Mildred ignored him. Instead she frowned at Kathleen. "Why would anyone do that?"

"Because they're either very stupid and don't know horseflesh, or they're somewhere close by and mean to retrieve it at another time."

"Don't you think they might just move on and trade in your horse for another in some other town?" Ed asked nervously.

Both Mildred and Kathleen ignored him. "My guess would be the second," Mildred said.

"So would mine," Kathleen stated. "It's the one reason I don't mind putting up with the bounty hunter for a few days. He could be the only good protection I have."

But Ed wasn't so sure. "What if he comes back to this town and realizes we have no sheriff?" he asked, panic growing in his voice. "He could kill us all!"

Mildred and Kathleen both looked at him. "Why would he do that?"

Ed shrugged and nervously looked around. "I don't know. Why do rustlers rob?"

"To get rich, Ed. What would make him kill someone?"

Ed shrugged again. "For money?"

"Whose money?"

"We've all made money off the scenes we do, Kathleen. You and I have done a good job of that, to say nothing of all the other townspeople. In fact, the bank has grown fat taking care of our money." He looked around. "This general store was nothing until we all had money to spend in it. Since then, the stock has doubled, and the quality has risen, too."

Kathleen stifled another yawn. "Are you saying you think someone will rob the store or the bank?"

"We don't know, do we?"

"No, we don't. But it would be pretty hard to do in a town where we all are so alert to strangers, don't you think?"

"They could try to rob us while we're putting on one of our shows," Ed said, fear still lacing his voice.

"Our shows are done by us, Ed," Kathleen said patiently. "We would *all* notice a stranger in our midst."

"I know but—" he began.

Mildred's patience was at an end. "Enough, Ed. Let's get going. Tomorrow is my baking day, Evelyn's sewing day, and Kathleen's baking day. We have only an hour or so to spend here before getting back home."

Kathleen yawned, this time unable to delicately hide the action. "In fact, we should be able to run through it quickly. I'm exhausted." She thought of Charlie sound asleep in her bed and was jealous. Her mind was dulling. She needed to rest, to sit for just a little while. "Let's run through it quickly."

It took half an hour to organize everyone into places, describe the scene, and then do a walk-through of the action. All this was done inside the store. The townspeople had done so many in the past two years, they knew the stances to take and the guideposts outside that would be done on horseback for the best angle to the railroad cars that would be stopped there, witnessing the action.

She felt a sense of relief as she quickly made her good-byes and dragged herself away from the general store, almost stumbling in her exhaustion. She felt flushed and heated from the merest movement.

Halfway home, she looked at the soft grass on the side of the path and thought she needed to rest her cheek against the cool ground for just a moment, close her eyes and rest, breathe deeply of the clover and rest.

Her last thoughts became reality as she stumbled to the pasture edge and dropped to her knees. She didn't remember closing her eyes . . . .

A little while later, Charlie picked up the awkward bundle of femininity and cradled her in his arms for a long moment before he slipped her over the saddle of his horse as if she were a load of laundry. He led his horse down the road, sticking to the shadows as he walked Kathleen home.

Switching bowls with Kathleen had been a smart thing to do after all. He'd had a funny feeling, and had followed the gut instinct that had kept him alive so far.

But when this woman woke up, she had a few more questions to answer than she had griped about so far.

He was looking forward to the answers . . . .

Four

Warm sunshine fell on Kathleen's face, and she reluctantly forced her lids open. But when she looked away from the ceiling and into Charlie's stormy expression as he bent over her, she knew she wanted to go back to sleep instantly.

But she was not one to run away from a fight, especially when she was probably right about whatever it was he wanted to argue about. She wasn't sure what he was angry over, but she'd find out. Gathering her courage to face the man, Kathleen stared back, blinking occasionally.

"So you're awake," he said, satisfaction lacing the outright anger in his tone. "Or you're asleep with your eyes open."

"I'm awake," she said, slowly rolling over to sit up. Her stomach lurched and she held her head to keep the room from rocking back and forth. She felt awful. "Maybe I'm not."

"Maybe you're reacting to whatever it was you put in my bowl of gruel."

Her bed kept dancing on the floor, or her vision was blurring. She wasn't sure which. "I don't make gruel. I didn't put anything in your food."

"Really? Then why are you suffering so? I switched bowls with you and you fell asleep on the side of the road. Something doesn't seem right, does it?"

"What a smug attitude," Kathleen stated groggily, wishing she knew what he was talking about. She wished she could remember . . . .

"Only because I'm right and you're lying."

She looked up at him, careful not to move her head too quickly. If only her thoughts would clear! "About what?"

"About Vic, about the fact that you're a murderess, or at least trying to be, along with the rest of this hellhole's townspeople."

Dimly, she realized she had slept in her shift. Her dress hung over the side of the rocking chair. But that observation was overridden by Charlie's declaration. Those words certainly got her attention. "What?"

"I could be in the shape you're in right now if I wasn't suspicious by nature. In fact, I damn well thought you were trying to poison me like you were planning to kill the sheriff." His smile was deadly. "Until I spotted the herb you sprinkled in my stew. It's in the back of the pantry, in a small jar." His brows rose, but she refused to talk. She couldn't even think, let alone answer.

Charlie continued. "Then I knew what you were doing was just knocking me out for a time while you worked out whatever you and the rest of this murdering town could work." Charlie snorted in disgust. "No wonder people stay away from here. It's got *deadly* written all over it."

She let go of her head and looked up at him. Once she stood, her eyes focused quickly. Funny how anger kept everything in perspective. "Tell me something that is not written on our town sign, Mr., uh, Charlie. The town is working on that."

"That meeting you went to?" He sneered. "I never saw so many people in one spot who couldn't fight their way out of a wicker basket if it had a hole the size of a train in it."

She snapped to attention, then swayed and reached one hand for the rocker. She put her other hand to her head, trying to regain her equilibrium. "You *spied* on us?"

"Some," he said casually. There wasn't a guilty bone in his body.

She tilted her head and stared at him. Suddenly she didn't feel her queasy stomach or her headache. Suddenly every fiber of her body was focused on him. "What did you hear?"

"You think if you can convince the town, you can all have a hand in shooting another sheriff. I'm just not sure who's really assigned to do the dirty deed." Charlie placed his hands on his hips and glared down at her. "I don't even know the poor fool's name or where he lives so I can warn him!"

Relief flowed through her body in waves that eased tension from every muscle in her body. Kathleen plopped back down on the bed, the springs giving squeaks and screeches in protest. The bounce reminded her of her queasy stomach, but she chose to ignore it again.

"We don't have a sheriff yet."

Charlie's glare turned even more dangerous, if that was possible. "What the hell do you mean? I heard everyone rehearsing the poor joker's death."

She wished her brain weren't so befuddled. She

needed to give him an answer that would appease him, and she wasn't sure what that answer needed to be. "Yes, but you see," she began, and mentally fumbled around again. "He, uh, we were just rehearsing in case we got a bad sheriff again. That was all. That way, the people aren't so likely to really act out their feelings because they've already acted them out in their thoughts." She smiled like a brainless idiot. "See?"

Charlie looked at her for several long minutes. Her cheeks hurt from keeping the stupid-looking smile on her face. His eyes narrowed as if he saw straight through to her soul. Finally he turned away in disgust. "That's either the sickest or the stupidest thing I ever heard. I'm not sure which."

"It's true."

He gave a disbelieving grunt. "It's a lie, but I won't begin to figure it out right now. I'm dead on my feet."

"Why?"

"Because I haven't slept well for the past two weeks, especially in the last two days since I've had a taste of your hospitality."

She decided against telling him the obvious. "Didn't you sleep last night? After all, I was drugged," she said, reminding him of his own part in this disaster. It wasn't her fault that he decided to change bowls. "Either way, you could have slept very well last night."

"And not worry about your friends coming up to help you? For all I knew, you were going to bring them back here and shoot me like you were willing to do to the sheriff."

"You *are* crazy," she muttered, standing and heading for the door.

"Where are you going?" he asked sharply.

"To the outhouse, if you don't mind," she snapped just as harshly.

"I do. I'll go with you."

She tilted her chin in the air. "No, you won't. Unlike most of your species, I have need of privacy."

"That's tough, 'cause you got my company anyway."

Kathleen tried hard not to flounce from the room, barely keeping herself from slamming the bedroom door in his face. Besides, it wouldn't work. The old door had a hard time swinging on its leather hinges.

She squinted her eyes against the bright sunshine. Then she stopped and stared at the sun's location. "My word!" she exclaimed. "It's got to be close to noontime!"

"It is." Charlie was right behind her. "And some woman named Josetta came by, but I told her you wouldn't be doing any baking today. You'll have to give her another date for that."

"Josetta!" Kathleen groaned in exasperation. Now she'd have to set a new date and be a day behind. She hurried toward the outhouse. "If you hadn't switched bowls with me, I'd be halfway through my baking by now."

"And I would have been knocked out and probably dead by now."

"You would not. I tried to keep the dosage according to your body weight," she stated defensively.

"But you didn't know my weight."

"I knew you were heavier than me." Kathleen reached for the outhouse door and held it open. "I did the best I could."

He looked at her in disbelief. "You're just plain crackers, you know that? You think I should apologize for switching a bowl of sedative that shouldn't have been in the house to begin with!''

"It's a good thing you don't have a wife or children, Charlie Macon! You'd never be able to understand them either! You have no sympathy to understand others' motives!'' With that she stepped inside and slammed the door behind her. But she wasn't quick enough to catch the expression on Charlie's face. A few seconds later, the latch clicked in place.

Charlie stared at the door for a moment. That woman was lethal! She knew just where to hit to hurt.

His beloved wife had died four years ago. There hadn't been a day that had gone by since then that he hadn't thought of her and wished she was by his side. The chasm that was left in his life was something he didn't want to look at or acknowledge. It was too painful. He wasn't about to think of his daughter.

And damn Kathleen O'Day for bringing it up! Because of everything that had been going on in the past two days, he'd put those usual thoughts on the back burner and just concentrated on the problems at hand. It had been the most normal time he'd had since the funeral—if he could call bounty hunting for a man who killed one of two of his partners in the cattle ranch normal.

But Kathleen's comment made him aware of his loss again, and the past four years of his loneliness slammed into his gut and twisted like a serrated knife. It took his breath away.

Damn the woman.

When Kathleen exited the outhouse, she was ready to be angry with Charlie . . . or at least pretend to be. As long as he thought she was a flaming idiot, he wouldn't expect more out of her than what he got. Besides, she needed some peace in order to reorganize her weekly baking.

But what she got was something completely different. She got his anger, hot and bubbling out of his eyes and confirmed by his taut, stiff stance. What had happened in the five minutes since she went in and came out?

She hated mysteries.

Instead of asking questions and getting into another fight, Kathleen walked inside the house and grabbed the pail. With Charlie right on her heels, she ignored him and poured a cup of water from the trough onto the pump to prime it, then began pumping, filling the bucket in two or three pumps. Holding the bucket in both hands, she trudged back to the water trough on the side of the barn and fence and poured it into the large tub.

Then she repeated the process.

This time Charlie stood at the screen door, leaning against the jamb as if he were holding it up, looking deceptively lazy and casual. But she felt the heat of his gaze on her, still shining with anger boiling over and spilling into the room.

After the third and last trek, she sidled past him into the kitchen and accidentally splashed water on his boots.

Charlie didn't move.

After priming the indoor pump, she began filling her tin tub with water. She reached for the big bowl on the top shelf and sifted flour from the flour barrel into it with quick, jerking movements. "You could help, you know."

"I'm too tired. Besides, I don't bake cakes with ladies of the evening."

"Who are you joshing? You don't bake cakes at all, let alone are lucky enough to do so with ladies of the evening—if there were any around, which there are not."

His smile was as grim, and her throat felt tight. "If you don't like that explanation, then give me another, Miss O'Day." He took one of the kitchen chairs and sat down, tilting it against the far wall.

She glanced over her shoulder just in time to see him tilt his hat so far over his eyes that she could barely see the outline of his mouth.

"I have, Mr. Macon. You have chosen not to believe it."

He muttered an expletive.

She was brave enough for one more jab. "And since you let go the woman who helps me, I'll be at this all evening. So as I see it, you owe me."

For the next hour there was silence in the room except for the sound of grating carrots and the comforting sounds of wooden spoons against bowls and pans and the opening and closing of the oven as she stoked the fire, then began the process of baking forty-four carrot cakes. It was a process that took all day.

Charlie didn't say a word. The quiet was almost deafening at first. Kathleen decided to ignore him. If he had nothing to say, then neither did she! The man was rude and insensitive. Charlie reminded her of her brother—in fact, of most of the insensitive, brutish men she'd known in her life. As long as his needs were met he was silent and happy. And when his needs were not met, he was constantly griping and making everyone unhappy in general.

Well, she'd gotten away from her brother. Eventually she'd get rid of Charlie, too. She had to, or the town's life would be in jeopardy.

It wasn't until Kathleen took out the first batch of small cakes from the oven and set them on the wooden table to cool that she realized Charlie was not watching her. She tiptoed to his side and carefully looked under the brim of his hat. He was asleep!

Her first instinct was to let him sleep. After all, the guy had rescued her, reluctantly or not. Then she realized what she was thinking.

This man was the enemy! He was dangerous and she needed to get rid of him as soon as possible. Should she shoot him with the gun she kept under her bed? He'd probably found it and emptied it already. She had no other bullets besides the one in the gun. Her aunt had had it before her.

Run for help to kill him? The closest house was Mrs. Hanrahan's across the street, and the woman was in her eighties. Kathleen couldn't put the older lady through the anguish of it all. It wasn't fair. Besides, what if he was telling the truth? What if he was the only thing that stood between her and a killer? She and Mrs. Hanrahan were at the edge of town, a likely spot for a killer to hide out. And from what she'd seen so far, Charlie didn't act like any killer she'd use in a play. He wasn't deadly enough. He cared, or at least he seemed to.

But he wasn't saint enough to sleep while she worked.

She'd do something; she just wasn't sure what. Her mind was muddled with the herb she'd used in the food. But her determination to get through this mess was with her once again. Her expression turned grim. Without another thought, she dropped one of the carrot cake pans hard on the table, then slammed the door to the oven.

Charlie's chair legs cracked down on all fours with

the sound of a firecracker. He pushed his hat back on his head and glared at her.

She smiled sweetly as she rearranged the pans on the table. "Fall asleep?"

Charlie didn't answer. Instead he pulled out a watch from his waist pocket, clicked the lid open, and checked the time. With a definite snap, he closed it again. Just then the living room mantel clock chimed three o'clock.

Kathleen reached for the tub half-filled with carrots she'd dug up two days ago and had been soaking ever since. She finished grating the stack of bright orange carrots. Each top was set aside carefully as she began the process of grating.

After a few minutes, Charlie leaned back and covered his face with his hat again.

Five minutes later Kathleen dropped a clean pot to the floor.

A minute after that, she slammed the back door screen and headed toward the small henhouse for some eggs. He could stew on that for a few minutes and wonder where she was going. It was apparent he wasn't following. It was just as well. She needed a little time alone. She wasn't used to this much togetherness, especially with a man in the house.

A light afternoon breeze felt cooling on her oven-heated skin. Damp hair curled around her face in curling ringlets, while the rest of her felt limp and frazzled. But there was no help for it. She had only two days to get ready for the next train, and it took that long to prepare the cakes. Besides, with Mr. Sleepy watching every movement she made, she was going crazy as it was.

She looked around the chicken yard. Her kingdom for a little privacy. Remembering how it felt to have

Charlie stand at the outhouse door, she prayed the words again, this time with much more fervor.

Walking back to the house with the eggs held in her apron, she lifted her hair and allowed the breeze to hit the back of her neck. She never cooked this late in the day, and she couldn't bake too late into the evening either, or the house would never cool off.

When she opened the screen door Charlie was standing over the kitchen table looking over the small loaves of cake in their individual pans—and one *empty* pan. The telltale crumbs on his mouth told the story.

"You ate a complete cake!" she accused.

"Almost, until you walked in," he grumbled.

She narrowed her gaze. "Where is the rest of it?"

He opened his hand and showed her a little less than half of the carrot cake left. His expression was as defiant as that of a child caught stealing candy from the counter jug.

"All right, Mr. Macon." She sighed heavily. "Take your time and eat your cake. Then leave fifty cents on the counter." She turned and carefully placed each egg she'd collected in a blue-dotted bowl sitting on the windowsill. All nine of them sat there, looking pretty as a picture.

"Beg your pardon?" he asked, his mouth still full of crumbs.

"That cake cost fifty cents and is for sale. You ate it; please pay for it."

"I will not." He sounded affronted at the suggestion.

She turned slowly. "You will, too." Her voice was solid, strong, and demanding. "You are my guest here and every bite you eat costs me money. That means that you've just stolen from me. Especially since those cakes are how I earn my living." His brows rose in disbelief and she knew he was thinking of his accusation of prostitution. Her voice hardened. "I do not have time to chase across the countryside and make up what you eat, so you will pay your way or find somewhere else to stay while you chase your needle in the haystack."

"Lady, either you've got a lot of nerve or you're crazy," he said, but his voice wasn't quite as disbelieving as it once was.

"Both. I'm a survivor, Mr. Macon. I'm not a rich woman, but I'm a proud one, and I survive by baking. I give my heart to those cakes, and it's paid me back with respect for my ability with flour, eggs, and money to buy what I need. You *will* pay for it."

Charlie stared at her, locking eyes with her for a very long minute. The clock in the living room chimed four-thirty. With slow motions, Charlie reached into his back pocket and dropped several coins on the table. His eyes never left hers. "I just bought a bunch of your cakes."

Kathleen crossed her arms. "And what about the soup last night?"

Charlie closed his eyes, ending the staring contest. "Well, let me see, Miss O'Day. I will pay for your delicious soup or whatever it was, if you will pay me for transportation services in getting you off the side of the road and bringing you home, then undressing you and putting you to bed."

Heat flared in her cheeks. He would have to bring that up. "You're right, Mr. Macon. We'll call your dinner and my transgression even for yesterday. Tonight I'm making ham sandwiches with the fresh-baked bread I just made, so we'll start the bill from here."

"I'll go into town and eat," Charlie stated noncommittally.

"No," she stated quickly. "There are no restaurants in town. You'll need to go to Mason."

"Where's Mason?"

"It's the next town, about twenty miles away. It's where the cattle stop is," she explained. "It's a bigger town and has more visitors, so they're set up for company. They even have a sheriff."

His gaze sharpened. "I thought the nearest sheriff was in Waco."

"Oh, no. Mason has one. He's very nice." *Nice?* What was she saying? Charlie didn't need to know the sheriff was nice! She didn't need to make him any more suspicious than ne already was. She could have slapped herself silly over making such an error, but it didn't seem to register with Charlie. Instead he looked as if he was mulling the information over for his own use, rather than wondering what she was doing knowing the sheriff despite living in such a bad town as Blissful.

"What direction?" he finally asked around another bite of his cake.

Kathleen let out a sigh of relief and began cleaning up the kitchen. The last of the cakes were in the oven, ready to be pulled out in just a few minutes. She would do the rest tomorrow. That way her night wouldn't be filled with heat, too.

She set the empty pan Charlie had left in the bucket filled with soapy water. "Oh, just follow Bliss Creek on down a ways to where it hooks into Spring Creek. It's on the other side."

"Spring Creek?"

Continuing to clean, she nodded. "It goes from behind the mercantile through the side of Blissful until it winds up at the back of the barn. Then it meanders around. From what I understand, it pours into the Colorado about fifty miles from here."

Her heart pounded heavily all through the next hour as she cleaned and put the kitchen to rights. Being around Charlie did that to her. She chalked it up to her upset feelings about him, but the truth was she was more than upset. She seemed to have a reaction that was unique to Charlie.

All day long, bits and pieces of last night had returned to her, reminding her of his touch last night, reminding her of his tenderness as he held her in his arms and carried her from the horse to the house, then to the bedroom. Each time she was jogged, she awoke to feel his rough hands trying not to abrade her skin, his strong arms holding her close to the beat of his heart thudding in his broad hard chest.

As Charlie walked outside, rolled a cigarette, and took a stroll toward the back of the barn and beyond, where the creek lay, Kathleen finished the cleaning. When she was through, she'd milk the cow and then make them both something to eat.

Suddenly being by herself was not quite as important as it had been earlier. Truth to tell, she enjoyed knowing Charlie was on the property and she wasn't all alone. . . .

Charlie took a drag of his hand-rolled cigarette and stared down at the clear-running water. Oak, pine, cottonwood, and a few mesquite ran its border as far as the eye could see. It was fast, deep, and hummed with its own power. Nice.

He tried to make sense out of all the information he'd been given, but his tired mind just didn't want to work well right now.

And this led to the next town down the way—the one with a sheriff that Kathleen was very familiar with. He bet if he asked the man's name, she'd know it.

Yet she chose to live here, in a town that was known for its rough element. Why?

There were more whys. Why was she so damn pretty? Why wasn't she worried about Vic Masters? Why did she want him drugged last night?

He knew she was aware of his every move. Hell, he was even more aware of hers. Not because she had bullied him as he'd bullied her. *Hell, no.*

He was attracted to her as he'd never been attracted to any woman since his wife's death. Not the way a whore attracted a man with a sexual appetite, although he was sexually aware of her in every way possible. Just thinking about her turned him into wood.

Last night when he picked her up, he had smelled the scent of her skin, the very essence of her. He had the richness of her hair in his palms, flowing through his fingers like molten gold, making his calluses seem to fall away and every movement of his hand enrich his experience.

He felt the muscles of her back and arms—the strength of her legs. That strength was made possible by her picking up the buckets she'd picked up again this afternoon. It made her strong and ready to survive, just as she'd said. But over those muscles was skin that was as soft as bread before baking. It was heady feeling her skin, making him so aware of the feminine woman in his arms.

And when he took off her dress, her skin shimmered in the moonlight. He ached to touch her, to explore her inner folds and warm places. Instead he ran his hand lightly over her arm, reminding himself that this was what a woman felt like. What his wife had been like. But Kathleen was *not* his wife. No one could take her place any more than someone could take his place with her. Any more than anyone could take the place of his beautiful daughter, Becca.

Charlie flicked the cigarette into the creek water and watched it float away on the current. Tree leaves and limbs shadow-danced on the water's reflexion. He wanted to sit down on the bank, prop himself against the trunk of a tree, and close his eyes. He was bone weary and ready to sleep for days, except that he couldn't sleep while Kathleen was around. He didn't know what she might do next.

Last night he was afraid she might wake up while he was sleeping and do something silly . . . like kill him. But in the light of day, it was obvious that Kathleen wasn't that kind of woman. In fact, while he watched her bake her cakes, she'd thought he was asleep. He wasn't. Well . . . he wasn't until she went out to gather eggs. Then he instantly fell into a deep, snoring slumber.

But she hadn't done anything that might harm him. She could have. Kathleen had had the knife in her hand several times. It was obvious she knew how to wield it.

So now he had loads of questions and not enough answers. It was time to find out what was going on . . . in the town and in Kathleen's life.

It was obvious she trusted him, but why?

His pappy, worthless man that he was, had one saying that made sense: *Dirt shows up on the cleanest cotton.* Misdeeds by pious people were evident to everyone.

Certainly he could find some dirt on Kathleen.

It was a tough job, but somebody had to do it. Besides, it would keep the nightmares away . . . .

But there was more to it than that.

Five

When Kathleen finished wrapping the cakes in towels and bundling them into baskets, tins, and small wooden drawer-size containers, she was tired and depressed.

It took a lot of work to stay angry.

She milked Hilde, the cow, as the sun set, casting long shadows. Despite waking at noon with a muzzy headache, she felt as though it had been a full day. But she still hadn't found a solution to her uninvited guest. What was she going to do with him? She was just as frightened of having a killer around their small, unprotected town as he was angry about the death of his friend and partner.

If Charlie was right about a killer being in their midst, the whole town was in jeopardy. On the other hand, she didn't know if he was right. She hadn't noticed the horse with the crazy shoes, but Charlie had, and that lent his story a lot of weight. Logic and her friends at the town meeting told her that there were no other strangers around. If there had been, surely someone would have seen him and reported something by now. This town was not only small, but with a secret as big as theirs, they were gossips as well. No one wanted the truth to get out and ruin their moneymaking ability or their upcoming last chance to get the railroad to stop more often. Letting that information out would affect everyone in town.

But Charlie wasn't going to believe her if she told him that. He believed the publicity the surrounding towns had helped promote. If she didn't give Charlie some bait to follow, he'd hang around here all month, and Blissful would lose its only chance at being a regular train stop again.

Kathleen had no choice. She had to confront him and find out what his plans were, one way or the other.

As she walked out of the barn with the cloth-covered pail, the last of the sunset dimmed the western sky, turning it indigo with shards of warm pink. For just a moment she stood poised, marveling at the beauty of it and how much the land suited her.

When she'd lived in North Carolina with her brother, she'd never been outside long enough to marvel at anything. According to John, she was to stay inside and handle all domestic activities—unless she sat on the porch on a warm evening and kept out of the men's conversation. Her brother segregated her from anything that wasn't pertinent to a dim-witted female. In the beginning, it was wonderful. Overworked all her life, she needed the rest. Her father had worked everyone, including herself, to the bone. He didn't care who worked as long as it wasn't him.

Her brother, John, had gone off and made his fortune. He cut an indigo farm out of nothing, working the land and the dye with ex-slaves and giving them a small cut of the proceeds in exchange. It worked.

When her father died, John, ever the dutiful brother, moved her to his home. Then he gave an overseer the run of the property her father owned. He now had two farms working well.

He was conscientious with everyone except his baby sister, who he believed had no right to feelings and emotions. He was giving her a roof over her head and a household to occupy her time.

John believed that as a female, Kathleen was never meant to venture outside into the big bad world. And he met, wooed, and married a woman who fit his ideal. Christina was beautiful, sweet, cheery at any time of the day. And as dumb as dirt.

Christina sat all day giggling with her friends who came to visit and spent half the afternoon lollygagging in her chambers as she dressed for dinner.

John ate it up as if it were ambrosia. To him, Christina was a trophy. She was the mark and measure of a man who could afford the least useful toy in the world. If that was the case, he was rich beyond measure.

Kathleen gagged more than once a day.

Then came the ultimate betrayal by her brother. He managed to wrangle a proposal of marriage from Henry James, two farms over. Henry was ten years older than her brother and drank as much in a day as a whole household drank in a week. His teeth were rotten from sucking on sugarcane, his body odor so strong that even the stench of liquor couldn't cover it. Besides, he'd already gone through two wives. He had three children who, according to him, needed spanking on a daily basis. And he, humbly spoken, stated he was a man who needed a woman's touch.

But he was an able farmer and had a nice spread. It would go to his oldest son when he was gone. That son was no prize either.

Somehow Kathleen couldn't imagine touching Henry. The very thought made her sick.

Then, in the midst of despair of never making her brother understand that money wasn't everything, especially in Henry's case, Kathleen wrote about the problems to her Aunt Hattie, who was the only living relative she knew. Her aunt and uncle had settled in Texas twelve years earlier. Within a month she had her answer: *Come out to Texas and visit for the summer.* Her aunt was a widow woman now and would love the company. Enclosed was a railway ticket.

Kathleen did so immediately and never returned to her brother's farm, preferring to be with Hattie on the frontier forever.

Even with John's written tirades demanding she return instantly, she'd never left. And she wouldn't— not for John, not for Vic whoever, not for Charlie, not for the dying town. She would stay here until she was old and wrinkled and had a dozen cats sitting in her lap as she watched another sunset from her rocker on the porch.

There was a certain amount of freedom here that she could never have in the East: an ability to do and be the best she could. If she didn't meet the challenges, then it was *her* fault, not someone else's. She held the key to her own happiness.

She wasn't the least bit surprised to hear Charlie's voice interrupt her reverie.

"Thinking about the one that got away?"

Kathleen smiled without looking at him. Her gaze was still on the last shards of pink dwindling to deep blue. "I *am* the one who got away."

"I see," he said, a quiet note of surprise in his voice. "And where did you get away from?"

It wouldn't hurt to tell him. "North Carolina," she said softly.

"That's a beautiful state."

"It certainly is."

"And has the big Atlantic Ocean right there."

She nodded. "It does. I've seen it. Water as far as the eye can see."

"It's really something, isn't it?"

Kathleen smiled. "Yes. It reminds me of the Texas plains around Amarillo. All that golden grass waving in the breeze."

Charlie gave a low sound that reminded her of a yes. "You're a long way from home."

She didn't look at him. Instead she lowered the bucket to the ground and massaged her hands. "No, Mr. Macon, I *am* home."

He continued to probe, like a toothpick hitting a toothache. "Nobody back in North Carolina is waiting for you?"

She carefully kept her tone even. "If they are, they can wait till the cows come home a thousand times and then some."

Charlie leaned against the gate next to the little barn. It led into a small corral where the horses were penned. "Who?"

She was in the calmest mood she'd been in for a long time. She placed the pail on the ground and walked over to the corral fence. Immediately her old horse came over, nudging her hand for a pat. She stroked his nose. "My brother, John, still lives there with his wife," she said quietly. "He tries to control everything. And he was never sure what to do with me."

"Were you so hard to get along with?" Charlie asked, his voice soothing in its timbre.

She laughed. "*You* might think so, but no. I was used to working from dawn to dusk for my father. John wanted to pretend that we were always wealthy and that I wasn't raised to have a brain in my head. I was supposed to sew all day, stay out of the sun, and smile at people I didn't know." She smiled. "He didn't seem to think I should want to do more than that."

Charlie chuckled, low and deep and easy. The sound was musical and warmed her in places she was surprised to notice. "I've known you for only three days and I know better than that," he said. "What about your parents?"

That sad feeling she always got when she thought of them came to her again. "My mom died of influenza when I was twelve. My dad died six years ago on my twentieth birthday."

"I'm sorry."

He obviously didn't know her parents. The horse neighed quietly. "So am I," she said, but not for the same reasons he was. Her father did not have children; he had workers he grudgingly fed because it was expected.

"Then what happened?"

"While I lived with my father, my brother went off to seek his fortune. When John returned, he'd won some land and began an indigo farm. It's done well for him." The fading sun moved a notch closer to the horizon, shooting shards of pink across the growing indigo sky.

"And you? With all these male relatives, how did you escape to Texas?"

"My Aunt Hattie married late in life and had come here years ago. She and Uncle Harold had a vegetable farm, doing a little cattle raising on the side. When he died, Aunt Hattie kept up the farm until the railroad decided there wasn't enough business in Blissful to allow the train to load livestock or farm produce here. They wanted us to truck our goods over twenty miles to Mason, where we would fill out a sheet ahead of time so they would know how many cars they needed. It wouldn't have done us any good because in a month our vegetables would have rotted on the dock. Or they would have gone bad in the wagon as we struggled to take them down the road to sell.''

"But it stops now.''

"Only once every other week and only for ten minutes. The men are fast, and load our stuff well and quickly. But we need more of a stop than that so we can open our hotel again, get our cattle to market without the families separating for trail rides, and get visiting money back into our coffers.''

"So that's what happened,'' he murmured, then frowned.

"It used to stop twice a week to allow heavy loads like produce and cattle on. But it doesn't now.''

"Why?''

"Because the bigwigs in the railroad offices can get our produce on down the line. And soon maybe they'll change that stop, too, and there will be none within hundreds of miles.'' She sounded disgusted but she didn't care. Those holier-than-thou men could just eat her produce if they didn't like her attitude.

"No, I mean why did they change their mind and begin stopping once a week? This town has the worst reputation in the West.''

He was getting too close to the truth. What could she say? Her mind scrambled for another topic. "Who knows? We're just glad it's one time a week.'' She turned and looked at him in the dim light. She could smell the scent of him. It wasn't sweat, but it was musty. Natural male. Interesting. "What about you? Where are you from, Charlie Macon?"

"Oklahoma." He leaned back again. "You know that golden grass you were talking about in the panhandle?" She nodded. "Well, it's the same way in Oklahoma, except that the dirt is a rich red." His voice warmed with the texture of his thoughts.

"You miss it," she guessed.

"Yes." It was simply said but it resonated with a thousand unstated words.

"Do you have family?"

He sighed heavily, the sound standing between them like a lost memory. "I lost my wife four years ago. My daughter, Becca, lives with her grandparents in St. Louis. She's such a pretty thing. She looks just like her mama."

Kathleen searched his face and saw the pain there. He was feeling every word he said. "But why?" she asked. "Why would you leave your daughter with her grandparents?"

"Because she needed a woman's touch. She needed a mother."

"She needs a parent who loves her."

"Her grandparents love her."

Silence that served as condemnation fell between them. She had so much to say on the matter, and he had to give her credit for not jumping in and telling him off.

Slowly, the tension eased with every dram of light that was lost.

In the dim light, Charlie pushed the brim of his hat further up his forehead and narrowed his eyes as he looked at her. She was just about his shoulder height. That was a respectable height for a woman.

In fact, everything about her was a respectable size. His gaze drifted lower to encompass her breasts pressing tightly against the faded gingham dress she wore. They pushed against the fabric, begging to be free. Calling out . . .

He sighed. There he was, getting off track again. "I'll tell you what, Miss O'Day. You don't want me here and I don't want to be here. I've got a ranch to work and a life to get back to, pronto. As soon as I find Vic and take his hide back to jail so I can see he's hanged nice and proper, I can get on with my life and you can get on with yours."

"I told you—" she said, stiffening in anger even as he was speaking. He could tell she had a lot to say on the subject, but he didn't want to go through all that again. It was time to lasso the calf and brand him for his owner.

He held up his hand as if stopping traffic in town. "Now just hear me out before you go all hot on me. I'm trying to solve our problems, not add fuel to the fire, ma'am."

Kathleen crossed her arms and stared back at him, her green eyes as level as a playing field. "And your suggestion is . . . ?"

"I suggest you tell your neighbors that I'm a long-lost relative come to visit. I'll snoop around until I find the son of a bitch I'm after, and then I'll wave adios to you with a smile and a criminal in tow, and ride off into the sunset."

"Have you been reading those dime novels in the front bedroom?" she asked, accusation in her voice.

"No, ma'am. I don't believe in them." He stared at her disapprovingly. "And I might add that I'm a bit surprised that you would read them."

"I don't. I inherited them from my aunt. She loved them and couldn't wait for the train to arrive with the latest issues," she said, relaxing a little. But she still had a wary look in her eyes that he could see, even in the dimming light. "What choice do I have?" she asked, bringing him back to the problems at hand.

He was proud of himself for persuading her to go along with his line of thinking. So far he was doing a pretty good job. That wasn't bad for a man whose wife used to say he never communicated enough. "You can fight me every inch of the way, but it wouldn't solve your problem," he suggested. "I would still be around here, snooping into the townsfolk's personal business and seeing who has what guests. I'd still be doing what I'm going to do, which is find Vic Masters. Only, I'd be doing it in a way you probably would have a hard time explaining." He gave a knowing smile. "Especially if you are not Vic's lady of the evening."

"So what is new about that thought?"

He was going to have to spell it out, even though she knew where he was going with his thought. He just had to be patient if he wanted to have his way. "If you help me, I'll try to maintain your reputation while I find Vic. If you don't help me, I'll do it anyway, but your fair community might not look at you the same way they do now."

"Is this blackmail?"

"No." He crossed his arms and stared her down. *Damn the woman.* She wouldn't back down.

But the tension around her beautiful green eyes seemed to ease considerably. "If I give you a family role to fill, will you keep to it?" she finally asked.

At just that moment a star in the heavens twinkled brightly just above her head.

"I promise. To the best of my ability," he said as if it were a vow. "And will you promise to allow me to act like a relative in public without gettin' in the way of my investigation?''

"I promise," she answered, and as Charlie watched the words roll off her tongue, watched her form sounds with her lips, he felt himself harden with a bright bolt of desire. She made him remember he was a man, planting sexy thoughts in his head he hadn't thought in a very long time. She had the prettiest lips he'd ever seen . . . .

He looked away. What the hell was the matter with him? He wasn't used to these feelings and he sure as hell didn't like them interfering with him now.

"Now what?" she asked.

"I guess you'd better tell me your plans and I'll tell you mine. Then maybe we can cook up a story that might stick."

A slow smile broke across her face. "I think I might be able to help there," she said softly, reaching for her milk bucket again. "I've been known to weave a good tale when the need arises."

"I believe that," he said, fascinated with every sensuous movement she made—and to his mind, they were all sensuous.

"Don't jump to conclusions, Charlie. They would be the wrong ones for sure."

"Of course they would," he soothed. "Just because I heard your plans to kill a sheriff that wasn't even hired yet doesn't mean I don't trust you."

"And don't get too smart-mouthed, either," she said, walking to the milk bucket and then heading toward the back of the house. "Or it won't work for either of us."

"I'll make it work," he said, following her up the steps and into the kitchen, his eyes moving back and forth with every swing of her hips.

"Then shouldn't you be a sweet brother and carry this bucket instead of me?"

Charlie chuckled and reached for the bucket handle as she slipped inside the screen door. "Brother, huh?" he asked, setting the milk on the table without a single slosh. "We don't look alike," he mentioned, his gaze scanning the length of her hair, barely kept in check by a yellow ribbon. Her creamy skin and flaming hair had to be a family trait.

Kathleen tilted her head and studied him. "Hmmm. It's obvious we don't have the same father, but we could still share the same mother. Especially if we worked it out ahead of time."

Charlie's brows rose. "Not the same daddy? Why?"

"Because my name is O'Day and you are a Macon. Irish and German."

"I could be an O'Day."

She shook her head. "No. You're not dark enough to be what my mama used to call black Irish, and you're certainly not fair enough to look as if we had the same parents. So we'll settle for what most people would believe."

"All right," he said, intrigued in spite of himself. "What else?"

"Well," she began, her brow furrowing with thought. "You can be my brother, John, from North Carolina. You have come to Blissful to see if I want to come home and help with the new baby your wife will have in another month or two. Of course"—she smiled—"my answer is no. But you decided to spend a couple of weeks with your dear sister before you go back to the farm, where you grow indigo and cotton."

"Let me guess," Charlie stated dryly. "Your brother really does want you home with him and his new bride."

Kathleen stood straight, her eyes dancing with fire.

All the words that poured through her look finally died before they reached her tongue. "Yes."

He couldn't help goading her. He wanted to watch her reaction, to see what she would say or do that was unexpected.

"That's it? Just yes?"

She nodded her head. "Yes, John."

"I don't like the name John."

Kathleen gave a shrug. "I'm so sorry. But you have no choice."

"Can't I be your other brother? The one named Charlie?"

"No."

"Sure I can." He gave her his best smile. It was too bad it was so dark that she couldn't see the full effect. "Why, I bet you'd take to me like a bean stalk to sun if my name was Charlie and I was your long-lost, favorite brother."

Kathleen turned and reached for the matches, then lit the lantern standing on the kitchen table. The smell of sulfur filled his nostrils while the gleam of golden light became brighter and spilled to the dark corners of the room.

"No."

"You could at least think about it."

She moved aside the small rag rug, bent down, and opened the root cellar door. Then she headed down the stairs with the bucket she'd just filled with milk. "No."

She was the most stubborn woman Charlie had ever met. His wife could have taken lessons from this one. Why did she have to be so contrary? "I'm Charlie Macon, your long-lost brother from South Carolina I was raised by my grandmother while you stayed with our daddy."

Her voice echoed through the small cellar. "No."

"Don't I have any say in this?"

"No." Her head popped up from the opening and then she stepped up and faced him, hands on her hips. "Please listen to me carefully, Charlie Macon. If you want to stay here as a relative and find your man, you'll have to do it my way. Most of these towns-folk know me, and they *all* knew my aunt. They know the history of my family fairly well. The story I told you is about the only story we can get away with. Since that's the case, we will use it. Anything else will be seen through and you'll be branded a liar. More important, so will I. I am not willing to lose my respect, my reputation, or my place in this town. I am not willing to lose anything so you can find your man."

She took a step closer to him and a light whiff of woman hit him. He took a deep breath, his thoughts going everywhere but on the words she just spoke. "Do you hear me?"

He shook his head to dispel the images that flooded his mind. Suddenly the words made sense. "Yes. But I don't like it."

"Neither one of us does, but that's the way things are. At least for now."

The creak of wagon springs and the neigh of a horse filtered through the open windows, stopping both of them in their argument.

Charlie looked at Kathleen and she returned that look. *Who?* he mouthed.

"Brother, dear"—Kathleen laughed—"it's proba-bly Zeke, a neighbor I would love for you to meet!" she exclaimed, acting delighted at the prospect, but her eyes warned him to play his part to the hilt. Kathleen ran into the living room and threw open the front door. "Zeke? Is that you?"

"Yes, missy," a gravelly voice answered in the dark-

ness. "I was jes' checking to see if you was coming
to the town hall meetin' on Friday."

"Of course," she said, still acting delighted. "But
come in and meet my brother! He just rode in." She
opened the door wider. "I know he'd love to meet
you, too, Zeke. He needs to know how much my
neighbors care for me."

After carefully scraping his dirt-laden boots, Zeke
stepped into the parlor. He wore worn bib pants and
a threadbare plaid shirt that looked as if it needed
one more washing before completely falling apart.
His hat brim, now in his hand, was as wide as the
land outside, and practically as shapeless. His bald
pate shone even in the dim light coming from the
kitchen.

His glance skittered around the darkened room.
Charlie stood in the entrance to the kitchen, taking
up the whole doorway. Zeke, looked him over, staying
on the other side of the room. It was up to Charlie
to put him at ease.

Charlie pulled his hands out of his pockets and
strode toward the older man. He reminded Charlie
of a weasel: small and skittish, ready to bolt immediately. But the man's watery eyes glowed in the dark,
reflecting the dim light. "Hi, I'm John," he said with
a smile in his tone. "Kathleen has written me about
you. Thanks for helping her settle in this community."

Zeke's hand bolted out, touched Charlie, then
released quickly. "Nothin' to it," he mumbled, clearly
anxious to get out as quickly as possible. "We all try
to keep an eye on each other. Any neighbor'd do the
same."

Charlie recognized the voice. It was the same voice
that had discussed killing the sheriff the day Charlie

stood under the window and listened to the conversation. The day Charlie had tracked Vic here.

"Well, I'm glad to meet you." Charlie tried to sound happy the scrap of an old man was standing in his "sister's" parlor when he should be behind bars in some prison . . . if Blissful had a prison. "I'm trying to talk my sister into returning home with me."

Zeke's eyes widened into big holes of watery light. "Home? Home where?"

"Why, North Carolina, of course."

"No!" Zeke stated, clearly astounded. He gave a big swallow. "You're joshing me!"

"Yes," Charlie stated calmly. "After all, she belongs with her family."

A match sizzled and the room lit with golden light.

While they had been sizing each other up in the dark, Kathleen had found the matches and lit the ornate oil lamp sitting on the lace scarf covering a Victorian table.

"There," she said with a smile as both pairs of eyes turned toward her. "Now, Zeke, don't you worry. My brother understands that I love it here and want to remain. He's just doing his brotherly duty by making sure I know what I want. After a wonderful visit for a week or two, I'm sure he'll understand that this is where my heart is. Then he will return home to his wife, who is ready to make him a brand-new father for the first time." She smiled brightly. "My brother is making his own family."

"But I always have room to take care of my sister, sister."

"How sweet," she said, but her eyes didn't show her gratitude. Instead they wanted him out of the room.

Charlie had nothing to lose by leaving. He could always eavesdrop and learn more. " 'Scuse me," he

said, placing his hat back on his head. "I'm needin'
to check on my horse. After all, I gave my sister a
week to say her good-byes. Then I'll just take her back
home, whether she likes it or not."

"John!" Kathleen's voice exclaimed.

"Spittoon in the kitchen corner, Zeke," Charlie
said just before walking around the kitchen table.

"John!"

But he was too busy leaving the room to be detained
by her admonitions.

Thank goodness she couldn't see the smile on his
lips. He'd bet the town would have something to talk
about at the next meeting. And it wouldn't be killing
a sheriff they didn't yet have . . . .

Six

Kathleen had never felt such anger as she experienced watching Charlie's back disappear into the kitchen. That man was a gunfight looking to happen! Who did he think he was baiting? And why? Did he get sadistic pleasure out of baiting her for no reason?

Zeke danced around the room as though he were dodging slings and arrows, his gaze darting everywhere he wasn't. "Did you tell him? Does he know about us? About the town? Are you goin' back with him?"

"Stop jumping around, Zeke or you'll bounce through my floor," she whispered crossly.

"Well, then, missy, tell me what's goin' on!"

"My brother wants me to go home to help take care of his wife and child. But he has plenty of help and I'm staying right here."

"He can't make you?" Zeke asked, disbelieving such a thing as a woman could stand up to a man of John's stature.

"Of course not!"

"Then why not write you a letter? Huh? Why not?"

She tried to be patient, but it took everything she had to concentrate on Zeke and not on Charlie . . . John. "Because John wanted to see me. I'm his sister. We miss each other."

Zeke's sharp black eyes narrowed. "You never said you missed him. Not ever."

"I don't say everything I feel, Zeke. No one does," she said. "Except you."

"Since you didn' see fit to bring him to the last meetin', are you gonna bring him to the next one?"

"No. He's only here for a visit."

"But he's your brother, ain't he? Why don'tcha trust him?"

Zeke was nothing if not sneaky. And he was always more astute than people gave him credit for. This was just one of the times he proved it. "I don't trust him because he wants me back at his home, and might use the danger of our, uh, situation to do that," she said softly. "I'm not taking any chances on giving my brother ammunition to use to get me back to North Carolina."

"He don't talk like he's from there," Zeke said, still suspicious.

Kathleen wished Zeke weren't quite as astute as he was.

"Well, he is," she snapped. "My father was from north New York. Maybe John acquired his accent."

"Don't you know?"

"I never paid attention," she said with an edge to her voice. "What did you come here for, Zeke? Certainly you didn't know John was here yet."

"No, but I thought I'd let you know that Mabel was writin' something for the next robbery."

"After this one, we won't be doing a robbery for almost a month. She knows the schedule."

"I know, but she said she had an idea and that she wanted to start on it now. It must be a doozy, 'cause her cheeks were high with color, like she was sick. Never saw her lookin' that way unless she was sick or somethin'."

She angled toward the door. "Well, I appreciate your telling me." She wanted Zeke gone so she and Charlie could work on their story a little more. Zeke had brought up some interesting questions they needed answers for.

Zeke looked a little disappointed. "I was headin' home and jes' thought I'd tell ye what's goin' on an' all." His gaze flew toward the kitchen. "I thought if ye wasn't busy, ye'd make me one of your famous sandwiches an' I wouldn' hafta cook up somethin'."

She relaxed. About once or twice a month Zeke dropped by for supper. With Charlie here, she'd forgotten it had been a while since Zeke had tasted her cooking. "Sorry. But with my brother here . . . "

"I know, I know," he said, disappointment lacing his tone. Then he gave an instant grin that made him look like an Irish leprechaun. "I need to go check on Mrs. Heine anyway. She's been after me to taste her wunnerful German dumplin'."

"Tonight's the night." Kathleen laughed. "Meanwhile, I'll see you tomorrow night at the meeting."

"Right," Zeke said. Then he cupped his hands and shouted toward the kitchen as if it were a mile away. "Good-bye, there, Mr. John."

No answer.

Kathleen wondered where Charlie was, but she wasn't about to let Zeke know she was concerned. "He probably stepped outside," she said.

"Well, tell 'im I was polite," Zeke said as he made

it to the door. Now that he had another destination in mind for dinner, he obviously wanted to get there as soon as possible. "See you later. An' call on me if you need me."

"I promise I will," she said, equally as quiet. "Tell Mrs. Heine hello for me."

"I'll try. It won't be easy seein' as she don't speak much English and I don't speak no German."

"You've found a way to communicate so far, Zeke. Don't let a little thing like a language barrier stop you now."

His answer was a laugh and a wave of his hand as he hitched himself up on the wagon and headed back out toward the dirt track.

She felt rather than heard the closing of the back screen door. Then Charlie stepped out from the shadows and back into the parlor. "What robbery?"

"Robbery?" She acted confused, as if forgetting the conversation with Zeke.

He wasn't a patient man. "Answer me."

"You weren't supposed to be listening to a private conversation."

"You aren't supposed to be planning a robbery."

"I'm not." She busied herself by rearranging the shawl on the back of her sofa, covering the worn spot it hid. "It's not what you think."

"Then what is it?"

He just wouldn't let it go. She stood and faced him, her eyes as level as she could make them, considering he was several inches taller than she was. "We have a writer's group of women, and that's the next challenge to write about," Kathleen stated evenly, thankful that she had thought up that answer earlier.

"That's a crock."

She raised a brow. "Really? I doubt if you would

know a crock of anything without sampling it to the bottom of the bowl.''

"And what would you do?''

"Lift a lid and sniff, Mr. Macon. Then I'd know whether it's the truth or not. My explanation stands. And if you were a family man in a close-knit community, you'd know that.''

"I thought this was supposed to be the worst town in the West?'' His words were thrown out like a gauntlet.

She was up to picking them up and fighting back. "That doesn't mean that we don't fight back. And someday we'll win, Mr. Macon. This town has families and children and women who care. The very same women who won the rest of the West.'' She stood tall and proud as fire burned in her leaf-colored eyes. If he'd been any closer he'd have felt the heat of her body. "Not the men. Women. Men just keep fighting like children who won't share toys. Women keep the peace and insure the family goes on. And in time we'll do the same in this small community, Mr. Macon. In spite of you men and your childish ways.''

He gave a half smile. "You've told me off good and proper, Miss O'Day. Do you feel better?''

"Not until you agree and apologize for accusing me of more crimes. After all, you're the one after a bad man. The key word is *man*, Mr. Macon.''

Charlie's gaze narrowed, knife sharp. "You're asking for an apology because I questioned you about a robbery?''

She stood defiantly. "Yes.''

"Well, you'll get it when hell freezes over,'' he said, his voice rising with each word until the last word was strident as it echoed through the room.

"When you apologize is up to you.'' He would change his mind and they would both know who was boss here. She hadn't lived with her father and brother for nothing. They had taught her just what stubborn was, and Charlie or John, or whatever he wanted to be called, would find that out.

Kathleen walked to the spare bedroom door and opened it. "Sheets are in the bottom drawer, window gets stuck, and there's a blanket at the foot of the bed. Food is in the cellar, as you've already discovered. You are on your own, dear brother. Don't expect anything from me until you apologize."

Being sure not to touch him, Kathleen walked around his large male frame and into the kitchen. After picking up her favorite large knife, she went down the cellar ladder. She sliced off a hunk of ham, then unwrapped the cheese Mrs. Donaldson had made and sliced off some of that, too. All the while, anger fed her movements. She sawed through her freshly baked bread until there was just enough for her, then strode up the ladder stairs with her hands full of her dinner.

Charlie waited at the top. "What is that?" he asked, eyeing her full hands.

"My dinner."

She stepped around him again and headed for the table, spreading her bounty out. Grabbing a wooden plate, she arranged her food on the freshly cut bread, topping it off with freshly made warm butter.

"You wouldn't even get some for me?" He looked crushed and hurt. "I wouldn't do that to you."

She closed her heart to the gentle censure in his voice. It was a ruse, something he did when he wanted his way. Not this time. "That's your option, John. My option is to choose not to wait on you for any reason until my sense of decency is assuaged."

"You won't tell me about a robbery you're involved with and I'm supposed to apologize?"

"Yes. I told you I wasn't involved with anything.

And this town is just trying to retain its own dignity. You have to take my word for that or leave—or apologize.''

He gave a sigh that filled the room with regret. "I'm damned if I understand this, but I'm sorry."

Kathleen lifted her sandwich and held it in front of her mouth. "Thank you for that." And then she took a big bite, closing her eyes while she chewed.

When she opened her eyes, he was staring at her meal. "Will you make me one of those?" It was said in a nice, gentlemanly tone.

"No. But you know where everything is. You can do it yourself."

"But I apologized!" he said, clearly hurt and not quite sure what he'd done wrong.

"I know, and I accepted." She daintily talked around another bite. "That doesn't mean I have to wait on you."

"That's no way to treat a brother or a guest."

"We both know you are neither, so please don't press the issue. Besides, I never waited on my brother, either. He's a big boy and can do so himself." She took another bite. "Or hire someone."

"I'll hire you," Charlie said.

She looked up, startled. Why on earth would he hire someone when the food was just down the ladder in the cellar? As she looked into his eyes, she saw the glint there. He was teasing. He was playing. For the first time she saw his sense of humor and it gave her a warm feeling. Her body relaxed, eased, and she felt as warm as his look. "Why, Charlie Macon, you devil, you."

His twinkle spread to a grin. "It's about time you noticed. I thought I'd have to grow bigger horns."

Before she could finish the thought, Charlie made

his way down the ladder. A low curse, several scratches of matches, and two or three minutes later he was upstairs with his hands full of ham, cheese, and bread.

Kathleen didn't bother telling him he'd chosen the two-week-old bread she'd kept for the birds. He'd find out soon enough. Instead she cleaned up her place, then gave a delicate stretch.

"Good night, brother. I'll see you in the morning."

"Good night, dear sister," he said without looking up. He was sawing on the old loaf of bread, his jaw clenched. "Sleep well and don't try anything."

"Don't worry. Just behave yourself." She walked into her bedroom and shut the door quietly. The thought of a hungry Charlie trying to make a sandwich out of a stale brick of bread almost made her feel sorry enough to help. Almost. It was a good thing she removed herself from temptation. He deserved his cold dinner.

She slipped out of her dress and hung it on the wooden peg on the back of the door, then reached for her nightgown on another peg. Within minutes she was in bed, snuggling down and staring through the open window as a light night breeze ruffled the curtains. It was a beautiful night—a night to share with someone.

Not with Charlie.

A night to be outside and enjoy the clear, starry skies.

Not with Charlie.

A night to feel the breeze on her skin and thank her lucky stars that she was in Blissful.

"Not with Charlie," she whispered to the darkness. The darkness never answered back.

Slowly, inevitably, her eyes drifted closed and she fell into a deep, comforting sleep.

*   *   *

Charlie finally cut the crust off the bread and used only the middle to make his sandwich. Then he abandoned that idea, instead rolling the ham around a piece of cheese and biting into it with gusto. He was starved. Along with it he drank a large cup of fresh milk, the foam tickling his upper lip. Without giving it a second thought, he cut half a loaf of carrot cake and walked outside to sit on the steps, stare at the moon, and eat the sweet in darkness. It was delicious.

He felt no compunction about eating the cake. After all, Kathleen hadn't helped at all in his meal; why should he help with hers? But a tiny niggling piece of guilt grew in the back of his thoughts, taking away from the full enjoyment of sitting on the steps on a perfect evening and knowing that he didn't have to curl up on the hard ground. Instead, just one thin wall away from Kathleen was a bed with his blanket on it.

Charlie finished off the last of the cake crumbs, relishing every chew of it. For just a moment he wanted to get the rest of the cake and eat it, too, but he thought better of it. After all, he'd wanted only enough to ease the hunger that had come over him, not to irritate her so much that she called on the town to hang him.

Feeling all was well with the world, he stood, stretched, and made his way back into the house. He latched the back door, then turned down the lamp wick until the flame died, doing the same in the parlor.

Then, with steps as quiet as he could make them, he tiptoed across the room and found his way to the bed. After taking off his boots and setting them carefully on the side of the bed where he could reach

them in a second, he lay back on the bed and pulled
the worn horse blanket over his clothed body.

He was asleep before he got to think one more
thought.

Kathleen stood at the indoor pump and galvanized
tub, her slim back rigid and her movements jerky.
Her hair was balanced haphazardly on top of her
head, and curling tendrils drifted down her back and
shoulders, as if it was too much volume to be deco-
rous. Morning sunshine poured through the kitchen
window and door, lighting her hair to the brilliant
color of a dancing forest fire.

"Good morning," Charlie said, his smile evident
in his voice. It was his best night's sleep in a week of
Sundays. He wasn't on the ground, worried around
being killed in his sleep or scared that the woman in
the next room would set off an alarm that would
bring the townsfolk running for all the wrong reasons.
He'd slept for a straight ten hours and it felt great.

Kathleen didn't turn around. She scrubbed something in the tub and her motions kept her bobbing
up and down, making the thin material of her skirt
mold and form to her waist and rounded bottom.
It was a delightful sight to watch—hypnotizing, like
staring at his mama's wound-up metronome when he
was a kid. Only his immediate reaction wasn't that of
any kid he knew. He felt hard as a rock just looking
at her.

"This just won't work," she said, slightly out of
breath and her voice flat. "It just won't work at all."

Charlie adjusted parts she couldn't see with her
back turned toward him, then poured himself a cup
from the pot on the potbellied stove. "Why not?"

"First of all, don't scratch in the kitchen," she said

without turning around. "It's probably from that flea-bitten blanket you brought into the house without my permission. Now I'll have a devil of a time getting the fleas out."

"Sorry," he mumbled around the cup. She was right. He should have left it outside to air. He'd do that today, just for her. Then he'd use her quilt until it was time to leave. A clean covering—one that smelled like fresh lavender and springtime sun. And Kathleen. "I'll use yours."

Kathleen turned then, staring him down with a look that could have frozen a pail of water. The sun was right behind her, lighting her hair as if she were wearing a halo. "You will leave now."

His brows rose. "Why?"

"Because you bring bugs into my home, you scratch in the kitchen, and you interrupt my sleep."

Now he was confused. "How?"

She waved her hand in the air as if dismissing the question. "It doesn't matter. You just do."

"Well, hell, woman. That's not enough. You just introduced me to your buddy, Zeke, as your brother. I'm going into town today as John, and I'm not leaving this place until I find Vic or find out that he's moved on. When that happens, I'll leave. Until then, get used to it." As if to emphasize his words, he scratched at his chest through the shirt and undershirt fabric. If possible, her look became even more disdainful.

If Charlie could burp on command, this would be the perfect time to do so. *Darn.* Some people had all the talent.

"This isn't working out."

"You keep saying that, but I don't think you know what you want."

"I want someone who helps instead of makes a mess. I want someone who can pull his share, not make extra work for me. I want someone who will fit into the community, not have it in an uproar.''

''Well, lady. Why don't you give me your pattern, but make sure you give me an exact size. I'm not the best seamstress, but I'll damn well give it a try.''

Tears sprang to her bright green eyes, making them glisten like emeralds. ''I . . . I . . .'' Instead of finishing, she walked to the door and stepped outside. A few minutes later, Charlie saw her walking across the field to Bliss Creek beyond. She was obviously distressed and there was nothing he could do to help her. Hell, he couldn't do anything with a crying woman. They were beyond his ken.

It brought back memories of his marriage, and how helpless he'd been then, too. But his darling wife had given him a piece of information that was most useful today: *I just want to be alone for a while, darling. Occasionally let me figure out my own thoughts without your help. It will be better that way.*

Well, he'd stay away from the redheaded woman in the yard, too.

His eyes touched on the galvanized tub. It was filled with something she was cleaning. He dipped his hand in and pulled out a piece of fabric. It was the kitchen rag rug, dirty from his boots. The first night he'd entered her home he'd tracked mud from one end to the other. Reaching in again, he found the one that was in her bedroom at the foot of the bed by the rocker. He'd forgotten that.

''Damn,'' he muttered softly under his breath. *Women.*

Like a man resigned to his fate, he rolled up his sleeves and began scrubbing the material against the metal board. Then he clumsily rinsed it under fresh pump water and carried it, dripping, to the backyard clothesline. With as much creativity as he could muster, he draped the rugs over the lines. With a prayer that they would stay where he put them, he went back inside.

It was time to clean up and act like a brother who wanted his sister back—not some mad dog in heat who felt guilty for being in the way of a woman's already lonely life.

"Damn." He sighed once more in resignation.

Kathleen allowed her eyes to adjust to the dim light of the barn. The smell of dry hay and freshly milked cow filled her nostrils. It was reassuring to see that things were the same here. They were supposed to be. It made her believe all was right with the world.

Well, almost.

Everything *would* be all right once Charlie Macon found his man and left. Meanwhile, she had a life to live and a town to help save. She had to remember that.

Wind rustled leaves just behind her and she turned to look out the back of the barn. A deer stood perfectly still, looking more like a painting from one of the town magazines than like a real animal. A buck, his head tilted up, sniffed the wind. He must have felt safe, because in a moment he began grazing again.

As silently as she could, Kathleen reached for her rifle, kept behind a slicker hanging on the wall. It was there for emergencies when she was away from the house . . . and her pistol. Soon the heat of the summer would make it impossible for her to have meat unless she bought it from Mr. Horst, the butcher. This was a golden opportunity.

She raised the gun and took careful aim. With her finger tightening slowly on the trigger, she was about to have deer meat—until the screen door slammed and the stag bolted in the blink of an eye.

"Kathleen?"

Anger welled up inside her breast until she thought she would explode with it. "How could you do that?" She turned to confront him, barely managing the words. "How could you be so loud and unruly?"

Charlie's hands came up in surrender. "Whoa, now wait a minute, lady. I didn't mean any harm. I haven't done anything that deserves shooting."

"That's what you think," she said, her anger still burning through and staining her thoughts. "If I had the nerve, I'd serve you up for dinner instead of the buck you just helped get away."

He looked blank. "Buck?"

"You heard me."

"Where?"

"At the stream." The gun was getting too heavy for her, and she slowly lowered it to aim at the ground. "Or it was until you slammed the door and startled it right out of my sight."

Charlie's hands drifted down to his sides. His frame was outlined by the doors and the sunlight, tall and straight and handsome in a manly kind of way. "I scared away the buck."

She sighed heavily, her exasperation as close to the surface as ever. "Yes."

Charlie walked toward her slowly, as if not to remind her of the gun in her hand. It was all right with her. Her arms were tired. She'd been scrubbing and cleaning all morning before milking and finding the eggs and stacking wood up to the side of the house for cooking later.

Her anger, so heated, was now drained, leaving her feeling deflated and out of sorts. She wasn't sure why.

When he reached out and took the gun barrel in

his hand, she let the weight go completely. "That's a girl," he said, as if gentling a horse. "Where do you keep this?"

"Behind the poncho," she said, waving her hand in the general direction. But her eyes never left his.

"Over here?" he asked as he placed the rifle, butt down, behind the material.

She nodded, but didn't answer.

"Do you always keep it here?" he asked softly, walking to stand in front of her, his belt buckle almost touching her just above her waist.

"Yes," she whispered, looking up into his face. Something was building, something new and foreign, sending her nerves to a new, heightened awareness.

For the first time she noticed the delightfully sexy crinkles at the corners of his deep brown eyes and the soft smile that framed his mouth into something wonderful. "Were you going to shoot me?"

"No. Yes. Well," she finally said, "maybe. I was angry at losing the buck."

"And at me for bringing dirt into your spinsterlike home."

"That, too," she admitted.

"Kathleen," he said, stumbling for the right words. She placed her hands upon his chest.

His heart beat so rapidly against her palms that she felt as if her hands were moving with each beat. Astoundingly, she realized her own heart was working the same way—like a bird battering against the ribs of its cage.

"Kathleen," he said again, but this time it was a whisper.

She looked from her hands on his chest to his face. "Yes."

It was the answer to his unasked question.

Charlie bent his head, his hat giving even more

shadow to his features. Kathleen waited, craving what was going to happen next. He was going to kiss her and stop all the speculation that her day thoughts and night dreams had been preoccupied with. She wouldn't have to wonder anymore, but would know they were wrong for each other. Know for a fact.

And then his mouth slowly moved to cover hers, his lips so gentle yet firm. Her arms crept up his broad expanse of chest to his shoulders, then held on for dear life as he took control and the world spun out of control.

His tongue met and danced with hers, lightly, tenderly. His arms circled and enfolded her against his chest, their beating hearts coinciding with each other.

And as suddenly as she didn't want to know they were right for each other, she also knew she was doomed.

Damn the man. He did good.

Seven

Charlie pulled away reluctantly, his breath hot against her cheek. "Damn. I didn't mean for that to happen."

Her quickening heart wouldn't stop fluttering. Her thoughts swam in a warm pool that didn't allow her to focus on anything but Charlie holding her safely in his arms.

She swallowed, slowly licking her lips to keep the taste of him on the tip of her tongue. "Neither did I."

"Don't do that!" he ordered gruffly, but his gaze was as hungry as she felt. Instead of showing anger, it sounded like an endearment. Charlie's thumb took the place of her tongue, his nail outlining the curved bow of her lips. She felt his touch and knew she had never been caressed before this. Ever. The kiss behind the house with the young farmer next door to her father's place had never had more than the delicious secrecy going for it. She had thought kissing was overrated and had never bothered again. Even when she arrived here, she had two or three beaus from town. None of them were worth the effort.

But Charlie was. He had just proved it by showing her that this was what a kiss was supposed to be like. No wonder women threw away their reputations and common sense to be with a man. For this.

Her eyes focused on his and thousands of thoughts, emotions, and yearnings passed between them, acknowledging and underlining everything they left unsaid.

One thought came to mind: she would never know this feeling again. It was too strong, too scary, and far, far too addictive. And he would leave her here with nothing but memories she'd regret.

"Talk to me. What's going on behind those green eyes?"

"That this won't happen again," she whispered, not moving away from his arms, not wanting to. "It has to stop."

"I know. Brothers don't do this to sisters." His slow, sexy smile melted her heart.

"And now that we've gotten this kiss out of the way so we both know not to do it again, what do we do next?" she asked, still trying to catch her breath.

There was a derisive twinkle in his eye, one that held merriment as well as regret. "I know what I'd like to do." His voice lowered to a rough whisper. "I'd like to take you to bed and undress you, one layer at a time. And then I'd stroke your skin, touch you in places that would please both of us . . . "

"Kathleen?" Sarah Hornsby's quavering voice called from the barnyard just as a horse neighed.

Kathleen jumped back as if struck by lightning. A flush stained her skin to a delicious peach. Her eyes searched the doorway as if an apparition were standing there. There was no one.

"I'll walk behind you," Charlie said, his voice slightly hoarse. He took her shoulders in a soft but firm hold and aimed her toward the door. "After all, I'm your brother, John, just helping you in the barn."

Kathleen nodded, trying to swallow as she pulled herself together. Her hands jerked up and ran through her hair like a comb to settle it back into its own unruly pattern instead of the one Charlie had made. She was sure there was writing on her forehead telling everyone she'd just been thoroughly kissed.

"Kathleen?" Sarah called again, this time fear lacing her voice. "Where are you?"

"I'm here, Sarah!" she called, stepping out into the sunshine. "I'm checking the stock."

Pretty Sarah Hornsby looked like a scared bird about to take flight as she sat perched precariously on the edge of the bench seat of a small wagon led by two old roans. Relief at seeing Kathleen was only momentary, returning to fright as Charlie, several feet behind, stepped from the shadows.

"Oh! I'm sorry, I didn't know you already had company." Sarah's voice was high, like the cheep of a martin.

Kathleen smiled, feeling as stiff as a board. "Oh, Sarah, this isn't just any company. This is my brother, John."

Sarah's eyes widened as they lit daintily on the man stepping forward with a frown on his face. Her gaze skittered back to Kathleen. "My goodness! Your brother. Why, how nice," she said.

"I think so, too," she said, relieved at the expression on Sarah's face. She believed her; Kathleen could tell. Otherwise she wouldn't have looked at Charlie at all. Sara was tiny, like a perfect little doll. She was such a timid woman. Of course, her husband had a lot to do with that. He was a big, silent, imposing man who hardly let Sarah out of his sight. The only place she could go was to church, the quilting bee, and Kathleen's to pick up carrot cake and bread. Kathleen always felt as if there was an inner strength in the woman, but for the life of her, she didn't know where it was. "Won't you come in? I'll put on a pot of tea."

"Oh, I . . . " she began her usual protest. Kathleen should have known Sarah would bow out, since there was a man present, but the woman surprised her. She straightened her shoulders as if gathering her courage around her. "I think I would like that," she said, wrapping the reins around the wooden brake handle. "Would you help me down, please, sir?" She looked straight at Charlie then, her eyes meeting his as if she were braving the executioner.

With far more gallantry than Kathleen had seen from him, Charlie stepped forward, touched the brim of his hat, and took her outstretched hand. "I'd be most obliged, ma'am."

Sarah walked toward the back of the house as if she were a queen, her hand resting lightly on Charlie's arm. And he acted as if he were escorting one. Where the manners came from on his part, Kathleen had no idea. But a quick shaft of jealousy meteored through her and landed like a sharp rock in the pit of her stomach.

She deliberately looked where she was going as she made her way into the kitchen, filled the kettle, and set it on the fire to heat. She heard Sarah's quiet "Thank you" to Charlie.

His quiet answer was, "No thanks necessary."

Imagine, manners from a cowboy and a bounty hunter. By the time she looked around, Sarah was seated at the end of the table and Charlie was hanging his hat on the peg by the back door.

"How is everyone in your home, Sarah?" Kathleen asked, placing the teakettle on the back burner before reaching for the carrot cake to slice off a piece for each of them.

"Thomas is fine, just fine." She looked startled at the question.

Come to think of it, Kathleen hadn't bothered to ask her about her husband before. He was boring. "He is busy with culling the chickens out for market right now. It's the busy time, when he has to find all the layers he can and get his crop up. He and two of our kind neighbors are also trying to complete a coop that will hold more than two hundred chickens at a time. Imagine that! It will look like a long hall, with chickens on both sides and doors and chimneys at both ends for a draft in the summer and heat in the winter."

Kathleen tried to keep her attention on the conversation. "Oh? That sounds as good as any home in Blissful."

"Doesn't it though?" Sarah said, accepting the piece of cake on Kathleen's Blue Willow–patterned plate. "But we lost too many last year from the freeze. Thomas wants to be prepared."

"If he keeps that up, he'll be the biggest producer of chicks south of Dallas."

"I imagine so," Sarah said, but there was wistfulness in her tone. "It must be so nice having your brother visit. Will he be staying long?"

"Not long enough, ma'am," Charlie answered, still standing near the door. "If you don't mind, sister, I'm going to let the horses into the corral."

"Thank you . . . John. I'd appreciate that."

The women waited in silence as Charlie left the kitchen and walked across the yard to the barn.

"He's very nice-looking, Kathleen. It must be wonderful to have family."

"It's very nice. But in this case, John wants me to go home with him." She wanted to make sure the story was still intact. "His wife is having a baby soon and he thinks she may need help afterward." The kettle sang and Kathleen prepared the tea.

Sarah looked surprised. "Will you return to us?"

"Not if he has his way." Kathleen laughed, knowing her real brother wouldn't want her ever to leave the house, let alone the state.

"This town would miss you very much. You've been such an inspiration to us all. Why, in a few weeks, we might have the railroad stopping here for large loads. You've accomplished so much, Kathleen. You must be very proud."

Kathleen brushed off her accomplishments. It wasn't settled yet. "The whole town has done it, not just me. Besides, I'm not going anywhere."

"Yes, but we all know the idea never would have gotten off the ground if it hadn't been for your leadership. Why even Thomas admires you greatly!"

Thomas was a stuffed shirt who had much in common with her real brother. He meant well, but to him, women weren't really worth more than the means to a clean shirt and for taking care of a house. How scared-of-her-own-shadow Sarah could love him was beyond Kathleen. "I'm touched. And we still haven't gotten the railroad to agree yet. But I do have my fingers crossed."

"And you'll succeed. I know it. My goodness. You're helping bring forth Thomas's big dream. In three weeks he'll have stock enough to send a whole carload to Fort Worth!"

"Congratulations."

Sarah stared into her cup for a moment. "Do you miss your family, Kathleen?"

She made sure her smile remained. "I'm so busy, I'm not sure anymore. Aunt Hattie was part of my family and I miss her, and it's wonderful to have my brother here for a visit, but I don't want to return to my home state. Texas has me now."

They chatted for a few more minutes, and Kathleen didn't think she'd ever seen Sarah more animated than she was today. Whatever brought it on, it made her even more beautiful. Color was high on her cheeks, and her smile was bright and easy.

As they both saw through the screen that Charlie was returning to the house, Sarah leaned forward, petting the purring Fancy, who scratched her back on the chair rung. "Does your brother know about the town?" she whispered, as if he could hear from a hundred yards away.

"No, and I have no plans to tell him. He wouldn't understand, and he certainly couldn't keep the secret," Kathleen said, reminding herself of their role as brother and sister. She wanted the information to get out as quickly as possible so she wouldn't have to do much explaining in the weeks to come. Blissful was a small town and everyone knew each other, but not everyone saw each other on a regular basis unless it was meeting time. This method of communication would help.

As Charlie stepped into the kitchen, Kathleen smiled at Sarah and asked in a loud voice, "So, Sarah, where do you go from here?"

Sarah promptly answered, her gaze darting to Charlie often. "I promised I'd go see Margaret this afternoon. As a matter of fact, Kathleen, if you don't mind,

I said I'd collect her order, if you have it readied I brought both our baskets in the back of the wagon."

"I'll get them," Charlie said with a smile as he turned around and left.

"He's so handsome," Sarah said, as if unaware she was speaking aloud. She cleared her throat. "Does he take after your mother or father?"

"What?" Kathleen was lost in watching him walk to the wagon. He had a stride that was cocky and all male. It was a strong, confident saunter, one that most men didn't have.

"Your brother," Sarah said. "Does he take after your mother or father?"

"We had the same mother, but our fathers were different," she said absently, her eyes glued to the swagger of Charlie's shoulders. "His father is from German stock. Mine was Irish."

"Oh, my," Sarah said, walking to the door and blocking Kathleen's view as she extended her own. "I'm so sorry."

"Don't be." Charlie disappeared behind the rear of the wagon.

Kathleen began selecting the right cakes and breads from the pie safe drawers she stored them in and placed the selections on the table. This was her prime opportunity to tell her story so Sarah could pass the word. "We've adjusted to it. But he's bossy, and if he knew about the town he'd drag me back home by the hair and keep me there, sheltered inside that house and taking care of his offspring."

"You wouldn't marry?"

"No. He already tried that. It's the decision that brought me here. John wanted to marry me off to a farmer whose one wish was to have a live-in nanny. I was his fourth choice for a wife, and would have been his third wife."

"And you didn't want marriage?" Kathleen looked up. Sarah stood in the light, her expression earnest and questioning. The young matron was serious.

"Not every woman wants marriage, Sarah," she said gently. At the look on Sarah's face she felt she needed to elaborate. "At least not without a strong commitment and good reasons," she amended. She had wanted marriage, but she'd also wanted love—love for her, not for her brother's finances or the hope of a piece of his land as her dowry.

Sarah sighed, her hands dropping to her lap. "You're so strong, Kathleen. You live out here alone. You support yourself. You even fight your family and win. I admire you very much."

It was beginning to make sense. "Did your family choose Thomas for you?"

Sarah nodded. "And a husband for each of my sisters. I have two, one younger and one older."

Charlie walked through the door holding two baskets with hand towels neatly folded in the bottom. Without looking at him, Kathleen took the baskets and filled them with the homemade sweets and breads. After they were packed, she tucked a towel securely around the edges. "There. Ready to go, Sarah."

Kathleen walked her guest to the wagon, then gave her a light kiss on the cheek. Sarah allowed Charlie to help her up, giving him a shy smile as a reward. "Thank you for the conversation and the friendship, Kathleen. You and your brother are welcome to come visit anytime."

"Thank you, ma'am," Charlie said, tipping his hat once more as she drove out of the yard. "That's a fine compliment, and it's good to know the friends my sister has made while she's been visiting here."

Sarah looked at Kathleen. "You have your work cut out for you."

Kathleen gave a short laugh. "Always have," she said.

As she drove off, Charlie stared after her. Kathleen watched him, deep in thought, and felt jealous. She reminded herself that he was supposed to be her brother, and the confusion of her feelings eased a little . . . only a little.

With her head bowed, she walked toward Bliss Creek just behind the house. She hoped Charlie wouldn't follow her. She needed time alone, time without Charlie around to influence her thoughts. Kathleen had some thinking to do.

Now that the cat was out of the bag and he had been explained to at least two people in this godforsaken town, Charlie wasn't the skeleton in the closet anymore. Instead, she was the one with the big secret.

Charlie watched Kathleen walk across the yard and toward Bliss Creek. She'd survived for three years without him watching over her; she probably knew what she was doing right now.

She was ignoring him.

Feeling chastised for something he wasn't sure of, he decided to do the same thing. He walked into the house to the room that was supposed to be his. A tangled mess of sheets decorated the floor where he'd kicked them during the night. The red-and-blue-gingham patchwork quilt was crumpled in a heap at the bottom of the bed. The feather pillow was punched into a ball and pushed to the side wall.

"Damn," he muttered. It looked as if a dozen restless kids slept there. The way he was feeling right now, that wasn't too far from wrong.

What the hell was his problem? *Stupid question.* He knew the answer but didn't want to acknowledge it. That stolen kiss in the barn had his head spinning like he was a school kid again. Kathleen's touch packed a powerful punch. In fact, he didn't remember ever feeling so much over a simple kiss.

Since his wife had died, he'd had a woman or two, but only to release his own sexual frustration. He knew what to do and how to do it and not let his plumbing get rusty. But it was more for the physical relief than for the excitement of sex. Now all of a sudden all his attention was focused on Kathleen—the same woman he had thought was a lady of the evening just four days ago!

"Damn."

He wanted her. That must be apparent even to her. And when he kissed her it was apparent she wasn't experienced—or she was a damn good actress.

Miss Kathleen O'Day had more than beauty and sensuality. She was charming and intelligent and seemed genuinely to care for people.

And the way she acted with Sarah, so gentle and caring. The woman reminded him of a bird about to take flight. What a scared woman! But Kathleen was patient. He'd bet she'd be patient with everyone. Hellfire, half the time she was even patient with him! He saw the flicker of impatience that she quickly tamped down. But she never lost her temper. At least not yet.

But after the kiss they shared, walking away from him the moment they were alone was insulting.

Well, he could be just as insulting. He could pay attention to his business. It was his reason for being here. Vic. He had lost track of that somewhere between making sure he wasn't drugged by the woman and wanting to bed that same woman.

"Damn. I'm crazy," he stated under his breath.

He was healthy enough not to answer. Instead he slammed out of the house and into the barn, where he saddled his horse and rode away. He didn't know where he was going, but riding was better than sitting and silently stewing over a woman he had no business stewing over.

Being Kathleen's brother wasn't a role he could endure for long.

Kathleen grabbed her fishing pole from the side of the barn and continued toward the creek. It was early fall, and Bliss Creek still rode high on its banks, more resembling a river right now. It was never empty, but when it ran full to overflowing, the sound was deep and chuckling, like someone whispering delicious, dark secrets in her ear—or as she imagined it would be if someone spoke lovingly to her in bed.

With hands used to hard work, she dug into the side of the riverbank and grabbed several worms from the damp, fertile loam. After threading them onto her hook, she swung it around and dropped it into the water, watching the cork dip and sway with the current. She sank to the mossy ground and leaned against a tree, her pulse calming with the sway of the leaves and the easy current moving past the bend.

She had to keep her mind on the real problem of getting the railroad to stop in Blissful on a regular basis—not on Charlie Macon. The real problem concerned the livelihood of so many people, including herself. The whole town depended upon her to resolve this dilemma. The time was coming . . . just a few more weeks.

Charlie's problem was as distant from her own as chalk from cheese. If this Vic really was in Blissful, surely someone would have seen him by now and reported it to her. Someone in the town would have recognized a stranger and tossed him out on his ear. Especially right now. The townspeople couldn't afford to lose their focus on the common goal. And they wouldn't, because she wouldn't let them.

Her livelihood and independence depended upon it.

Kathleen shivered. The thought of her real brother visiting here and requesting—no, demanding—that she return to North Carolina was brought into reality by Charlie's playing out his role this morning.

A tug on her fishing line brought her back to the present. It tugged again. Kathleen pulled on the pole, then on the line until she dragged a fighting bass out of the creek. Bass for dinner.

Throwing the bass farther up the bank, she turned back to the creek once more. She dug up another worm, loaded her hook again, then tossed it back in the water.

Her thoughts drifted back to the same problem, but this time she was resolved it would end quickly.

She would play along with Charlie, giving him time to find his man. If he didn't find him within a week, he'd have to move on. Horse in the barn or no horse, he was out of here by the end of next week.

It was amazing how much better she felt by putting a time limit on Charlie's visit. After all, he was a disturbing influence on her. The kiss had proven that. Two days of thinking about it and one minute of trying it told Kathleen it could not be repeated. Not under any circumstances!

The line tugged again . . . .

Charlie rode into the barn. He'd been gone a little over an hour. Before he went hunting for the small buck now on the back of his horse, he'd ridden around the town, looking at the layout of the houses. No one came out; no one waved except a wizened old man in a field he was earnestly plowing with a worn-out mule.

It was eerie.

The two stores, a general store and a feed store, were closed. The bank had a lock on the door. The doctor's office looked deserted, as did two other storefronts. A hotel was securely locked, although the balcony above looked as if it were home for someone. A large tub of pink and purple flowers smiled at the late-afternoon sun. There was a shawl caught on the railing.

Interesting.

After hanging Teaser's tack on the wall, Charlie brushed him down and led him to the corral, then headed out the back door of the barn. He hung the deer on a rafter, letting it finish bleeding. It was a peace offering for his spooking the deer she'd have shot earlier. Not that she would appreciate it.

He had a few questions to ask Kathleen when she came back from the creek. He sniffed the air, and his stomach growled in response. The tantalizing scent of fresh-baked corn bread came from the house. Kathleen was already home.

As he reached the small outdoor pump, he heard the sizzle of frying. He recognized the smell: fresh fish. His mouth watered. Home-cooked food. It was his lucky day!

He slipped off his shirt and pumped water into the large scrub pan, then sluiced his face, neck, and chest with the icy liquid. The cold raised goose bumps on his skin even though it was a hot afternoon sun. He rubbed himself vigorously.

Questions could wait until after dinner—just in

case she got mad enough not to let him eat. Besides, any information he needed couldn't be acted upon until after supper anyway. Then, after dinner, he'd calmly talk to her about the town, and this time he expected answers. He would remain aloof and in control, being the man he was meant to be.

After all, if he couldn't control a little gal who baked for a living, he wasn't much of a man.

And nobody could say that about Charlie Macon.

Eight

Charlie pushed his empty plate toward the middle of the table, and leaned back in the wooden kitchen chair. He'd eaten as if he hadn't had food in a week. What was more, he never said a word, just stuffed his face. And Kathleen never corrected him.

She sat quietly, daintily eating her fish with a knife and fork, cutting it into tiny bites and acting as if she was savoring each and every bite. The copper-penny carrots and fried potatoes weren't bad either. In fact, the thinly sliced potatoes were crisp and brown and touched with just the right amount of salt and pepper. Delicious.

Charlie gave a satisfied sigh. "You're pretty handy to have around when there's fishing to be done," he said. "And handy with a frying pan, too."

She smiled and stood up. "Thank you, Charlie. I am, aren't I?" It was the first set of words she'd spoken since she'd told him to sit down and serve himself. She sounded amiable enough, he thought. *Good.* He wanted her amiable so she could answer some questions. "I forgot to tell you, I have a buck hanging in the barn, ready to dress."

"Why, thank you for that, too, Charlie. If you don't mind, perhaps you can dress it, too."

"Certainly," he said magnanimously, not looking forward to it but knowing it was the least he could do. Especially if she kept feeding him like this.

Without another word she walked to the back door and reached for the shawl that was stationed on the wooden hook by the door.

"Hey, wait a minute!" he said, coming down on all four legs of the chair. "Where are you going?"

"I have a quilting meeting," she said, wrapping the shawl over her arms and reaching for the small fabric packet of needles and thread from the single drawer near the pump. "I'll be back late."

"But I have questions!"

She stepped toward the back door, holding the screen. "Since I did such a wonderful job fishing, cleaning, and cooking, won't you clean up, brother, dear? It seems only fair."

"Did you hear me?" Charlie asked, his tone belligerent. Was she ignoring him?

"I heard you," she stated calmly. "And I trust you heard me, too. I will be late; don't forget to clean up properly. And will you milk the cow for me? I'd be so obliged."

"You want help, you pay for it," Charlie said, standing.

"Exactly." She smiled briefly—smugly. "You want help, you pay for it," she repeated. "Although this is my home, you have room and board. You also have an ingenious cover from which to search for your friend. So, cleaning the kitchen, dressing the deer, and milking the cow seems little enough repayment for the work I did for you just this day, to say nothing of the other days."

Charlie's mouth worked for a minute, but nothing came out.

Kathleen smiled again, calm as a pond on a breeze-less day. "Have a nice evening and we'll talk in the morning."

"But . . . " Charlie said, finally protesting the quick change of events. However, he was too late. He was talking to an empty room.

Kathleen was out the door, down the steps, and around the front of the house before he could prop-erly think of a protest.

"Double damn," he muttered under his breath. She'd outmaneuvered him. Kathleen had been slick as oil and twice as stinky, but she'd managed what she set out to do: get her own way.

He wondered where she had to go in such a hurry, but it dawned on him there was no hurry at all. She'd known all day just exactly what she was doing.

But where had she gone? Had she really gone to a quilting meeting? Should he follow her?

The thought was a good one. But if he was seen, he'd look like a damn fool brother for checking up on her at a quilting bee. It wasn't worth it. And the way the people in this town protected each other from harm was nothing short of a miracle.

Besides, he thought as he stretched, this was the first time he'd rested in all the time he'd been chasing Vic like a fox to his den. He scratched his chest, remembered the dirt he'd had to scrub from the rugs, and thought of a nice hot bath. Why not?

But first he had some cleaning and milking to do. Much as he didn't want to delve into his thoughts, the whole set of circumstances reminded him of when he was married and his wife wasn't too far away. He wasn't alone then. Instead he was part of a family, something that made him feel as if all was well, even when it wasn't. It was great, that togetherness. It made everything worthwhile, complete. A smile tilted his mouth. It was a good feeling. . . . As long as he didn't think more about the feelings, he was fine.

Instead Charlie began cleaning the small kitchen, taking a bite of the carrot cake sitting on the counter while he did so. This one had pecans. It was the best damn carrot cake he'd ever had.

Kathleen sat on a sealed barrel of pickles and repaired the shirt Timely wore when he had played sheriff. No sense wasting a good shirt. Sixty-year-old Timely Greer grinned at her from across the store. He'd been acting for over two years. A little shoe dye on his hair one time or henna another, or leaving it long and gray another and he was different-looking each play. His wife had died last winter from influenza. Kathleen tried to help him when she could. This was one of those times.

"Can we attempt to do this one more time? Perhaps we can even do it right." Kathleen kept her patience better than any one of the players deserved. "And Bitsy, do you think it would be possible not to giggle? Pretend Orville really is going to kidnap you and take you into the woods."

"Kathleen! Really!" Bitsy exclaimed, her sallow skin brightening with the thought. Kathleen couldn't figure out whether or not the idea was appealing. "A little deportment would be preferred right about now."

Kathleen stuck her finger with the needle again. "I agree," she said, sucking the tip of her finger. "Let us all walk through our parts once more and then we can all go home." She began tying off the thread. "This show is very important. There are rumors that one of the board of directors from the railroad will be on the train. They want to see exactly why we sell so many tickets on this stretch. He doesn t believe his ears, so we will have to convince him by his own eyes."

Margie's eyes widened. "Oh, my."

Zeke looked startled. "Why didn't no one tell me?"

E. Z. spoke up. "They coulda tole you but you woundn' 'member anyway."

"That ain't true."

"So I take it the word didn't get around?" Kathleen acted surprised. "My, and I thought we told everyone everything," she said. "Communication is very important to all of us. Please don't hesitate to pass on information when it has to do with the town's future. At least until we have the railroad stopping properly."

Everyone mumbled as they sat back down and ran through the play one more time, telling each other what they were saying and where they were supposed to walk. After two years of doing these, most of the men and women knew the routine. It was the story that was important.

Kathleen was surprised at how well she could choreograph these plays, making sure that as one action phased out, another action began in another section of the arena. She loved fitting it all together, and she loved the fact that she could do this while still maintaining her dignity. Most professional actors and actresses weren't allowed in people's drawing rooms. They were one step above thieves and rogues. Except for this.

Although she wasn't fool enough to think this would last forever, she would miss it when the plays were over. There would be only this one and another one before the railroad board would give them a regular stop on the schedule.

Zeke tripped over a direction or two, but otherwise everyone seemed to know what they were doing. Their relief was evident when Kathleen said, "That's wonderful. Thank you for your patience."

Jacob, the owner of the store, stood behind the counter beaming as they finished rehearsals for the night. He was a middle-aged man who stooped, as if concealing his height. His four young helpers were also milling around, showing gingham and dark plaid piece goods to a few of the women or enticing the husbands with spanking-new buckets that just came in.

This was his favorite time of the meetings and the main reason he allowed the rehearsals to be held in his place of business. Now some of Blissful's townsfolk would buy things they might not have seen if they'd just rushed in and out with a list of supplies. Now was the time Jacob made some of his largest profits.

Kathleen bit off the thread attached to Timely's shirt. He'd noticed only one rip, but she'd found three more. "Here you go, Timely. All fixed until your next 'death,' " Kathleen said, holding out his shirt by the collar.

He looked relieved. "Thank you, little Kathleen," he said, reaching for it. He'd always called her *little*. Since she was five and a half feet tall, it didn't seem to pertain to her height. No one, probably including him, knew why. Whenever she asked, he just shrugged and said, "It fits." Timely took the shirt and carefully folded it and laid it on the barrel next to her. "I'll remember to take it home with me," he said before his attention was caught by Susan motioning to him from across the room.

Timely lived on the edge of town right by the rail-road water tower. The house was as unique as it was small. It had just enough room for a bed, a table, two chairs, and a large sea chest. To quote Timely, he couldn't cuss a cat in there without getting hair in his mouth. It was made completely of broken bottle glass he'd found and stuccoed together with a home-made brick compound. He also commented in his slow drawl that he loved watching sun- or moonbeams shine through the glass bits and light up his home, turning it into a rainbow wonderland. At one time Kathleen thought Timely was slow mentally as well as physically, but she was wrong. Timely was just slow to react with any quick move or snap judgment.

Susan wanted him. It didn't matter that she was obvious in her attempt to snatch him. Every time she saw him, her bosom heaved in anticipation. At every meeting, gathering, barn-raising or rehearsal, Susan found some way to let him know she was available and waiting for him to say the word.

Timely never said the word, but he was so polite to her, she couldn't get mad. Neither could anyone else. Instead the close-knit town just watched and smiled and wondered who would win the tug of wills. Right now, most of the bets were in Timely's corner. He spoke less.

Ed nervously took the actors through their paces one more time. This evening they decided on murder-ing one of the "soiled doves" by a gunfighter, thanks to Charlie's accusation of Kathleen. They were going to stage the vignette off the balcony of the hotel next to the railroad station. The building hadn't been in use for years, but served as the perfect exterior background for their plays.

The soiled dove was going to be played by Amy McLendon. Kathleen hadn't seen her since the eve-

ning Charlie had entered her life. She'd gone to
dinner at Amy's house to celebrate the first anniversary of their plays. They accomplished so much in
such a short time. Two more weeks and she was supposed to join the small delegation from Blissful to
attend the Railroad Commission meeting in Fort
Worth. Mentally, Kathleen crossed her fingers, just
as she always did where the commission was involved.
Blissful had to be a regular stop if they were to keep
the town alive. If the railroad said no, Kathleen knew
the town would be dead within a year. Most people
would move away to other communities throughout
Texas, where their produce could get to market faster
and easier. It wouldn't be long before the land would
be worthless, useless to sell. Maybe they couldn't even
give it away . . . .

All their hard work for nothing.

E. Z. came up to Kathleen and watched everybody
walk through the scene. After a few minutes, he spoke
softly. "What happened to the stranger in town?"

Charlie. She'd forgotten she'd told E. Z. that she'd
had him as a visitor. It was a mess she had to clean
up. Smiling, Kathleen began. "Well, he was looking
for a man who wasn't in town. Anyway, he left the
same day my brother surprised me."

E. Z. stared at her a moment, and she wanted to
fidget under his gaze. But if she did, he'd know she
was lying through her teeth. That wouldn't do.

"You sure 'bout that?" he finally asked. "Thought
he was lookin' for some gunfighter he tracked right
to here."

Kathleen gave a shrug. "He still is, I imagine. But
he wasn't at my house, so he moved on."

"You believe that?"

"Yes," she stated with finality. But every nerve in
her body sang with tension. If E. Z. thought Charlie

and John were the same man, he'd think there was still a gunslinger wandering the county, and that would put him in danger. Since E. Z. was wanting to live forever and had said so on many an occasion, he'd be the first to blow the whistle to get the gunfighter out of here—if the man was still here.

Kathleen still believed that the man Charlie called Vic had moved on. After all, he'd changed horses with her over a week ago, and no one had seen her horse—although no one would claim it anyway. It was swaybacked and ancient and didn't want to leave home to go farther than a mile. When it reached its limit, it turned around and headed back to the barn, no matter what the rider said or did.

Kathleen ought to know. It had happened to her more than once.

Mabel, her usual sallow color high and her laughter loud, apologized for flubbing her single line. "Oh, my! A lady of the evening!" she was supposed to say loudly as she stood on the railroad platform when the train was stopped. Instead she shouted, "Oh, my! A lady of the baby!"

Kathleen gave a sigh. No one said Mabel was bright, but just average intelligence would be nice. She looked a little closer. The giggle and laughter were normal for her, but the high color and flirtatious ways were different. The way Mabel kept smoothing her skirt and watching the doorway and windows would lead one to deduce that someone might be watching, or at the least, arriving soon.

Kathleen couldn't help gazing at the spot where Mabel was looking, over by the window. For just a moment, she thought she saw a shadow move. Her spine stiffened and ice water zinged down her arms. Was Charlie watching? Was he spying on her? Had Mabel seen him and decided to flirt?

She didn't think so. Mabel was a featherhead but she wasn't stupid enough to be that stupid. At least she didn't think so . . . .

Her heart beating quickly, Kathleen pretended to be interested in a piece of fabric near the window. She walked around the tables stacked with pots, pans, and cooking utensils to finger the gingham by the large side window. But out of the corner of her eye, she saw a shadow move just outside the window directly across from her. Her gaze darted into the darkness, searching.

Nothing.

Her mind struggled with the list of characters they were using for the show. Was someone missing? Had someone left? She glanced around, mentally counting heads. Everyone who was supposed to be here, was. Two of the husbands stood by the open door and spoke in a low voice. Kathleen heard the word *branding* and knew they were discussing the most frequent topic of conversation in the area: cattle.

Taking a deep breath, she relaxed her shoulders and allowed her heart to slow down. She was jumpy because of Charlie's—John's—hunt for a criminal. For all she knew, it was Charlie looking through the window to see what he could see. Or one of the children whose parents were here. The fact was, it could be anyone. She was just jumpy because it never dawned on her that her little town could be in any danger.

Several of the cast members began clapping, letting everyone know rehearsal was over for the evening. *Thank goodness.* She was anxious to get home and find out what Charlie was doing and if he'd seen fit to take a walk in this direction.

It wasn't that she didn't trust him with the town's secret. Well, yes, it was. She didn't trust anyone and probably wouldn't until they had the new railroad contract signed, sealed, and delivered to the mayor, Fredrick Johnson, who also happened to be the town barber.

Until then, she wasn't willing to tell anyone, and wished not as many knew about Blissful as did already.

Two more weeks . . .

As the mercantile emptied, good-byes were exchanged and soft words and laughter filtered through the warm night air. Kathleen watched. It was almost nine o'clock, yet the day's temperature hadn't dropped more than a few degrees. This was almost fall, and it was looking to be a warm winter.

Jacob stood on the porch and lit his pipe, his body outlined by the glow of the light inside the store. As far as Kathleen knew, he stood there every night and smoked before going upstairs to his apartment and going to bed. Lean and slightly stooped, he was a gentle man. She'd always liked him.

"Kathleen?" he asked, seeing her standing in the middle of the road and looking up at the sky. "Are you all right?"

She pulled her light knit shawl over her shoulders as if it were armor. "I'm fine, Jacob. Why?"

He took a long draw on his pipe and it glowed in the dark. "You seem to be miles away from us tonight."

She smiled ruefully. "That's a sweet way of saying I wasn't paying attention."

"That's a no-nonsense way of wondering what is on your mind."

Kathleen tilted her head back and stared at a million stars shimmering in the velvet sky. "I don't think I've ever seen a more beautiful sky than here in Texas," she murmured. "Not even in North Carolina."

"I heard your brother came to visit," Jacob said. "Are you pleased?"

"As pleased as any of us are to see relatives when we cannot tell them the truth about our town."

Even in the dark she could see his grin. "I felt that way about my daughter's visit last year. But it was winter and she didn't stay long."

"She was lovely, and she loves you very much."

"Yes. She loves me so much she wants me to move back to Dallas and live with her."

"But you said no," she said. "You said your home was here."

Jacob nodded. "Yep."

"And she left, unhappy."

"Yep."

"Are you sorry?"

"No."

The quiet of the night echoed through the now empty streets. It was a comforting silence, one that she had grown accustomed to over the past two years. The occasional screech of an owl, the swish of a bat's wings, or the distant bark of a dog greeting its owner were the only sounds to break the silence.

"You won't be sorry either, Kathleen."

She looked back at him. "Sorry about what?"

"Sorry about not going back with your brother. You were meant to be in the West, Kathleen. You're the strength and spirit of the women out here."

She gave a light laugh. "Me and every woman in this town."

"That's right." Jacob's pipe glowed bright for a moment. "And that is why you are here. You are all rare."

She realized where this was going. "And your wife was right for Blissful, too, Jacob."

"Yes. She would have been," he said. The regret

in his voice told her she'd been right about where his thoughts had led. His wife had died the year after he moved here from Dallas and opened his store. It had started as a cold that would never leave her, finally turning her lungs to mush. She died in her sleep. No doctor, he'd been told, could have saved her. Not the one in Mason, one town over. Not the one in Dallas, where there were several to choose from.

"Will you ever go back?" he asked, circling back to the original question.

"No."

"I didn't think so."

Again the silence. Everyone who was at the store earlier was now certainly in their homes. Probably in their beds. Except Kathleen and Jacob.

And maybe whoever was looking through the window tonight.

"Jacob?" She hesitated a moment. But that flash of an image wouldn't leave her thoughts. "Did you see anyone outside tonight?"

"No. Did you?"

It had been such a fleeting image of movement she wasn't even sure she saw it. But her instincts told her she had, and it wasn't a welcome sight. In fact, it seemed downright malevolent. Or she could have been spooked. "I'm not sure."

"If there was anyone, it could have been any neighbor or child or friend waiting for the rehearsal to be over." Jacob moved toward the steps of the boardwalk. "Come on, young Kathleen. I'll walk you home."

"That's not necessary, Jacob," she said in a chiding voice, but suddenly she wanted him to do that more than anything. She had tried to tell herself that it was Charlie sneaking around, trying to find out what was going on, but she didn't believe it. Charlie was curious, but now that he had the cover of being her brother, he would have walked in.

She'd ask when she got home, but she was pretty sure it hadn't been Charlie.

Jacob came to stand beside her and looked up at the same stars she'd been counting just minutes ago. She swallowed all the words that came to mind. She wasn't as brave as she thought. Instead she said what was in her heart. "Thank you, Jacob."

"You're welcome, Kathleen."

They walked along the road in companionable silence. Jacob stopped once and tamped his pipe against the heel of his boot, then stepped on the ashes before walking on.

Just as they turned the bend in the road and she saw the dim gold of flickering light from her parlor window, Jacob decided it was time to talk.

"Kathleen, do you think you'll pick one of our fair town's swains to marry someday?"

"Me?" she asked, startled. "Why?"

"Because my Dora used to say that every woman's dream was to have a home, husband, and family. Isn't it yours?"

"Certainly," she teased. "I already have two out of three, Jacob. The town has become my family in a way I've never had before."

"Yes, but you need your own. Until you have that family by blood, you don't have one."

"Perhaps someday I'll find the other two."

He gave a husky chuckle. "In the order I mentioned, please," he said.

"But of course," she said, laughter filling her voice. "Or the townsfolk would never speak to me again."

Jacob stopped. "Kathleen, you know you can count on me if there's anything I can do to help you. Please call on me." He hesitated a moment, and Kathleen knew he was embarrassed, but she wasn't sure what to say or do to ease the situation. "I feel like a father to you. You're the young woman I wished I'd raised. And I know my Dora would have loved you, too."

Placing her hand on his arm, she gave a squeeze. "Thank you, Jacob. I appreciate the thought. The only thing I can tell you is that I'm glad I'm here in Blissful and can't be forced into a marriage that I do not want. That is so important to me."

"I can see why. You're so independent. Your brother must be just as, uh, independent as you are to keep pace." His voice held a hint of a chuckle.

Suddenly she was so very tired. It had been a long night and she still had to deal with Charlie before crawling into bed and going to sleep.

"Jacob, my brother is sweet and loves me," she said slowly but firmly. "But he has a different life. Just as you do and I do. And in time he will leave here and go back home. Without me, because I am not leaving the life I built because my brother, or anyone else, thinks it is time to do so."

"I see," he said slowly, which told her he didn't see at all. She repeated her convictions as if he would understand the second time. "I am not changing to please anyone. Not my brother, nor the townsfolk of Blissful. And if I never fall in love, then I may never marry. Not everyone is cut out for it. I may be one of those who do better living alone."

"With your aunt's cat."

She nodded. "With my aunt's cat. Fancy is a wonderful companion."

"I'm sorry if I intruded into your personal life, Kathleen. I just don't want to see you unhappy."

"And you think unhappy translates into lonely?"

she asked gently, finally understanding what he was saying.

"Yes."

Now she understood. He missed his wife terribly. "Is your daughter so lonely?"

"Yes. But she won't 'lower her standards,' as she calls it, to find a man who will make her happy." He sounded so miserable. All Jacob wanted was a family. Instead he lost his wife and his only child, a daughter who married to give him grandchildren and was now widowed and alone, too. No wonder he was worried about Kathleen. He figured if he could get her married, there was hope for his daughter. In a convoluted way, it was his chance at happiness—at fulfilling his own dream.

What she hated to admit was that she wanted that, too. Someday.

A home.

A family.

Someone to love.

Someone to love her.

Was that so impossible?

Shaking her head to dissolve the thoughts that tumbled around at the mention of marriage, she went on tiptoe and placed a chaste kiss on Jacob's gaunt cheek. "Thank you for walking me home. Take care, Jacob."

"See you this Saturday," he said, squeezing her hand, which rested on his arm. "And bring your brother around to the store. I'd like to meet him."

"I will. Soon," she promised. Her glance skirted the darkness. "Take care going home, Jacob."

"Don't you worry 'bout me none, young lady. I will." Jacob didn't turn around to walk down the darkened path until she was on her porch and opening the door. Kathleen strained her eyes and watched the white of his shirt disappear into the darkness and was thankful for his company and generosity. She hadn't felt safe tonight, and it was the first time since she'd moved here that she'd felt that way.

Perhaps it was because there was a storm in her breast that was awakened by the male storm in her home.

Would anything ever be the same again or would the whole town change with the coming of Charlie and the coming of the railroad?

She didn't know, and not knowing her thoughts jumble together and dart into areas she didn't want to think about.

Damn Charlie for coming and making her face things she wasn't ready to face . . . .

Nine

At first, the silence in the house was deafening, with only the hoot of a nearby owl searching for food to break the mood. Was Charlie gone?

Then she heard it: the gentle sound of splashing water came from the kitchen. She sniffed the air, instantly smelling the pungent odor of cigar smoke mixed with her rose-scented soap. She followed both the splash and the odors until she stood in the kitchen doorway. The sight was worth the stare, especially when Charlie couldn't see her.

Her battered copper tub had been dragged in from the summer storage place in the barn and set up in the middle of the kitchen floor. From the warmth of the room, Kathleen knew Charlie had heated water and filled the tub with it.

The seat of a kitchen chair had been turned into a makeshift table and now held a tall glass of water, a saucer holding a still-smoldering half-smoked cigar and a white bath sheet she'd put on his bed earlier.

Charlie gave a contented sigh and stretched out, wiggling his toes over the end of the tub. Lucky for him, bubbles from Kathleen's good soap kept her from seeing the rest of him.

He needed a haircut. His shaggy hairline curled like a baby's at the back of his neck. For some strange reason she refused to contemplate, she wanted to bend down and kiss him there, right at the indentation. She could almost feel his skin with her mouth, with the tip of her tongue—could almost inhale the scent of him that erotically surpassed any soap or dirt or heated sun. Charlie Macon definitely had sex appeal.

As she watched in fascination, he lathered the soap between his callused hands. Leaning forward, he ran his fingers through his toes, scrubbing them afterward with the small piece of toweling she used as a washcloth. All the while, he hummed an offbeat rendition of "Coming 'round the Mountain."

It brought a smile to her heart.

Charlie continued to wash himself, never looking around to her. "Bet you didn't know I'm next to godliness." Charlie's voice broke the sound of the splashing water.

He'd known she was there. "No, I surely didn't," she stated, her tone calmer than she was on the inside. "I didn't know you went near water, let alone took a good long soak."

He dropped the washcloth in the water and took a deep pull on his cigar, then placed it back in the saucer. Then he tilted his head back and made smoke circles with his mouth . . . the mouth that Kathleen couldn't see because he was facing the other way. She wanted to see his face badly—that and other parts of his anatomy. Very badly, but she wasn't sure how she could.

"Did you have a good meeting?" he asked lazily.

"A wonderful meeting."

"Do much sewing?"

She remembered Timely's shirt and smiled. "I did a pretty fair amount."

"Let me see," he said, and it was the excuse she was waiting for.

She stepped around to the side of the tub and held out her fingers. She had long ago lost the soft, well-cared-for look of a pampered woman with money. During the two years she lived with her brother, she'd gained that look, but it had been fleeting. The garden and just plain living had taken their toll on her skin, but she didn't care. She liked working with her hands.

Charlie's dark brown eyes claimed hers and held her attention, making her feel as if he were reading her mind. But he wasn't. She knew it, or he would be blushing instead of her.

Charlie reached out and collected her hands, then ran a wet thumb over her finger, where she'd pricked herself twice. It sent a delicious chill down her spine. "Careless," he said.

"Probably." She was staring at his solemn face. She didn't have the nerve to glance where she wanted to, although curiosity was killing her.

"Well, brother," she said, pulling her hands away from his and taking a seat on the nearest empty chair. The wet heat of his touch invaded her. "What have you done this evening?"

He ticked off his accomplishments on his fingers, one by one. "I milked Hilde, gave her fresh water and new hay, cleaned the kitchen, gave the damn cat some milk, and heated my water for this bath." He chewed on the end of his cigar, a wicked gleam in his eye. "And waited for my saintly sister to return home safely."

"Knowing there was a killer out there, you let me walk home without you."

Silence echoed through the room. His eyes, mischievous just seconds ago, turned to steel. "I've been worried sick since you left, but I knew if I followed you that you'd scream and yell and carry on. Besides, I knew the neighbors wouldn't let you wander away without them close by. You all seem like a close-knit group. And close-knit groups aren't Vic's style. He likes 'em one at a time."

She stared at him, realizing just how hard it must have been for him to remain here. "You never left here."

"Never left here, sister mine." His gaze sharpened. "Why? Did you think I did?"

She knew he hadn't. She'd known all along. There was no reason to think that he'd lie. And if he hadn't been there, then someone else had been peeking in the window. Maybe it was one of the bigger boys, or a husband who was waiting outside for his wife to finish up with rehearsal. Anyone. Anyone but a gunslinger.

She smiled. "I was fine. Jacob decided to walk me home so he could smoke his pipe a little longer, I suspect."

"His wife doesn't like smoke?" Charlie asked, bringing her attention back to him. There was a sharpness in his tone that surprised her.

"His wife died a couple of years ago."

"And he's looking for a new one?"

Kathleen stared at him a moment. He held the washcloth in his hand, rubbing the soap against it and making lather spill over his hands. His brazen look returning to her was the only sign of his irritation. "If you have something to say, just spit it out and I'll deal with it directly."

"I'm wonderin' if *you* have something to say," he said, but the easily spoken words belied the look in his eyes.

"This has left the conversation arena," she stated. It was amazing how quickly desire, once reared and ready, could run and hide. "Let me know when you wish to converse again."

"I *am* conversing."

"No." Standing tall, she walked toward the back door. "You're accusing me of misconduct without coming out and saying anything. I resent that, Charlie."

His mouth clamped tight around the cigar. "So I hit a nerve?" His tone was smug.

"Yes, the same nerve anyone feels when face-to-face with a full-fledged, braying jackass," she stated quietly but vehemently.

"Well, I'll be . . . " he began, but he was too slow.

Kathleen was out the screen door and walking toward the barn at a fast clip. She had better things to do than stand there and spar with him. And to think she'd gone all wishy-washy over seeing him sitting naked, broad-shouldered and handsome in her tub!

Well, he'd cured her of that quickly enough. All he had to do was act like the jackass he was and those thoughts sped away with the speed of reason.

Lucky for her.

So what if he didn't know what he was missing by kissing her again? It was his loss and certainly not hers!

The nerve of him to hint that some sweet man he didn't even know was sweet on her! She didn't need accusations like that to float around. It wouldn't take long to ruin a reputation, and hers was too hard-won to allow him that. She had fought like a tiger to earn a say at the meetings. A rumor about impropriety with any member of the town would mean all her good works and customers would be gone.

To say nothing of the fact that it wasn't true.

Slipping into her uncle's old boots, she reached for the pitchfork and began mucking out the stall where the new horse was. Each pitchfork stab made her feel better. Each load of manure removed gave her a sense of accomplishment.

Each movement worked off the feeling of sensual delight she'd been envisioning.

Maybe, if she was good, she could do this all night and be rid of the thought of him by morning . . . maybe . . . .

Charlie sank the tip of his cigar into the water and listened to it fizzle. He and the cigar had a lot in common. She'd left him hanging, damn her! She'd left him not knowing whether she was taken in by the jackal who walked her home or hated his guts but was afraid to say so for fear of letting the damn town down. So he pressed and lost the answer. "Damn," he muttered, tossing the soaked cigar on the saucer. Suddenly the water felt cold and the house seemed empty and lonely.

"Damn," he said again. But he wasn't about to get out and ruin his first real bath in a month of Sundays. No, sir. He was staying right here until he damn well felt like moving. And that might be just as she opened the door and stepped in. It would do her some good to shock the hell out of her that way. Shake her up a bit.

That thought gave Charlie some satisfaction. After all, it wouldn't have taken much for her to explain how she felt about the guy. She could have defended herself. It wouldn't have cost her anything to tell him she wasn't interested in the damn man, now, would it? A thousand and one questions popped into his head, and all of them were without answers.

And him being so good by staying here and working *her* little piece of land so that she wouldn't worry! Why, he'd even cleaned up the kitchen, as she'd told him to.

And this was the thanks he got.

"Damn."

But somewhere under the flush of his skin and the heat of his newfound anger, he knew she was right. He'd been riding her and making her second-guess what he wanted to know instead of just outright asking. He wasn't used to being called on that. Hell, most women knew the game and went along with it. Most women understood he was just acting manly and was waiting for an answer to the specified unasked question. They gave him the answer he wanted and then, with the answer he wanted to hear, he could relax and go about his business.

Most women. Not Kathleen.

Kathleen demanded that he be direct and ask the question on his mind. That was unfair. She was just a woman, damn it, and should act like one! He was the man around here. Didn't she see the difference? Why, it was exactly for reasons like this that men had clubs in the big cities, and hunting shacks on the range. Women complicated every issue that came up by doing or saying the unexpected. At least with a man-to-man conversation, he knew the rules.

With women, there didn't seem to be any. Just like now. Kathleen needed to learn how to converse man-to-woman. She must have lost that knack by living here with her ancient aunt and attending nothing but sewing meetings all the time.

That was it. She was behind the times.

The West, without the normal conventions and attitudes of the more "civilized" cities back east, made people act strangely. Women grew stronger than they normally would, more capable. And as for men, well, they became even more independent, except when it came to women . . . .

He frowned. What the hell was he saying? Since Kathleen had walked out the door, he'd bamboozled himself with double talk so he'd feel better about what he'd just said and the way he'd acted toward her. But he was wrong. She was right. She had every right to expect him to be direct.

"Damn," he said for the last time. It was a hard thing to do—admit he was wrong—and he was only thankful that Kathleen O'Day wasn't around to hear him recognize the truth.

Now the bathwater really was cold—as cold as Bliss Creek behind the house. The cooling night air had seeped into the kitchen back door and scattered big goose bumps on his arms.

Kathleen hadn't come back from wherever she was, and sharp worry about her safety entered his thoughts. He'd almost forgotten why he'd come here. Although Charlie doubted it, Vic could still be inside the town somewhere. Surely someone would have said something to Kathleen by now, and he was sure she'd say something to him instantly. Whether she admitted it or not, Kathleen was worried enough about her reputation to make him an honorary brother. So this little community, tainted as it was, must still have close communication among its members. After all, he'd seen several people come by here in the past couple of days. It proved that not all the shooters cared what went on, on a day-to-day basis. In fact, it made for a great deal of puzzlement. Some women, like Sarah Hornsby, didn't seem prepared to meet a desperate stranger on the small dirt road between their house and Kathleen's. Odd, come to think of it. And so far, the only men he'd seen were older than she and twice as ornery. Very odd.

He'd look into that, and it might help him solve the problem with this town and get back to his own life. That would please both of them. It was as obvious as the stubble on his chin that Kathleen wanted him out of her life as quickly as he wanted out of hers.

He swallowed that lie without flinching.

Keeping his eye on the towel draped over the chair back about five steps away, Charlie stood and let the chilly water sluice off him. Just as he was about to step out of the tub, the screen door squeaked, then slammed back in its casing.

Surprised brown eyes met wary green ones and locked. Charlie didn't move. Neither did Kathleen. Slowly, very slowly, he eased one foot onto the rug on the linoleum floor and kept one foot in the tub, straddling it.

Kathleen's eyes darted down to the vee of his legs, then back up again. The only giveaway of her appreciation was the heightened peach color on her cheeks.

He gave a long, slow grin. "Didn't expect you back so soon," he said, knowing full well she'd been gone half an hour or so.

"Water cold now?" she asked dryly, keeping her eyes on his while walking to the chair and picking up the towel draped there. She handed the wad of material to him with a casual air, then walked past him to the stove.

"How could you tell?" he asked, glancing down to see if he looked as chilled as he felt. *Nope.* Big Charlie and the twins had looked damn good, even if unappreciated.

She filled the giant pot with more water from the pump and placed it on the stove burner before stoking the fire once more. "Your arms are all goose bumps."

"That's a true story," he muttered, briskly wiping himself with the towel. When he was finished, he wrapped the cloth around his waist and stood watching her. "Are you gonna take a bath, too?"

"Yes." She grabbed the bucket and began filling it with Charlie's bathwater. Then, walking to the door, she flung it out to the garden beside the house— the very garden Charlie had stepped on to hear her conversation that first day.

After watching her smooth, feminine movements in fascination, he started to offer to help. But the determined set of her full mouth told him he'd be better off getting the hell out of the kitchen and out of her way. And putting some clothes on.

He felt deflated. Most women who saw him naked as a baby thought that he was a fine physical specimen of a man. Obviously Kathleen wasn't one of them. He wasn't sure why it mattered. After all, she hadn't had enough experience to know what good was. What the hell did she know?

Still, he'd wanted to impress her. He wanted her to be as aware of him as he was of her. *Hell, Charlie,* he thought to himself. He wanted her. Period.

Just admitting that thought annoyed the hell out of him. With a definite stomp, Charlie walked through the living room and into his bedroom. He changed into his only pair of clean jeans and a shirt, then stepped into his boots. Then, slipping his sack of tobacco and wraps in his pocket, he stepped out onto the front porch and tried to concentrate on the beauty of the night instead of on Kathleen's firm bottom swaying back and forth in motion with the bucket.

Stars, peppered between clouds and black night sky, twinkled so brightly he could almost reach out and grab a couple into his fist. Instead he leaned one hip against the railing and expertly rolled a cigarette. Striking a match, he lit the area on the porch while lighting his newly rolled smoke.

He was confused. That much was certain. He'd come here on a mission. Somehow, along the way, he'd lost track of that fact. It was Kathleen's presence that had made the difference in his goal. Ever since he'd come here, she'd taken over his mind and thoughts. She demanded his every waking moment to deal with, deal around, deal through. He'd had to deal so much he was dealing with dread.

Damn it!

He had to clean up his thoughts and get back to work. He needed to focus on the real problem and think like a no-good rustler to catch a no-good rustler.

He heard a splash and knew that Kathleen was probably stepping into the tub . . . naked.

That thought burned a vivid impression into his brain, showing him what he already knew she looked like under those prim gingham dresses she wore. With her rich auburn hair falling down to her waist and creamy skin covering a trim but full figure, she probably looked like one of those masterpiece paintings in some fancy museum.

A song, hummed softly and sweetly, wafted to him on the night air. More gentle splashes.

His reaction was as strong as the picture his imagination conjured: a naked and wet Kathleen soaping places his mind could only guess, her body shimmering a dull gold in the dim lamplight, smelling like the rose-scented soap that knew her body more intimately than he ever would . . . .

Charlie flicked the cigarette out into the front yard and turned neatly, walking through the living room and into the kitchen, stopping exactly where Kathleen had stopped earlier.

He was right. Piled high on her head, Kathleen's hair looked like a river of molten gold and icy red. Loose tendrils twisted down her back and white shoulders. And her skin was just as creamy and golden as he thought it would be.

Damn. His heart beat so heavily it was like a drum echoing throughout his body, blocking out all other sounds.

Kathleen lifted a sponge and let it dribble water over her soap-coated shoulder and arm. "It's my turn now. Leave the room, Mr. Charlie Macon," she said in a deep-throated voice that washed over him like hot lotion.

It took a moment for her words to register through the sound of the blood rushing in his head.

"Why should I? You didn't." His voice sounded low and gravelly.

"I made a mistake," she corrected, still absorbed with her ablutions. "An error in timing, if you will. You're here because you meant to be." She let the sponge drop back into the water and reached for the soap in a saucer next to her. "I'm here because this is the only room in the house that has the bath set up." She slipped her foot out of the tub and braced it on the opposite rim. "One of us has to leave."

It was hard for Charlie to find his voice. He tried. He honestly tried. Instead he heard someone clearing his throat, and knew it had to come from him. He was the only one trying to speak.

Kathleen's mouth was pursed as if she were sipping

a glass of something cool and enjoying the hell out of it.

He wanted that mouth on his. On him.

"I, um," he finally managed.

"Out," she repeated softly. Her lashes fluttered down to dust her cheeks; then she looked up at him again—lazily, sexily, tempting as Eve.

"No." There. He finally managed to find his voice.

Very slowly, she tilted her body and looked at him over her shoulder. If he lived to be as old as Methuselah, he'd never forget the way she looked at him that moment. He would carry the image of her to his grave and beyond. He couldn't breathe. The image sucked the breath out of him. His heart beat so fast he thought it would jump out of his chest and run away. Charlie had never craved anything as much as he lusted after Kathleen right this minute.

"Charlie," she said, her full mouth moving slowly, with such sensual art he was stupefied.

"No," he said, as if leaving would be asking for his death.

She sighed, and the lamp seemed to flicker at the same time, dancing on her hair and skin and helping to shadow and outline her luscious mouth. The whole room seemed to bend and sway with the flame.

As if he had no other choice, he walked around and stood facing her. She watched his movements as if he were a snake and she were the victim. But there was a gleam in her eye, a subtle green tone that changed to an even darker shade. She was challenging him. At least he thought she was.

"Welcome home," he said softly, in a lilting voice. "Why, thank you, Kathleen. It's good to be home." Her expression softened, a smile flirting with her mouth. "And how's my dear sainted sister doing? Can I wash your back?" Her green eyes widened at the

thought; she seemed very intrigued, tempted. Hope
rose in his chest. "Make you a pot of tea? Call for
help?"

"Help," she finally whispered.

"When?" His voice dropped several more octaves.
"Now isn't soon enough."

"Sure it is. I'm not harming you in any way. I'm
not pushing you around, beating you, starving you,
or even calling you names. There's no need to rush.
The room is filled with a rose scent and the water is
probably still hot and soapy, judging from the bubbles
that haven't popped yet." He tried to smile, nice and
friendly, but it felt more like a leering grimace. Hell,
it *was* a leering grimace. "So why don't you stop
fretting and enjoy the rest of your bath. I'll just sit
here and relax with a smoke."

He took a chair, flipped it around until the back
was toward Kathleen, and then straddled it with his
arms poised on the back.

"A gentleman leaves," she managed, her voice softening to a whisper that raked along his spine like a
loving caress. She was knocked off balance, not knowing what she wanted or why. He saw the confusion
in her gaze.

His eyes burned at the sight of her breasts rising
and falling with each breath. His humor quickly disappeared. "Now you know what I've always known: that
I'm no gentleman. We're both singing out of the
same hymnal."

"Please," she said, but it wasn't to placate. Instead
her eyes made a demand; he just wasn't sure what
the demand was.

"Yes?"

She gave a sigh of resignation. It was inevitable.
They both knew it. She was going to rise out of the
water and he was going to stare and they would both

remember the moment for the rest of their lives. Even though miles apart, when they sat on rocking chairs at the end of their lives and smiled into their grand-children's faces, they would still remember this moment and smile.

For always.

And he was waiting for that moment—ready to file it away in his memory bank and take it out on lonely, starless nights under the sky and over ground harder than he was right now.

Another sigh. But this time there was a daring in her eyes. A look that said, *Capture this moment, bucko, because you'll eat your heart out for the rest of forever after-ward. This is something you will* never *have.*

"I'm waitin'," he managed with a sardonic drawl.

It was just as much a dare as her look was. And she took it.

Slowly, ever so slowly, she bent her legs until her feet were flat on the bottom, and placed her hands on the sides of the tub. With a blush that covered her body in peaches and cream, Kathleen rose slowly. Water sluiced off her body, running into the tub and dripping from her elbows and breasts. A slightly rounded tummy was shaded by the light, only to end in a thatch of dark red hair. Her breasts were firm and full and high, accentuating her slim waist and full hips. Areolas the size of silver dollars were the color of light copper. Her nipples stood out as if waiting to be suckled. She looked slim and firm and creamy and soft. And feminine. So damn feminine.

His breath caught in his throat and he was heady without it. Image turned to reality, lasting a long moment and not lasting long enough. She was far more beautiful than any fantasy he had projected earlier. Far better than anything his imagination could conjure up in a million years. It took his breath away and made his brain turn to mush.

Kathleen bent from the waist and daintily reached for the towel, wrapping it around her and tucking it in at the hollow between her breasts so that it hung just above her knees.

"You didn't dry off very well," he managed in a gruff voice.

"I didn't dry off at all." She stepped from the tub and walked directly to her room, not stopping to argue, to weep, or to challenge.

Charlie closed his eyes and finally found the wherewithal to breathe. She didn't have to do any of those things. It wasn't necessary.

She'd won the battle of wills already.

Ten

Damn Kathleen. Things would never be the same.

Charlie lay in bed, hands behind his head, staring up at the painted clapboard ceiling. He'd been in bed for over six hours, and so far not one wink of sleep had closed his eyes.

The memory of a naked Kathleen rising from the copper tub, water sluicing from her body in the most enticing way, wouldn't leave his mind. It was one of those moments that would remain with him all his life, bringing to the surface emotions he didn't know he was capable of . . . or could name. In fact, some of them he didn't want to know about. It was the sorting of those emotions that was keeping him awake.

For the first time in his life, Charlie was afraid. And the fear was inside him instead rather than a danger he could see, hear, or smell.

That made this danger more deadly than any before it.

*   *   *

Kathleen stared at the painted clapboard ceiling of her room and wondered what she was going to do for the rest of the time Charlie was here.

Although she'd always been a little "spicy," as her mother called it, she had never been so wanton, so disregarding of convention. She didn't know what had gotten into her to act so brazenly! She was embarrassed at her willfulness and ashamed of the way she behaved. Just thinking about her wanton actions made her stomach clench and redistribute her supper.

She'd never look Charlie in the eye again. Ever!

It wasn't going to be easy not to ever see him again, but she'd break her neck trying. Maybe she could do her baking at night, when he was sleeping. Only then would she be able to keep her sanity and her pride intact. She could milk Hilde before dawn and after dark. She could sleep all day and do her work at night. Late night. Very late night. Anything as long as she never saw Charlie again. *Ever!*

The full moon crested the hills, and light poured across her bed in silver streaks. She tried to close her eyes and get some sleep. With any luck, she could sleep until Charlie left the area. Maybe, but she didn't hold out much hope.

How could she have been so brazen? How had she found the nerve to stand and display herself so?

Where on earth did she get the idea she could pretend Charlie was her brother and get away with it?

Her nerves were so tight she felt like old Zeke's drawn Indian bow. Tighter.

What was she going to do? Kathleen tossed in the bed again, turning her back on the moonlight and squeezing her eyes closed. But her mind refused to stop churning.

So much in her past had made her afraid of men. Her mother, who had such a brave front for everyone else, was always secretly afraid of her father. But she braved him for the sake of her children. When her mother died, Kathleen lost that buffer and protector, as well as the loving softness of her mother. There was no one to protect her from anger, not from her father when he was in one of his drunken rages or her brother when he turned nasty and cut with his tongue as well as the back of his hand. Not even from the boys on the next farm who taunted her when no one was around, letting her know that if they ever caught her alone at the right moment, she would never be marriageable.

And then there was Henry James, the man her brother wanted her to marry. His children were often dirty, always mouthy, and occasionally bruised and mending broken bones. Wasn't a father just as responsible for his children as a mother was? If not, why not?

So despite everything she'd learned about men, here she was with a male in her home—one who didn't belong and who wasn't married to her or related in any other way. And she was condoning it.

Not only condoning it, but playing the game of tease and strumpet—no better than some of the characters she wrote into her plays for the town. A lady of the evening, indeed!

Resolve slowly replaced her disgust. This mess with Charlie had to be straightened out tomorrow. She had to face Charlie and let him know he was no longer welcome in her home. If he wanted to find a criminal, he needed to look elsewhere. It was as simple as that.

And as for her decadent behavior, she would just have to pretend it never happened. If there was a thread of the gentleman in him, he would never mention it.

As the cock crowed, her eyes drifted down and sleep finally came.

When she awoke, she felt groggy and lethargic. Hilde's demanding moo was the noise that filtered through her dreams . . . her nightmares. She was dreaming that Charlie had taken her in his arms and kissed her, thoroughly and completely.

That wasn't a dream she wanted to repeat.

Sitting on the edge of her bed with her feet dangling, Kathleen brushed her hair over her shoulder and stared out the window at the rolling prairie beyond. Her problems had not changed since she went to bed. She still had a cow to milk, orders to fill, and a man to confront. In that order, she hoped.

With the same emotions that she was sure a condemned man felt, she rose, dressed, and walked out of her bedroom. Her eyes darted everywhere, looking, seeking Charlie. But he was nowhere to be seen.

With a sigh of relief, she grabbed her egg basket and the milk pail and headed outside. Reprieve—at least for the moment.

When she returned, her worst fear was sitting at the table. Charlie held a mug of strong coffee in his hands, staring into the depths of it as if the cream swirl held a message.

He didn't look up.

She didn't break the silence. After placing the pail next to the basement trapdoor, she began washing dirt and straw off the eggs, carefully and one at a time. All her attention was on the eggs. Her nerves, however, were tuned to every breath Charlie took. If he accused her of anything or made an advance, she would crack an egg on his thick skull . . . just before hurting him where he was most vulnerable. She would take no sass, no smart or sarcastic comments about last night.

Not one word . . .

"Sorry about last night," he mumbled into his cup. "You didn't deserve that kind of behavior and I apologize."

She turned, still holding the eggs tightly in her apron front like a basket. "I beg your pardon?"

He looked up then, and he looked as exhausted as she felt. "Don't make me say it again, Kathleen. I don't deserve that much punishment for my sins."

"I wasn't sure I heard you correctly," she said, then cleared her throat. "You're apologizing?"

"Yes." He lifted the cup as if it weighed a hundred pounds and sipped at the thick brew.

The egg in her hand cracked, the sound echoing loudly in the kitchen. With careful precision, she allowed each finger to relax. "Thank you," she finally managed, sounding stiff and formal instead of the way she felt, which was relieved. His words were a salve to her already bruised ego.

"You're welcome," he stated in a low voice that sounded sincere, if a little pained.

Her dignity felt as if it were still intact. She looked at him closely, feeling far more charitable toward Charlie than she had during the night, when guilt had flooded her every thought. "What is wrong? Are you not feeling well?"

"I'm fine," he stated, but there was a low level of irritation in his tone.

And after such a nice apology, too. She yawned against her will. Exhaustion. This was what it felt like.

Since leaving her father's home, she hadn't had this syndrome. But Charlie made her completely lose sleep for the first time in four years. As soon as she yawned, so did he.

Interesting. She watched him for a moment and knew this wasn't a hangover or a bad mood. Charlie was just as tired as she was. Suddenly she smiled; then a soft laugh lit her lips. And when he looked up in wonder, her laugh became a little louder. "Tired. You're tired, too," she finally managed.

His rueful laugh joined hers, a low, masculine, rough sound that was wonderful to hear. Slightly self-deprecating, ready to take a joke, laugh. "Yeah, I guess so," he finally admitted. "Sleep wasn't a friend of mine last night."

"Me neither," she said quietly.

His eyes widened. "Really?"

Her heart beat rapidly. She turned away and began counting the eggs—or at least pretending to. "Now, don't you read anything into it, Charlie. There was nothing but a restless night."

"Yes, ma'am," he said, but she could hear the grin in his voice.

Darn, she shouldn't have said anything! The most embarrassing moment in her life and she brought it up again. Hadn't she spent enough awake time worrying about it?

Charlie must have recognized the symptoms. She heard his chair scrape back and prayed he was leaving the room quickly. Instead, she felt his hands, coffee-mug warm, touch her shoulders, and she stiffened.

"I'm sorry I embarrassed you last night, Kathleen. I never meant to do so. And I'm sorry that you still feel that way and cannot look me in the eye." His hands tightened, heating her skin beneath the fabric of her dress. "Can we start again?"

"I . . . " She caught her breath. "I guess so." It sounded so lame, but she couldn't think of a single thing to say. She just wanted to disappear into the cabinet.

His palms stroked her skin enticingly. "Turn around. Please."

How could she resist? With slow moments that rivaled those of a turtle, she turned. Charlie kept his hands on her shoulders, and his eyes found hers and locked. The darkness of them searched her face, touched her cheekbones and forehead, caressed her hair and neck. "You're beautiful, Kathleen O'Day."

She didn't feel like it. But she certainly wasn't tired anymore either. Her heart raced at his touch, her mind running away with thoughts that had no business being born. His hands were heated like an iron now, branding her skin with his imprint. More than anything else, she felt *alive* with his nearness.

As if she had refuted the fact aloud, Charlie shook his head in denial. "I mean it. You're beautiful. Clothed, tired, unclothed, wet, dry."

Kathleen began to pull away, but his hands tightened ever so slightly.

"Don't be embarrassed. You should be proud."

Her skin flushed as if brushed with warm feathers. "Don't insult me."

"If the truth insults you, girl, then I'll be silent. But it shouldn't. You're a magnificent woman, and I just want you to know that you should look me in the eye and tell me to eat my heart out because someone like me will never be equal to someone like you."

She blushed a deep red. Not that she would admit it under penalty of death, but the words were so needed and welcome. Someday she wanted the man she loved to say them. But, especially now, she would take them from Charlie and feel wonderful even to think they were true. "You're crazy."

He raised a brow. "Really? Why? Because I'm saying what we both know? That I am a lone cowboy with a broken-down ranch at the end of the earth, and you're a Southern lady who works just as hard as any Texan, making a cozy nest for yourself. Why, I bet you even read, don't you?"

"Yes, but—"

"Don't but me. Do you play that pianoforte in the parlor?"

"Yes, but—"

"And are you not earning a very nice living by baking heavenly cakes? Blissful cakes?"

"Yes." She began the *but* again, then nipped it in the bud. His words were strokes and healing balm to her injured ego. She had felt so ugly and so very, very soiled after last night. All those feelings of inadequacy she'd known growing up had bounced right back into her life. But if Charlie thought that she was worthy, then perhaps . . .

"And don't you run this place by yourself?"

"With help from my neighbors," she said softly, finally opening her eyes and looking back at him.

"Do they live here? Do they come over to milk the cow, catch fish and cook it for dinner, weed and water the carrot patch?" His voice was soft, soothing, and mesmerizing.

Her chuckle felt good. From the softness on Charlie's face, he liked the sound of it. "I give up, Charlie. You've convinced me. I'm wonderful and far above most of the women in this town or any other town around from here to Waco and Huntsville."

His grin was delicious. "Atta girl."

"I'm beyond reproach," she stated even more firmly, getting the hang of it. "I can do anything any other woman can do and some things half the men of this town cannot do."

"I agree."

"I'm so good," she continued, "that I could easily be the teacher in this town. And then I could run the railroad in my spare time."

That brought Charlie's laugh. Kathleen didn't want to tell him she honestly thought she could—and much better than the men who ran it now.

Before she could protest, Charlie's hands slid from her shoulders to her back and drew her close to his own hard, lean body. "Kathleen O'Day, you are priceless. And I have no doubt you could run the railroad. And if you did," he said, giving her a warm hug, "I bet the train would stop in this lovely little town and you'd sell even more carrot cake than you ever dreamed of. And the train would make a profit."

Her heart was beating so fast from his touch that she could barely catch her breath. Light-headed from his nearness, she tried to focus on something—anything—other than Charlie's twinkling eyes. She had inhaled deeply when he hugged her, and the scent of him was filling her up. The feel of him against her was at once reassuring and dangerous. All of that rolled together made Kathleen feel confused and flustered and . . . she wasn't sure what else.

He pulled back, his smile still in place. But when he saw the expression in her eyes, his own smile slipped slowly into a more somber look. "Dear God, help me," he muttered, just before bending to capture her lips with his own. Just the touch sent her reeling. She had been kissed once before meeting Charlie, and now kissed by Charlie twice. She didn't know if she could ever do this again and live to tell the tale. She was giddy.

Her hands clung to his shoulders this time, holding

on for dear life. But when he deepened the kiss, her fingers found their way to his neck and felt the beginning of his hairline. Springy healthy hair, slightly curled, flicked against the pads of her fingers, sending off other sensations in her body. How could anything feel so good? she wondered. But she couldn't think to come up with a reply.

His mouth caressed hers, his tongue gently flicking against her lips, asking for entrance. She loosened her mouth, slowly at first, and he entered to search and stroke her tongue. She felt dizzy with his touch; then he began his quest in earnest.

His hands pulled her torso even closer to his until she felt every button and belt loop indenting her skin through the light material of her dress. She barely breathed, yet needed no breath. She barely moved yet felt every pulse beat in his body. She felt as if she were flying.

She clamped her arms around his neck, holding on as he edged toward the safety of the kitchen chair. He bent, sitting down and keeping her in his lap. His hands held her waist tightly, nesting her against the hardness of his legs and strength of his chest. Her own pulse seemed to fill her with the primitive beat of blood coursing through her in a rush of current so strong she was almost blinded by it.

"Ease to me," Charlie said, his voice near her ear, gruff yet soft. His hands showed her what he wanted as he adjusted her on his lap.

She began to protest, unsure what she was doing and how right or wrong it was. This was Charlie, the man who was uninvited . . . .

His hand came up and stroked her brow, then closed her eyes with a featherlight touch. "Shh," he whispered just seconds before his mouth closed over her parted lips once again.

This time the kiss was as silky-soft as a butterfly's wing on a hot sunny day. She didn't move.

Suddenly she felt as if she'd been captured, just like a butterfly, by his sweetness, his gentleness. And she was thrilled he pressured no more than this, for surely she would be forced to flee. But where? her muddled mind asked, and the question echoed through her without answer. She didn't need one. Kathleen O'Day had just found heaven and wasn't about to lose it yet. Not yet . . .

Charlie's callused hands were so sensitive that he felt every sip of her every breath as she sat so still and sweet and open to his probing mouth and seeking hands. Her waist was even tinier than he thought it would be, the sensuously sweet flare of her hips making him ache for release. *Not yet,* he told himself over and over, concentrating on the words in order to keep his mind off the sweet luxury of her flesh beneath his palm. *Not yet.*

Without thinking, he slid his palms slowly up the soft cotton of her dress and soothed her back, curved toward him and so very flexible. She was strong and slightly muscled, yet there was a femininity about her that belied her physical strength.

Her mouth opened under his guidance and he felt her inner softness, knowing full well he wanted so much more than this. Her honeyed mouth reminded him of other warm and wonderful caverns just awaiting his touch.

He groaned and the sound echoed between the two of them like a chamber filled with bittersweet memories.

It had been so very long since he'd held a woman— a real, feminine, sweet woman who responded hon-

estly to his tenderness and caring and delicious delays.
A woman who wasn't sure what the next move was,
but was happy to spend this moment in his arms, with
just him and nothing else to clutter the demands
made upon them both.

He'd been so wrong about Kathleen! This woman
was tough and honest and so very sweet. This was no
lady of the evening. Hell, she didn't know what could
happen from this point on any more than his own
sweet—No. He wasn't going to the memory of
another woman while he was with Kathleen. This
wasn't a time for sadness or regrets. This was a new
time. A new place. A new woman. A new him.

And Charlie was just vulnerable enough to feel the
difference, and horny enough to want to savor the
moment.

Her fingers climbed through his hair, massaging
his scalp until suddenly she held his head between
her palms and kissed him with a fervor he didn't know
she was capable of, with a strong and unsophisticated
manner that was as startling as it was endearing.

God, he wanted her! His fingers dug into her back,
pulling her as close as he could, needing to feel the
pressure of her breasts against his chest, her breathing
matching his. Her small frame yielded to his pressure
and she curled into him, taking his breath away with
the utter sensuality of her. He wanted to absorb her
into him, to keep her there forever—or at least for
a moment or two.

When she finally pulled away, she stared down at
him with wide eyes the color of green meadows after
a spring shower.

"I cannot do this," she protested, her lips wet and
full from the pressure of his own mouth. Such beautiful lips.

"No," he said. He was agreeing with her without

letting go. He never wanted to let go. Instead the image that came to mind was plunging into the honey-sweet depths of her, feel the tightness surround him, and look into those eyes as he drowned in the feelings that overwhelmed him right now.

"We have things to do," she said, her voice barely a whisper, breathless, with the still-quickened heart-beat of a caged bird thudding lightly against his chest.

"Yes," he said, finally willing to admit to the reality even while he felt the pulse at the base of her neck with his tongue.

"I'm not what you think I am."

She was still thinking of his ugly names for her when they first met.

"I know," he said, nuzzling her neck and feeling a pulse point there, too. His ear brushed her breast and he couldn't help himself. He bent his face to rest on the soft roundness of her for just a moment before taking her nipple, dress and all, into his mouth and breathing hot air onto it.

Her breath caught in her throat. She didn't stir. Somewhere far off, he could hear a slight gasp, but it didn't override the overwhelming need that washed over him. He gave a gentle suck through the cloth, felt her nipple react almost exactly as she had, by pouting prettily for him.

"Stop," she whispered, but it was so light a sound he wasn't quite sure he heard it over the heavy pound-ing of his heart.

"Mmmm," he said, and it vibrated through his mouth against her breast.

"Oh, please," she whispered, again so lightly he wasn't sure whether he heard the words or just imag-ined them.

"Yes," he said, his hands cupping both breasts now, and he realized how wonderfully they filled his palms.

Knowing that if one tasted so sweet the other would taste just as honeyed, he searched for the other breast. Nuzzling as a child seeking sustenance, he worked across and found what he wanted with a satisfying sigh. His mouth circled once more and he breathed deeply, then blew on the material he'd just wet with his mouth. Once it was warmed, he suckled gently until the moan came from her this time. It was low and deep and rose slightly at the end as if she was afraid of what came next. But he couldn't stop now. Wouldn't. Not for all the bounty from all the Vic Masters types in Texas.

"We have to stop," she said, but this time her voice wasn't the soft whisper it had been earlier. It was the rough and deeply emotional sound of a woman who was mouthing exactly what she didn't want to do. Out of honor. Or disgrace. Or the frustration of not having done the deed.

"When?" he asked, just before nibbling on her breast again. Even with the fabric between them, he loved the feel of her.

"Soon. Very soon," she said.

He dropped one hand to her leg and let her get used to him touching her there. Then, slowly, he allowed his hand to drift up her leg to the apex of her thighs.

Like a shot, her hand dropped and stopped his. "No."

"Just let me touch."

"No." But the pressure of her hand lessened.

"I won't hurt you. I promise." He covered her nipple once more and blew hot air softly. "Stop me when you've had enough. In a few minutes."

"I . . ."

He let his hand run up the rest of the way. The

pressure of her hand was on his, but not hard enough to stop, only enough to warn.

With careful fingers, he found the slit in her undergarment and touched the soft mound it covered.

Kathleen gasped. Her hand was still over his, but she didn't move. Just as when he had taken her breast in his mouth, she sat perfectly still and waited like a poised doe in the sight of a hunter.

With a slow and gentle touch, he allowed his finger inside the fleshy folds, rubbing his knuckle back and forth ever so slightly.

The gasp turned to a low moan that filled the room when he followed with the same sound of longing.

He was filled with the need to pleasure her, to have her feel what could only be described as a tiny death. That need was more forceful to him than his own release. This was her time. This was for her and her alone. He promised it to himself.

"Feel it, sweet baby. Feel it and enjoy it," Charlie said as he continued his small manipulations and felt her quivering in his arms.

A breath escaped her mouth, ending on a keening sound that reverberated in his soul. He loved the sound; he loved knowing he was the one giving her the feeling that produced the sound that made her quiver in his arms.

His mouth covered her breast again, and this time he suckled a little harder through the material. Kathleen strained toward him, wanting to envelop him in her body. He felt it. He knew it. He reveled in it.

His knuckle worked back and forth, never losing the rhythm that seemed to please her so well. Neither fast nor strong, it was half-time with his own quickened heartbeat.

She stiffened, moaned, then clamped her hands

on his shoulders as her body remained poised on his lap as if ready to flee at any moment.

But he knew what was happening and he loved it. He'd done this to her. No one else. Just him. And she would never forget that. Never.

With a rush of wind and all the tension escaping her body, Kathleen collapsed against him. Her heartbeat pounded against his cheek, her breathing stirring the hair at the nape of his neck. Each breath of hers sounded like a small circlet of sound that placed a halo on his head for his own massive restraint.

Carefully he pulled his hand away from her most intimate spot and brushed down her skirt for her before holding her to him with both hands. His spirit cried out for its own release, but he ignored it.

"Are you all right?" he asked, knowing full well she was more than all right. She was far more comfortable than he was. She'd had release. He was still sitting here with reality in his lap and a fantasy that was unfulfilled . . . for the moment.

She pulled back and looked down at him, her eyes dilated with an intensity of emotions.

Then her gaze narrowed.

"Charlie Macon," she said softly but in a very firm voice that didn't match the moment at all. "I don't ever want to see or touch you again. Do you understand?"

"What?" he asked, as if words weren't making sense. They weren't.

"You heard me. You can sleep in the barn tonight for all I care, but I don't want you anywhere near me." She stood and pointed toward the back door. "Now get out!"

Eleven

Kathleen spent the rest of the day in the fields with her uncle's long-sleeved shirt, floppy hat, and trusty hoe. She had already prepared the soil for the next crop of carrots and vegetables, but until the seeds she ordered came in, she needed to keep out the weeds that wanted to grow as plentifully as the crop. It was wonderful therapy.

If she had thought never to see Charlie again after the indiscretion she'd created in the bathtub on rehearsal night, she was wrong. That was not a very good reason never to lay eyes on him again. Why, it was just another ordinary if slightly embarrassing incident in all the other slightly embarrassing incidents of her life.

But after this morning . . . well, that was a horse of a different color.

Now she had good, substantial, rock-hard reasons never to see him again!

Now she had compounded what had been a very

tiny indiscretion into a major sin, if what her sister-
in-law had to say about sins—major and minor—was
correct. The guilt of her actions was so heavy she was
crumbling beneath the weight of it.

Now she had the right to slip out of the house and
never return until Charlie left this part of the world.
She could only hope it wouldn't take more than a
week. Until then, she'd hide somewhere, anywhere,
as long as he never knew her whereabouts.

But, having known Charlie this past week, she had a
feeling that a week wouldn't be long enough. Charlie,
rather than giving up his cover to find Vic, would use
her absence to his advantage. He'd probably go door
to door, hat in hand, and plead for help in finding
his dear sister. And trying to find out who could have
carted her off against her will—for certainly it would
be against her will! How could she leave just when
her dear brother came to visit?—and not returned
by now. And all the while he was visiting, he'd be
checking each and every house in Blissful for the
nefarious Vic Masters.

And then the entire town would be searching for
her and no one would get any work done, her cakes
wouldn't be baked, Josetta wouldn't get paid, and the
train committee might not meet . . . .

No. As much as she might not want to see him ever
again—and that was a mighty much—she knew she
had to find another way. She could not drag the town
into her own personal problems. She could not allow
anyone, not *anyone* to know what had just transpired
right in her own kitchen. *Under any circumstances!*

If that meant smiling at Charlie for the next week
while helping him find that Vic whoever as fast as he
could so he'd leave town equally as quickly, then so
be it. She'd already done as much damage as she

could . . . well, almost as much damage. She might as well repair the fences and go about her business.

Tomorrow afternoon was the play. Everything was arranged and she had to be there ready and waiting to sell her wares so she could buy more seed. Fall was coming. In another week, with luck, she'd get in the third crop of carrots and vegetables this year. It had been a mild early spring and a mild early summer, considering some she'd experienced.

Last year the heat was so strong, it came off the prairie in waves, enveloping everything and sucking the water out of everything, including her skin. If it hadn't been for the light breeze blowing between the front and back doors and the coolness of the cellar, where she retreated with a book in hand and a full, lit candle during the late afternoon when the sun was at its zenith, she never would have made it through without fainting full away. Between the cellar and Bliss Creek behind her, she'd managed just fine, thank you very much.

And if she could face a hot Texas summer by herself, enlist the support of the townspeople of Blissful, convince the surrounding area into the conspiracy, and talk the railroad board of directors into a water stop, then she should be able to face Charlie Macon again, no matter what horrible things she had done.

So there.

After the sun set, she milked the cow and washed up, grabbing a bowl of cold beans before entering her room and closing the door on the world.

But just in case, as she undressed for bed, she said a quick prayer, then crossed her fingers. Turning over to face the window breeze ruffling her sheer lace curtains, Kathleen closed her eyes determinedly and told herself to go to sleep. She would handle whatever came up tomorrow.

* * *

Meanwhile, in the other bedroom, Charlie stared at the ceiling and pretended he had no unfulfilled desires and fantasies. He lied.

Aside from the ability to make a tent with a sheet over him, his entire body hummed with the desire to possess Kathleen. But it wasn't just carrying her to bed that mattered to Charlie. There was something so elusive about her, something that called to him until he felt the pull like a siren's call.

What he had done to Kathleen in the kitchen chair, he'd never done before. Ever. It amazed him that he was so selfless in insuring that she felt that overwhelming rush of fulfillment without his own needs getting in the way. And when she stiffened and held on for dear life, he had felt more powerful than a herd of buffalo pounding down the plains. *He* had done that for her. No one else. He doubted Kathleen would have allowed anyone else near enough to initiate such intimacies.

Despite his own private agony, he was damn proud of himself. And he couldn't wait to see Kathleen again. Maybe next time he would experience a new kind of fulfillment. Maybe she would reciprocate, he thought as he finally drifted off to sleep.

Before dawn the next morning, Charlie was awakened by his bedroom door slamming against the pegs in the wall. He sat straight up in bed, reaching for his gun as he did so.

But the wraith framed in his doorway stopped him in midmove. Kathleen stood framed in the doorway holding a candle in a saucer. Her nightgown of pink and white gauzy material swirled around her like a lonely cowboy's finest apparition. Her hair was down and loose, lying on her breasts like he wanted to. But her face was spawned of the devil himself: beautiful and definitely untouchable.

"I will be milking Hilde in a few minutes. But before I go, I want you to know that what happened last night will never happen again. Never. Do you understand?"

His heart sank. She stood in front of him so he could know without a doubt that what he wanted most of all was not within his reach. He hid behind sardonic humor, using it as a shield for his own emotions. "Does that mean you don't love me anymore?"

Her eyes widened and even from the bed he could see the brilliant green color. "Never did," she finally said. "Never will."

"Speak in haste, repent at leisure," he said softly, leaning on one elbow, his bare chest and stomach exposed. The sheet remained draped at his hips. "You're a smart, churchgoin' lady. Never make bets you can't keep."

"Never fear," she snapped. "Sleep in. There's still an hour till daylight."

"Well, couldn't you have waited to tell me then, instead of waking me in the middle of a dream I was having about a sweet and wonderful woman who cared?"

Her smile never reached those beautiful eyes. "No time like the present."

"Kathleen O'Day, you have a mean streak in you."

"And you have a selfish one, Charlie Macon. You led me to the waters and made me feel too foolish to drink. I don't like that at all. So from now on, we'll just remain brother and sister, and both of us will know our role in this farce. In fact, don't think you're too good to do the chores. There are plenty to be done, and it's time you got to work, too, Brother John."

He looked at her warily. He was never certain what she was going to do next. "If you were smart, dear sister, you'd listen to your brother and stop behaving like a man." It sounded ludicrous. She had never looked so feminine as she did this very moment. "Let me make a few decisions around here."

Her brows rose knowingly. "Like what, brother? What happened here last night never would have happened between us if I were the man in the house. I would have stopped myself out of pride or self-control or honor." She began to turn away, the gown swirling around her. Then she stopped and looked over her shoulder. The picture was heart-stoppingly sensuous and would remain in his head long past this day.

"Oh, one more thing. We are invited to dinner at Amy's tonight. She and her husband, Troy, want to meet you. You have all day to memorize our history. We'll leave after I return from my quilting bee this afternoon."

"Of course, sister." Charlie's tone was mocking, but Kathleen didn't bother giving him any more of her valuable time. She left, her gown wafting behind like a softly undulating wave. The familiar, lingering scent of her filled his nostrils. It was soft tea roses and that indefinable ingredient that was so very Kathleen.

His physical reaction was instantaneous. *Damn the woman!*

Kathleen sat in Mabel's wagon and held on to her bonnet as Mabel touched the flank of her carriage horse with a quirt. The poor animal sped up the dirt road at a rate that was better if seated directly on the horse instead of allowing it to pull them in a flimsy carriage that was more for looks than for practicality. They were late. The train would arrive in half an hour. Her carrot cake was sliced and ready for sale. Amy had offered to sell them for her to the wide-eyed train passengers as the play was going on.

Evelyn and Mabel helped with the staging. Evelyn was warm and funny and friendly. She had a small daughter, six-year-old Trudi, who was just as sweet and funny as her mama.

Mabel, however, was the opposite. Usually staid and somber, she was a young widow who lived alone, with no children, and, until the plays began, she was a recluse. What she lacked in warmth and sparkling personality she made up in organizational skills. They were wonderful, and her distinct lack of humor helped keep the men in line. Kathleen did not know if it was because Mabel now had a more active role in the playacting that allowed those skills to come forward and be seen more, but it certainly seemed so. Lately she was more talkative, contributing and smiling far more than in all the past two years put together. The past two plays, she was Kathleen's second in command at the prompting, handling the upstairs when the "lady of the evening" went out to the balcony and began screaming for help. Kathleen would be downstairs, coordinating the men in the street, and Mabel would handle the upstairs acting.

They hit a rut with such a shock that Kathleen held her bonnet in place with one hand while holding to the edge of the bench with the other. An involuntary sharp cry passed her throat as her tailbone came down hard on the barely padded seat.

"Sorry," Mabel stated breathlessly as she kept the horse at a good gallop toward the town less than a mile away. "I just want this to be over with early."

"It cannot last longer than the train stays in town, Mabel," Kathleen protested, still holding fast despite her driver's attempt to rid herself of her guest.

Mabel didn't seem to notice her discomfort. "I know, but if we can get the visiting over with before the play, then perhaps I will be able to leave a little earlier this evening."

"You can leave whenever you wish!" Kathleen's voice rose and fell with the ruts and stone vibrations in the road.

"I know, but . . . " Instead of finishing her sentence, Mabel gave the horse another lash of the quirt and held as tightly to the reins as she did to her tongue

They were in the center of town, around the back of the hotel, and parked by the stable within five minutes of Mabel's having picked Kathleen up from her home on the outskirts of town.

With a strained smile, Kathleen gratefully accepted the hand of Adam, the young stable hand, and stepped down from the carriage.

Mabel didn't wait for help. Instead she jumped to the ground as if she'd done it all her life. They both slapped their skirts to rid them of some of the dust of the road before walking into the hotel lobby. The hotel was now closed, but the hope was that it would soon be open again, if Kathleen had any say in it. Old Mr. Heine used to run it. His wife now owned it, and she had her eye on Zeke to help her run it. Zeke was a torn man. He wanted to own it, run it, and enjoy Mrs. Heine's dumplings, but he wasn't sure the "noose o' marriage" was for him, he'd say quietly . . . very quietly.

But for now, Zeke was directing everyone to the main lobby while shouting for the stable hand who had followed them to bring around the horses needed for the play. The town needed to look busy, sleazy, and a lot on the wild side. That meant that people had to be coming and going. Gamblers, shady women, one or two good folk who looked as if they were in a hurry to get their shopping done and get out of the town—all had to be in place before the train arrived.

At the front door of the porch Kathleen recognized Ed's tall, bone-lean body above the crowd. His nervous frown was a trademark, and it was in place, so all must be well. He was coordinating the placement of carriages and horses, right down to empty luggage and trunks strategically situated on the wagon by the depot steps.

In the far-off distance, the high-pitched sound of the train whistle echoed in the warm air. It was a warning to all. Everyone needed to be in place quickly.

"Y'all hear that?" Ed called to the already bustling crowd in the lobby. "Be ready in two minutes!"

Hank and Zeke headed up the dusty stairs with Bitsy, who was playing the dance-hall girl, and Orville, playing the villain. Ed sat at the tinny piano and opened the window to insure the sound would carry. Timely, playing the sheriff as usual, ran out the door and across the street to the depot. When the train pulled in, he was supposed to be talking to the telegraph operator and waving at the passengers before seeing the commotion on the balcony. Then, after several warnings, he was to shoot Orville off the side balcony and into the large military tarp several of the townspeople were holding to break his fall. Orville would die killing Timely. It would be his twenty-fifth time to die. Jacob and Zeke had extended the balcony around the side for just that occasion. In fact, if the train was positioned correctly and Orville staged his death throes just right, he wouldn't have to fall into the blanket. Instead he'd just throw a pumpkin over the back side and curl into a ball in the dark corner while the squash plopped and split on the ground below, making the hollow sound of a dead body.

That is, if they could keep Bitsy from giggling through her own death. That high-pitched squeal that erupted from her mouth when something caught her sense of humor was enough to startle birds from the trees a mile away.

Less than twenty seconds later the train screeched and protested as it slowed down before pulling into the station. An engineer stepped down from the steam engine and unlatched the large hose from the water tower; then, with much grunting and groaning, he placed it inside the large barrel behind the coal bin.

With a heart that banged against her ribs with increasing pressure, Kathleen took her position at the curve of the window so she could cue the timing. Through a panel of ivory lace and dust she watched the rest of the Blissful townsfolk climb on board the passenger cars and begin hawking the wares they were selling, both for themselves and for others. The train would remain in the station for ten minutes. That was all the time they had to pull off the death scene of the century . . . this week.

As if to verify the fact that this town held tight to the reputation as the home of the devil himself, the passengers in all four cars craned against the smoke-smudged windows for a look.

Tinny music blared through the streets as Ed played something that sounded more like a fast-paced jig than a dance for a dance-hall girl. But it was too late to change the tune now. Besides, Kathleen would bet that the visitors sitting in the train wouldn't notice

the musical tune as much as just feel the rowdiness
of it.

A few townspeople bustled in and out of the shops
farther down the street, making it look as if it were
a perfectly ordinary day of shopping in Blissful. A
young boy playing with a hoop was called to the boardwalk by his mother, taken by the ear, and pulled into
the barbershop.

Timely strolled out of the telegraph office, acting
perfect in his part. The real Timely was sad and shy
and withdrawn. But when he played the part of the
sheriff, he changed miraculously into whoever was
the other side of the coin. His smile was knowing,
manly, as if he were sharing a bawdy joke with other
male friends, with a tinge of secret-buddy laughter
that meant a female was involved. He strolled along
the boardwalk, smiling and tipping his broad-
brimmed cowboy hat at some of the younger females
looking out the windows. His stroll was almost a swagger, a male comfortable in his manliness. His hand
rested easily on his holstered gun, his other hand
swinging at his side.

Kathleen cued Zeke, who stood on the steps to the
second floor. Zeke gave a signal to Orville, waiting
at the upstairs landing. "Now!" he whispered harshly.

The wood floor beneath Orville's boots creaked as
he rushed toward the front bedroom, where Bitsy
waited in her harlot's costume.

Kathleen crossed her fingers as she waited for the
first shout. Her part was almost over. Mabel would
take over orchestrating the rest of the scene upstairs.
This was her moment of glory—the first time she'd
ever done the end scene.

Kathleen grabbed her shawl and market basket and
headed out the front door of the hotel just as Ed
broke into a melancholy tune to fit the fight scene

coming up. Just as she stood at the porch steps, Bitsy ran outside the room door onto the balcony.

The action had begun.

"No! No! Please don't kill me!" she cried, running to the balcony and holding on as she faced the villain following her.

"Don't you tell me what to do! I saw you in there! Dancing with that dirty, no good . . . " He acted as if he slapped her while Mabel clapped her hands from the window toward the train, making a louder noise than any Orville could have made.

Kathleen stepped off the porch and ran across the street to the saloon, running inside as if the hounds of hell were after her and she was seeking shelter.

Timely turned from the passengers in the car, all his attention on trying to locate the screams. The passengers helped, pointing and shouting to the sheriff and letting him know where the danger was.

"Hold it!" he shouted once the passengers pointed out the argument.

"She's nothin' but a hussy!" Orville shouted loudly enough for the passengers to hear through the open-topped windows.

"I don't care. Everyone deserves a chance to live and to repent, young man. Including you! Now unhand the lady!" Timely ordered in his deep baritone voice.

"Lady?" Orville spat. "You're crazy, Sheriff! She's not worth your gettin' kilt fer!"

Kathleen glanced at her watch resting on her bosom. Time was closing in. The townspeople on the train had four minutes to complete their sales, help the customers duck any stray "bullets" from the gunfight, and hop off the train before it left the station.

"Don't do anything foolish!" Timely shouted.

"This is the sheriff talking!" That was just in case anyone on the train didn't know who he was.

Once Kathleen made it to the saloon, she watched from the window, where no one could see her. The balcony was directly across from her, tilted slightly toward the train station. Orville had Bitsy by the hair and was getting ready to slap her again.

Kathleen had a feeling that the sound of shock in Bitsy's voice was real. Orville had a fistful of hair in his hand.

"Stop, I say! Don't lay a hand on that young woman!" Timely shouted, stepping toward the board-walk nearest the corner of the saloon. The late-after-noon sun glinted off his shoe shine-dyed hair. He ran across the dirt street and stood by the horse trough and took aim at Orville.

The engineer's helper grabbed the water spout out of the train barrel and worked it around to hitch it back onto the water tower. He was a young man from Blissful who had worked with the railroad for the past two years. Knowing he would be slipped a silver dollar for his efforts, he took his time fitting the hose to the barrels for filling.

Orville looked down at the sheriff, his face as malev-olent as he could make it. He succeeded. Kathleen felt an instant of sheer terror, and she *knew* this was a play. If she hadn't known, she'd be ducking under the seat on the train just like some of the more faint-at-heart passengers!

"She ain't worth your life, Sheriff. I'm awarnin' you. Stay outta this!"

Bitsy gave one more bloodcurdling scream and Timely ducked behind the trough.

Orville growled, then shot Bitsy. Her death scene was dramatic and loud. She screamed again, then dropped forward to drape herself on the balcony Ed had just shored up two days ago with fresh lumber and nails.

Her moans were melodramatic, but they were drowned out by Orville's cussing.

Timely took careful aim. The sound of his shots echoed through the buildings and across the prairie. Then he slowly stood behind the trough as Orville registered his surprise before staggering toward his balcony death scene. Just before he fell over the rail, he gave a wild shot that just happened to hit Timely.

Orville died a splendid death. It was the first time he was the villain, and Kathleen had been timid about appointing him as such, but she'd been wrong. He was wonderful. The thud of the pumpkin smashing in the alleyway and echoing hollowly through the street was a realistic sound of a dead man dropping.

Some of the people in the windows of the train winced as they heard the dead body hit the ground. Others seemed to feel great satisfaction. Still others covered their eyes, then looked between their fingers at the scene of carnage outside their train.

Kathleen gave a sigh of relief when she heard the whistle blow, warning the hawkers on board that the train was leaving.

Within seconds, as Timely dropped his gun and staggered toward the middle of the street toward the alley, the red smear on his vest showed he'd been shot. The passengers moaned in recognition of the bullet hitting its mark. Timely gave a glance up at the "dead" Bitsy draped over the balcony and shook his head. Just as he dropped to his knees by the entrance to the alley, the train pulled out of the station and chugged down the track toward the bright orange setting sun. There might be bigger and better towns down the way, Kathleen thought, but not one of them would give a performance such as this.

As the train pulled away, the hawkers poured out of the station and shouted their success. The rest of the actors poured out of the hotel and alleyway. Once the train was out of sight, Bitsy undraped herself from the balcony and gave several curtsies to the crowd in the street. Orville came from his hiding place in the far corner of the balcony and did the same, taking Bitsy's fishnet-gloved hand in his and bowing.

The crowd roared in approval.

Kathleen gave a heavy sigh of relief. It was over for another week, and, the next time, they didn't have to kill the sheriff to succeed.

Twelve

It was over and Kathleen could breathe a sigh of relief. She glanced at her watch pinned to her chest. It was barely four-thirty on a beautiful Texas afternoon. Everything had worked like clockwork. Mabel had done well, as had all the players. Even the train passengers had dutifully fallen into the make-believe, taking an interest in the town and warning the sheriff of what was about to happen. In fact, this was one of the best plays they had put on. There wasn't one hitch to worry about or go over with the culprit.

Mabel quickly walked across the boardwalk and stepped down to the dirt road, her eyes on Kathleen as if she were a goal to achieve. Kathleen waited quietly among the dancing and shouts around her.

"I'm leaving now," she said in her no-nonsense way. "Do you want me to take you home?"

Kathleen smiled. "No, but thank you. I'll walk home in a little while. I still have to do some shopping."

Mabel snapped her head in the semblance of a nod. "Very well then. I will see you on Monday for the next meeting."

"Fine," Kathleen said, wondering if Mabel had a problem she hadn't discussed with someone. After all, she lived alone, much as Kathleen did, and sometimes it was very lonely to deal with life's darts and arrows. She placed a hand on Mabel's arm just as she was about to turn and climb into her carriage, parked across the street at the station. "Is everything all right with you, Mabel?"

She looked startled. "Of course." She narrowed her eyes and studied Kathleen. "Why do you ask?" she questioned suspiciously.

"Because . . ." Kathleen hesitated, finding the right words that wouldn't alarm the woman. "You seem so preoccupied today. And because you and I both live alone and I know just how hard it is sometimes to have no one to rely on. I just thought that if there was any way my brother or I could help, I would be most happy to."

For the first time since she'd met Mabel, the woman smiled with genuine emotion gleaming from her eyes. "Why, Kathleen, that is so caring of you. Thank you for your thoughts, although it's not necessary. I just have so much to do." Her smile turned positively impish.

Kathleen smiled in return, secretly relieved. She didn't know if she could be around the woman for a long period of time and still be sweet. "Let me know if there's anything I can do to help."

"Thank you," Mabel said as she backed away from her and aimed toward the carriage. She gave another quick smile, then turned and practically ran through the crowd to her carriage.

"Kathleen!" Ed called, coming toward her with his

arm around a beaming Orville. "Did this man not do a fine job?" he stated proudly. "Best death we've had since Timely died in that there explosion last year!"

"Timely almost died in that explosion for real," Kathleen said. "That's why we can't do that anymore." But she reached up and patted Orville on the shoulder. "And yours certainly is some of the finest acting we've seen, Orville."

He beamed as if a hundred candles were lit inside him. "Thank you, ma'am. I jes' did what I was told."

Ed laughed heartily. "You did better than that, Orville! You stole the show away from that ol' bag. . . ." He suddenly looked around until he saw Bitsy preening with several of the women by the alley.

"Ed . . . " Kathleen warned, and he grinned sheepishly.

"Anyway, Orville. I knew you could do it. Didn't I tell you so?"

"Yep. You talked me into it, all right," Orville said, still beaming.

"Well, I'm proud," Ed stated, still so elated he could barely contain himself.

"Kathleen!" Evelyn called from the boardwalk, and Kathleen was so relieved to be called away.

"Excuse me," she said as she left them still patting each other on the back and hurried over to her friend.

Both laughed in relief that the weekly show was over and they were free for several days. "I thought you might need rescuing. However, I realize I do not resemble a knight. . . ."

"You were right. How are you?" she asked, taking her friend's arm and walking slowly down the temporarily deserted boardwalk. Evelyn's daughter, Trudi was on the boards, jumping up and down with a friend of hers. Her bonnet had fallen down her back, and her pretty face was as flushed with the success of playing as were the actors' with the finish of their plays.

"I'm fine." Evelyn patted her gloved hand. "But I do not have my brother breathing down my neck, watching each and every move I make, or trying to get me to take the long journey to his home."

"Although you're painting an accurate portrait of John, it's not quite so bad." She laughed. The thought of last night popped into her head and she felt her skin heat to the color of a beet. "Although, I must admit, I will be so very glad to see him leave."

"I understand," Evelyn said. "Now, tell me. Have you seen that cowboy bounty hunter lurking around since your brother came to visit?"

For a moment Kathleen's mind went blank. Then she remembered. She'd told Evelyn and Ed about Charlie, but never referred to him again. "I haven't seen him since. Has anyone else mentioned a stranger in town?"

"Not that I know of." They slowed down until they stood in front of the general store, just a few feet away from the jumping girls. "Oh, someone came into the saloon two days ago when Ed was looking over the place for the rehearsal. It turned out to be a young man who believed that he could kill any gunslinger we wanted him to kill . . . as long as the town paid him."

"My goodness!" This was what she'd been afraid of. The town's reputation was growing so fast and spreading so far that gunslingers were now entering and feeling safe. It was a good thing they wouldn't be doing the plays for too much longer. It didn't sound healthy. "What did Ed do?"

"He told the young man that he'd better get out of town before he found a bullet in his back like some of the other gunslingers had." Evelyn frowned. "It's so sad to see the young believing that killing is a good way of life."

"And we help perpetuate that myth by putting on our plays," Kathleen guessed.

Evelyn looked relieved that her friend understood. "Yes."

"Sometimes I think we're safe here. But we're not, you know. If we were farther west or in the hill country, we'd still have the stray Comanche to contend with, or more gunslingers hoping to put notches on their gun handles. But we're civilized here and have been lucky that our reputation has kept most of the riffraff away. Still, it's frightening what's outside of our community. Maybe just in the next town."

Evelyn furrowed her brow. "Has there been any trouble in Mason?" she asked, referring to the town just twenty miles away. It was their closest link with another town.

"Last I heard, they've had some cattle rustling now and then, pies and food stolen from farmhouses, but nothing big."

"Am I a worrywart?" Evelyn asked, referring back to their plays.

"Some. So am I." Kathleen laughed. "But it will all be over soon. And we made it through the dark times of the past two years by putting those plays on. After all, it helped everyone. The railroad got more customers than it would have ordinarily. The towns surrounding us got the benefit of others stopping in their travels. And Blissful got to have far more prosperity than we would have if we'd waited for the railroad to come to us." Kathleen glanced back at the group of men walking down the middle of the street. "If we hadn't done the plays, we'd be starving, this would be a ghost town, and no one would have the money in our bank to buy more cattle, more plows, more people.''

"I know you're right, but at what cost?'' Evelyn asked. "I'm afraid that if one wrong young man comes, there will be others. I know that is one of your fears, too. What will we do?''

A heavy sigh escaped Kathleen's lips. "I don't know, Evelyn. I honestly don't know. But God will help with whatever happens.'' She hoped she was right.

"We need a real, honest-to-goodness sheriff, Kathleen. We haven't had one in two years and we're gonna need one. Soon.''

"But who?''

"Don't know, but we need someone.'' Evelyn's voice was flat with certainty. "The next young man who walks into the saloon might not heed Ed's advice. Instead he might shoot Ed and whoever else is there.''

Kathleen's worst fears were voiced . . . by Evelyn. Those were the same thoughts she'd had when Charlie had told her about the gunman he was following.

"We'll bring it up at the next town meeting,'' she promised, wishing she could gather everyone together now and do something—anything—to make them feel better. "It's only a few weeks away.''

Sighing, Evelyn patted her friend's hand and gave a rueful smile. "I'm sorry to bring this up on such an auspicious day. I just thought it needed to be said before we all go into euphoria too soon. Our next steps are crucial if we're to continue thriving.''

Kathleen knew she was right, but there was nothing to do for it today except think of a solution. Her glance rested on Timely. He could play sheriff but he certainly couldn't *be* sheriff. They were two different realities.

"Don't worry. We'll do something,'' she promised. Then, bending to reach her friend's cheek, she placed a light kiss there. "Meanwhile, I need to order a few things. I'll see you at Amy's this evening?"

"Yes," Evelyn promised before turning to find her own carriage. As she pulled herself into the seat and reached for the reins, she gave a final wave. Kathleen did, too.

It took ten minutes to order her seed and flour from Jacob's catalog. In the end she promised the money would be dropped off first thing in the morning. That would give her something to do tomorrow to get out of the house and away from Charlie.

The walk home was uneventful and usually relaxing. Instead, Kathleen was nervous. Every footfall took her closer to facing him. Finally, despite her stopping to pick daisies in Linda and Frank's front yard, Kathleen was standing in front of her own.

It was a small house as houses went, but it was well kept. The tin roof gleamed bright silver in the late-afternoon sun. It had a few dents here and there from some of the hailstorms that passed through occasionally, but it would last many more years ... as would the barn roof. The house was painted a clean, crisp white with green shutters and doors, and the front porch with its two deer-horn chairs with striped green-and-white cushions looked inviting and homey. And beyond, the run of large cottonwood and oak and pine trees proclaimed the Blissful boundaries.

And it was all hers.

She was proud of it and of her Aunt Hattie for keeping it before her and for being able to maintain it. And she could keep it up, she told herself.

It sounded downright lonely.

"Fiddlesticks!" she stated softly, walking around the house to the back door, the first door opened in the morning and the first one closed at night. She wondered briefly where Charlie was. He'd ridden out early that morning and hadn't returned when she'd left. Where would she find him and what would he say? Better still, what would *she* say?

When she entered, she gave her eyes time to adjust to the late-afternoon shade. With a door and a small window in the kitchen, it had more light than most kitchens, but it was still dim.

No Charlie.

She walked into the parlor and looked around. No Charlie there, either. His bedroom door was open and she could see he wasn't there, either.

Where then?

Dropping her shawl, she walked to the barn and looked inside. "Charlie?" she finally called.

No answer.

Walking through to the other end of the barn, she looked out toward the creek. Standing perfectly still, she thought she heard . . . another splash. He was swimming in the creek.

Delight ran through her veins at the opportunity that presented itself. *Get even time*, she heard her own brother say when they were young. Before she even thought it through, Kathleen hightailed it down to the creek, remaining in the cover of the bushes as she located him. Peeping through the leaves, she searched all the deeper holes of the creek. He was in the deep bowl of a pool at the bend of the river, swimming like a beaver, going under, then popping up, then doing a stroke, then rolling over on his back and floating.

Well formed, well honed. He was so manly and beautiful she wanted to cry, then yell at him for tempting her. She was too far away to see every part of his anatomy, although she had to admit her interest and curiosity were piqued. But what she saw was firm muscles and tan skin, and he was so *handsome*. Too handsome for his own good—or for hers.

Out of the corner of her eye she saw a color that didn't fit in with the thick green ferns hugging the bank. She spotted what she was looking for: blue denim and plaid against lush green. Staying low, she made a beeline for the pile of clothes. His blue jeans, red and blue plaid shirt, socks, and boots were all laid neatly in a pile. Keeping her gaze on Charlie, she rounded up her booty. Once everything but the boots was gathered in her arms, she headed up to the house.

Charlie kept splashing like a playful puppy.

Kathleen ran, hoping the wind in her face would keep her from laughing aloud. Once back at the house, she dumped his clothing on his bed. It felt so satisfying to do *something*—anything to be active and take matters into her own hands. It erased the night before.

With a lightness in her step and a giggle in her throat, she went about her chores, going into the kitchen to take stock of Hilde's milk. Charlie had apparently milked her this morning, and all she needed was a quick milk this evening before they left. She would feed leftover milk to the chickens because she would have fresh milk in the morning.

Tossing out what milk remained, she cleaned up the jugs and pails with soap and a scrub brush. Bending the supple branches of her gardenia bushes in front and in the backyard, she tossed the soapy water on them so both sides of her garden would benefit. Her Aunt Hattie's gardenia bushes were her pride and joy when she was alive, and Kathleen could do no less for them. Besides, the plants seemed to enjoy the soapy water as long as it was only a light cleansing. It kept the white flies from building their mold on the underside of the leaves. As the weather got hotter, the flies would multiply.

Kathleen did all this out of habit. All her movements were done by rote. But her mind was entirely focused on Charlie at the river. As the early evening sun coasted down the side of the hill outside, she waited— for something. A shout. A yell that proclaimed Charlie's anger and frustration. Cursing that would blue the air. A cry for help . . . anything that said he realized his clothing was missing!

Nothing.

She scrubbed the bucket, then went to the barn, sat by Hilde's side, and milked her efficiently and quietly. When she was finished, she went back in the house. And all the time she waited for Charlie. Any moment she expected him to show up. He'd say something. Be angry. Explode.

But there was still no sign of him.

Had he drowned? Was he caught in a tree root and unable to get out? Had he been bitten by a water moccasin? She'd seen only one or two of them in the years she'd been there, but she wasn't sure that there wasn't one down there right now.

The later it got, the more she worried. Finally she couldn't stand it any longer and walked down to the creek with quick, decisive steps.

When she got to the last stand of trees near the bank, she couldn't see him. Kathleen walked along the bank. It was almost dark now, and her gaze searched every ripple. The creek was deeply shadowed by cottonwood and oak limbs. Still no sight of him.

Her heart thumped so heavily she could have run the entire length of the creek bank and back again. She could hardly breathe. Making her way down the bank to the deeper hole where swimming with long, even strokes was possible, she kept her eyes on the water, searching every shadow and rock for the sign of a male. The creek was full this time of year, and the water barely rippled on the top although the current was swift and strong beneath the surface. Was he caught there?

"Looking for something?" Charlie's voice echoed through the small copse. She jumped, then turned around to look behind her.

She couldn't have missed him. He stood at the top of the steep bank, naked except for a pair of cowboy boots, hands on his hips as if he were the conqueror of the world. Heavy ranch work was obviously his friend. His anger seemed to roll down the moss-covered hill and envelop her in heat. "Or should I say someone?" His deep, clipped tone reinforced his black mood.

Tears of relief sprang to her eyes. "I thought you had drowned."

"How touching. So you ran to the creek to claim my clothes, thinking I wouldn't need them anymore? What a kind heart you have—probably willing to donate them immediately to help the poor!"

"No! I meant to take them, but not for that reason," she stammered. For the first time in her life she felt as if she couldn't think fast enough.

"You meant to take them with you, whether I was dead or alive?" he asked, one dark brow raised.

"No!" She turned to face him directly, suddenly absorbing his anger and turning it back to him. "Stop twisting everything I say! So far you've made me late for a dinner we were both supposed to attend. I feel bad enough already. Don't make me regret helping you out!"

"How in the hell have you delusioned yourself into

thinking you helped me out? By stealing my clothes? Or by returning much later to see if I was dead yet?''

It was her turn to demand an ear. Her chin tilted in defiance. "By giving you my brother's name as a cover for your search and giving you a place to live while you did what you said you were doing— although I never saw you do anything to find the big bad man, except harass me!''

Charlie stood stock still for a long moment. His hands dropped off his slim, naked hips. For once she wasn't taken with any one part of him, but with the whole of the man. He was all-over gorgeous, although she'd never admit it for the world. He was obviously unashamed and taken with himself enough for both of them.

"Well, if I find my clothing, I'll be more than happy to escort you to the dinner, which, I believe, begins in less than fifteen minutes." He dangled his watch fob from his hand. "My watch was in my boots."

"How convenient," she muttered.

"Now don't get hostile," Charlie said with a smile that proved he was glad she was as defensive as he'd been offensive. "I'll walk up to the house first and get my clothes. We'll be ready right after you get ready."

"Why am I waiting?"

"Give me a few minutes to get to the house," he explained.

"I've already seen what you have to offer," Kathleen reminded him dryly, although her mouth was drier than her tone. "There's little surprise there," she said.

He gave a grunt and a laugh. "That's what you think. But I'll play along."

He turned and strode back to the house. It was a

wonderful sight: a stark-naked Charlie, except for well-worn boots, striding with purpose to her home.

Great butt.

She couldn't help the smile or the soft giggle that erupted from her. Charlie might be all male—goodness knew he just proved that aspect of himself—but he wasn't infallible.

He was walking with his legs just slightly apart, as if he didn't want to rub something the wrong way.

It was the best entertainment she'd ever had.

With a still-silent Kathleen seated stiffly next to Charlie on the wagon seat, he clucked the horses and eased them onto the dirt road.

He felt as uncomfortable as she acted. Charlie hadn't been a house guest for a real, sit-down dinner for a long time. Women weren't dangling around his ranch, and on the few occasions he ate at the local hotel in town, he'd been alone or with some other ranchers. Not a woman. Not women.

He prayed he remembered his rusty skills at socializing. It had been a long while back since he had to remember anything social at all.

Although he hadn't wanted to go, he was clean, dressed, and spit-polished. He wouldn't embarrass Kathleen. For all his anger earlier, he was angrier with himself than he was with her. He had to be. Otherwise there was nothing he wouldn't have done before swimming in an icy cold stream, then standing on the top of a hill stark-naked. That was not the way to persuade a woman of any charm into his bed, that was for sure! He was damn lucky he persuaded her to look at him for even a moment without laughing! The . . . family jewels had shriveled a lot in the water; then the cool evening breeze did its work, and from the look on Kathleen's face, she wasn't awed because of his equipment.

But she hadn't seen him in the best light, he told himself. Somehow he didn't think it mattered. He'd show her just how wonderful he really was. He didn't know how, but he would, and he'd start now.

Amy McLendon and her husband, Troy, were as open and friendly as if they'd known him for years. Amy chattered from the moment they walked to the door of the lovely house just on the edge of the downtown area.

"The name Troy doesn't fit in this here country," her husband had said in a slow, soft voice as he held out his hand during the introductions. "But it's the name my pappy gave me, so I trust I'll continue to use it."

Charlie felt at home with the lanky young man immediately.

Amy served them cool glasses of milked coffee, sweetened with just the right amount of sugar. Troy added just a "tetch" of whiskey to the men's drinks as they strolled out to the porch for a cigarette before dinner.

The porch was dark, the sky brilliant with a full moon and dancing stars. Lamplight barely filtered through the single lace- and cloth-draped window, and after a few minutes, Charlie's eyes adjusted to the light and he could see the man he was with.

Kathleen disappeared into the kitchen with Amy almost as soon as the drinks were served, and he hadn't seen her since. Occasionally their voices rose in laughter, and he had to smile in return. For Charlie, the sound of their feminine voices and lilting tones was wonderful. It meant their surroundings were safe and the families were happy. That gave him a warm feeling in the pit of his stomach that he didn't want to go away. It was like Kathleen's carrot cake and warm milk, served with her sweet, sweet smile . . . .

"We're from Virginia," Troy finally said by way of making conversation. He leaned against the post and expertly rolled a cigarette. "Not too far away from the border."

"How long have you lived here?"

"Oh, 'bout six years now. Can't think of living anywhere else. This is home."

"I guess you know everybody in town."

Troy chuckled. "I guess I do."

"Ever see any strangers around?"

"I'm looking at one."

Charlie grinned. "Any others?"

"Occasionally. But they're not strangers long. They either belong to someone or move on."

"Any lately?"

"Are you looking for someone in particular?"

"No, not really," Charlie lied. "I was just wondering. With this town's reputation, it wouldn't be hard to imagine some lowlife coming into town to try to take over."

"That hasn't happened yet," Troy said slowly. "Although, I admit, it is a possibility. But I haven't seen anyone." He looked long at Charlie. "Why?"

"Because I'm trying to get my sister to move back with me, and I thought if there were any lowlifes around, it would be a good reason for her to leave. Her living all alone and all."

"I see," Troy said, drawing on his cigarette. "Where is your place exactly?"

Charlie tried desperately to remember exactly where Kathleen had said she was from. He couldn't. He dredged up every memory of Kathleen's conversations. Nothing came to mind. "Oh, well, not far from the Virginia border, long as you're not walkin'," he finally said with a chuckle he hoped sounded relaxed and easygoing—all the things he wasn't.

"Really? Pretty country around there—a little wet, but mighty pretty. Kathleen says your family farms. What crops do you raise?"

Something finally came to mind. "Used to be cotton, but there's not much call for it now that there are so many newfangled inventions around. Now I truck vegetables and grow indigo."

"Still prosperous," Troy said slowly. "I do some truck farmin' myself, but mostly I got cattle. Lots of cattle."

"Is it profitable down here?" Charlie asked. Oklahoma and the panhandle, he knew, were cattle country. But he thought the land between Houston and Fort Worth was more gardening land.

"Very. Not everybody shifts their herd up north. We have plenty of folks to feed down here, too. And I sell Santa Gertrudis milk cows as well."

Charlie was impressed. That new breed was doing well and catching on. It was also costly.

"And you're not worried about Amy and the other women in this town, women like Kathleen, being hurt or worse by the criminal element coming through?"

Silence hung in the air as Troy looked at him through narrowed eyes. Charlie waited, almost as if Troy's words would confirm or deny the state of the small town.

"Well," Troy finally drawled, "I'm worried about them all the time. But I own the land here, and my life is here, and Amy's friends are here. Looks like we'll just have to clean up the town's image," he said.

"Meanwhile, aren't you still worried?" Charlie pressed.

Troy flicked the cigarette into the darkness and watched it land. His hands gripped the rough porch railing. "Worried as hell," he finally admitted. "I taught Amy how to use a gun, and how to scream at the top of her lungs. I make sure my neighbors, good folk, know when I am home and when I am leaving. Then I practically insist she goes with me whenever I can. It's all I can do."

Charlie nodded. He understood all that. When his wife was alive, he had done the same thing. And when he had to be gone from the ranch, he worried. And when he was out on the range, he worried.

Or was it that he had been lonely without her company?

He didn't know which, but he was familiar with the feelings that Troy's words created.

"If the town needs any help while I'm here, let me know. I'd like to keep this place safe for my sister, too," he said before downing the rest of the drink and wishing there were more whiskey in the glass. Just the thought of leaving Kathleen in a town like this when his business was through made his gut wrench.

Just then, Amy's lilting voice called to the men. "Are you going to smoke all night, Troy, or come join us poor women and keep us company?"

Troy's eyes lit up and his lanky body straightened. "Coming, my dear. I cannot believe you think I would miss one of your meals." He opened the screen door and allowed Charlie in first. "After six years of marriage, you should know me better than that."

Amy went on tiptoe to give Troy a peck on his cheek. "I know a man who loves to eat," she said in a playful voice before walking over to Charlie and taking his arm. "So I have no fear your feet will be under my table. I'm just worried about John, who doesn't know I'm the world's finest cook. So I will lead him to the table, since you already know the way."

Charlie grinned, enjoying his hostess's flirtatious attention, knowing full well this was a loving couple and remembering that host and hostess took care of their guests to the exclusion of each other. At least that was what his wife used to remind him.

His gaze sought out Kathleen, standing by her chair in the dining area. She was prettier than any picture he'd ever seen. Her flame-colored hair was tied back decorously with a blue ribbon that matched the blue-and-white gingham dress she wore. He wanted her on his arm . . . in his arms. In his bed.

"Over here, Brother John," Kathleen said, patting the chair next to hers. "We shall face our host and hostess across the table and regale them with stories of our childhood."

Trying to keep his gaze from the material caressing her breasts, Charlie had never felt less like a brother in all his life. Apparently his mind realized it, too, for it began a chain reaction quickly and mightily, letting him know just who was in charge.

Kathleen's gaze locked with his, and it was as if she read his mind. In case there was any doubt, she blushed.

He grinned, satisfied his unspoken message was accurately delivered.

Funny how four people could be in the same room, and all standing with the wrong people . . . .

Thirteen

By the time dinner was finished, Charlie was certain Amy was the best cook in town. Dinner was delicious: slowly cooked venison, fresh greens, bowls of pinto beans with bits of rabbit, and gingerbread cake with thick dollops of fresh whipped cream for dessert. He ate two pieces.

"That's the best food I've had since"—Charlie began, but when he felt the sharp toe of Kathleen's shoe, it brought him back to reality quickly and he smiled broadly—"since my sweet sister cooked such a delicious stew for me."

"Why, that's such a nice thing for you to say." Amy laughed. "But since Kathleen probably cooked for you last night, it's not saying much. Besides, I've tasted her cooking and it's wonderful." She turned to her friend. "And you promised to give me the recipe for that chicken-fried steak you made last month."

Charlie looked at Kathleen in surprise. "Chicken

fryin' a steak? Why would you do that, little sister? Isn't steak good enough as it is?''

Her hand rested daintily on his arm and he felt the heat searing through the material of his sleeve. "Why, brother, I used to cook that same meal for our daddy," she said, teasing.

His brows rose. "Really? I don't remember you ever cookin' it for me," he said innocently. "Guess I wasn't around then, little sister."

Her expression looked a little strained. "Maybe not. You always were traveling around the countryside, spinning lies to all the women until they fell at your feet."

"Not too many of those," Charlie said, watching his host rise and walk to the small cabinet in the parlor. Troy pulled out a bottle of liquor and held it up in silent question.

Charlie nodded his answer.

"Why, you're much too modest, John. Before you were married, you had half the girls in the county panting over you."

"And you had several of the farmers wanting you in their kitchen, making dinners that would bring tears to their eyes," he stated graciously. But he hoped she saw the glint in his eye that reminded her of how she left him making his own dinners of bread and beef. Unless she was making a stew to knock him out for hours.

"My goodness," Amy said in wonder. "I had no idea, Kathleen, that you had such a romantic brother. He thinks so highly of you." Her voice held a tinge of envy. "You're very lucky."

Kathleen remembered that Amy had two brothers and a sister, and none of them ever answered her many letters. They remained together and at home in Cincinnati. Amy had admitted she craved family.

So far she had not been graced with children—and no one deserved them more than Amy. She was the most loving and caring person Kathleen knew. She was also blessed with a man who loved her more than he loved himself. Troy worshiped Amy even more than Amy loved him. It was nice to see. It reminded everyone around them how wonderful married life could be.

Charlie smiled as if Amy's compliment were only for him. Well, it was, he told himself. It had little to do with the fact that Kathleen was supposed to be deserving of being loved by her brother. Everything she said told Charlie that her brother was not a very nice person. "Kathleen's a very special lady. She's smart as a whip and twice as kind. Any man would be proud to have her on his arm. I don't want her to settle for any man. There's a special one out there for her."

Her hand on his arm tightened and he realized just how surprised she was at his words. One look at her face told him she was delighted.

Suddenly he felt bad for not telling her so earlier. After all he'd put her through, he'd never said "Thank you," or "Aren't you nice," or "Kiss my ass." In fact, the thought of her being with any man didn't settle well. He pushed that aside. She was what he said she was and so much more. Those thoughts brought heat to his own face. Come to think of it, seeing her naked once more was a delight he would love to experience. He covered her hand with his. "I mean it," he said. "You're always doing something for someone else, working hard, and taking capable care of your land and animals. And friends. I admire that in you."

Kathleen's blush turned her beautiful fair skin a light copper to blend with her flaming red hair.

"Thank you," she said softly, her hand tightening beneath his.

The room was quiet for a moment. Charlie looked into Kathleen's eyes and tried to tell her the rest of the feelings he felt bubbling up and clamoring to be told.

Troy cleared his throat.

Kathleen's head swiveled toward the others, her blush growing even deeper. Charlie was a little slower to look at his host and hostess.

"Sorry," he said slowly. "But I suddenly realized that this may be my only visit out here and I might not see my sister again. I need to tell her how proud I am of her now, before I leave."

Amy's expression turned into a soft smile. "Then you're not going to try to convince Kathleen to return with you?"

"I'm going to try," Charlie said slowly, reaching for his glass of liquor. "But I don't think my sweet-talking will land on cooperative ears."

"No," Kathleen said softly. "It won't."

"Good," Amy said with satisfaction. "Then I won't have to worry about whether or not her home will be vacant when you leave. This town needs Kathleen. She's been so good for us. . . ." Her voice dwindled off as she saw the look on Kathleen's face. Amy smiled brightly. "We now have some of the best carrot cake in the West, right here in Blissful, Texas."

"Har, har," Troy said, lifting his glass.

Kathleen and Amy dutifully followed the men's example, barely sipping at the deep golden liquid.

Standing with his drink in hand, Troy led the way outside to the porch, where they could smoke while the women cleared the table.

"Your brother loves you very much," Amy said.

Kathleen scraped the remainder of a plate into the

scrap bowl, set it aside, then reached for another. "Yes." Charlie had surprised her tonight and she was embarrassed by her own reaction. It was as if she couldn't take her eyes off him.

"Are you sure you don't want to go back to North Carolina?"

"I'm sure," Kathleen stated firmly. "Blissful is my home now, and I am staying."

"But you may never see your brother again."

"I know." She thought of her real brother. Unlike Amy's wishes for her own family, she didn't care if she never saw John again. "When he leaves, he will go home to be with his wife and new family. By next year, he won't be able to leave the farm to visit this far again."

It was all so confusing. Charlie was acting as her brother never had, and he was saying all the things Kathleen had wished she could have heard from John. He was treating her the way she'd wished she could have been treated by her own real brother. It was like a salve to her wounded soul, helping to ease the tightness that she experienced every time she thought of what could have been. Her father and brother were not the worst men in the world compared to others she had heard about since leaving home. But they certainly had so much room for improvement that just a kind word would have brought tears to her eyes then, just as they did now.

Amy placed the dishes in the tub and turned to her friend. "Are you all right?"

Kathleen wiped away dampness at the corner of her eye. "I'm fine, honestly. I just never thought I'd hear John say anything that wasn't about him. It was just so nice to hear after all this time." Now Kathleen was getting confused. John hadn't really said those words to her, but it had *felt* like he had, even though

Charlie was the one sitting there. All the warm feelings she'd always wanted to feel toward her real brother had come rushing up. "I mean, his letters are abrupt and brief and ordering me to do this or that, and then he says something nice and allows me to hear it firsthand."

"I know," Amy said with a sad look in her eyes. "But at least he has said it now. That takes a big man, Kathleen. And a kind one at heart."

Kathleen picked up the dishcloth and began wiping and stacking the dishes that Amy washed and put on the wooden sideboard. But her mind was spinning.

Her pretend brother or not, Charlie *had* been kind. Granted, he'd come into her life in a flurry and under all sorts of threats, but he had never, ever hurt her, had never threatened more than a bluster or two, and had been tender in taking care of her when she'd tried to put him to sleep with her stew. In fact, he'd been nothing but kind, if annoying at the same time.

And she'd felt less lonely and safer for having him around this past week or so. That was hard to say aloud, because she'd sworn she'd never be with a man. And this one wasn't even a wanted guest! He had practically forced his way into her home and then remained against all her pleas to the contrary.

It hit her as hard as an iron frying pan alongside the head.

Kathleen cared for Charlie. More than ever with any other man, she cared for him and about him. That was more frightening than thinking there was a killer loose in Blissful. She couldn't call it love because she had no idea what love felt like. And she certainly didn't want to know, either. That would only complicate the life she had scheduled for herself.

Her hands shook as she wiped the last plate and began reaching for the silver.

It couldn't be. Those kisses were kisses of anger, of frustration. Of plain old passion . . .

They had made her heart race and her pulse beat so hard in her throat she thought she'd heard drums playing in the kitchen. For a moment she couldn't catch her breath and felt as if she were gasping for air as a fish begged for water as it flopped on the bank of a river after being caught.

"Kathleen? Are you sure you're all right?" Amy asked, quickly wiping her hands on a rag and reaching for her friend to take her in a comforting embrace.

"I'm fine," Kathleen said, her words muffled against Amy's thin shoulder. But she didn't move away. "Honest. I think it was my brother's unexpected visit, keeping the town secret, the show, and the tension of the past week. It's just all piled up," she said. But the tears that flowed didn't stop, even with her good excuse.

"It has to be awful not being able to explain all the meetings and shows and things to your brother. I don't know if I could keep a secret like that if my family came to visit. . . ." Amy's voice drifted off. "But I understand, Kathleen. After all, the whole town depends on you to pull off this meeting in two weeks." Her hands patted Kathleen's back. That sympathy made Kathleen feel even sadder, and the tears flowed harder. "That's such a large responsibility. I don't know how you continue to march on and still tend to your own place. Why, there's no telling how I would botch things up if I didn't have my Troy."

Her Troy. That said it all. On top of Kathleen doing everything, she didn't have anyone to share everything with. To talk to. To care for. To be with.

A dog yipped in the distance, and one of the cows penned in the backyard gave a disgusting *mmmoooooo*, to remind her she wasn't the only one with problems.

Attempting to pull herself together, she took a deep breath and stood up straighter. But her hands still rested on Amy's thin hips as she looked her dear friend in the eye.

"I'm a silly woman who wants too much. I wish this part of my life were over and settled, but my dear mother used to say, 'Don't wish your life away. It is too short as it is.' " She attempted a smile. "I'm thankful for your shoulder, and I am so grateful for your friendship."

"Me, too." Amy grinned. "And I have your carrot cake money from today's train sale, don't forget."

Bless her, Amy was changing the subject and giving her time to recuperate. "How can I? Jacob has my seed in and I need to give it to him to pay for it."

"Round-robin," Amy said, her arms finally dropping as she saw her friend was once more in control. She reached into the sugar bowl and pulled out several dollars and many coins, pressing them into Kathleen's hands. "Here you go. Now let's leave this and join the men outside on the porch. It's a beautiful night and the stars are too brilliant to ignore."

Charlie's eyes followed her as the women stepped out on the porch. Thank goodness the darkness covered her tearstained cheeks. They sat on the handmade double rocker already there while the men leaned against the posts they'd chosen before the women arrived.

The conversation was soft, casual, and easy. Crops that needed to be tended, cattle to sell, and the cost of eggs were the topics at hand. No one was pressed to answer, and the evening wind seemed to keep them cool enough.

Finally Charlie threw his cigarette over the railing to the garden below. He stretched and gave a contented sigh. But his eyes gave him away. He had something in mind, for his gaze hadn't left Kathleen for longer than a minute. He seemed to be trying to say something, and for a while she thought that Troy might have spilled the town secret. But logic told her he wouldn't have done that. She'd asked everyone not to, so why would he bother? Troy had just as much to lose as the rest of the citizens.

"Well, sister mine, I think it's time we head for home. I have some chores to attend to early in the morning if I'm gonna leave your place in fair shape. And I need a good night's sleep to do so."

"Really?" she asked suspiciously. "What sort of chores?"

"Why, all those things you asked me to do before I took the next train for home. The barn roof needs patching. One of the trees by the side of the barn has died and needs to be chopped up before a good gust of storm wind comes and blows it into the barn. A step on the front porch squeaks."

"All right." She sighed, pretending she was tired just from hearing the list. It would be nice if Charlie fixed those things, but she didn't really think he would. It was just an excuse to leave.

To do what?

She didn't want to think about it. Standing, she curled her shawl around her shoulders, bent, and placed a kiss on Amy's cheek. "Thank you, Amy." She gave Troy's shoulders a light squeeze. "You, too, Troy."

"Come back anytime," Troy said, helping her down the steps to the wagon parked at the side of the house. But she was listening to Charlie as he said good-bye to Amy and then, by the side of the wagon, shook hands with Troy.

Within two minutes of saying their good-byes, she

and Charlie were in the wagon and on the dirt road leading in the direction of home.

Charlie was silent all the way. When they reached the small white house nestled in the copse of oak, he drove the wagon up to the back door and allowed her to get out; then he drove into the barn.

Kathleen stepped inside and touched a match to the kitchen lamp, then did the same in her bedroom. The house was warmer inside than out, and she opened several windows to allow the light evening breeze to filter through. Tomorrow would be another hot day, so nights were the only time to cool off the house. Besides, there was something wonderful about hearing the night sounds while safe in bed.

Going into the kitchen, she dipped into the bucket of clean water she kept by the pump and sipped on the cool liquid. Usually after a show, she felt relieved and relaxed. Not this time. Her nerves were on edge. She couldn't get rid of the feeling that something was about to happen. But what? There were no problems with the tilled ground or her animals. The garden seed had come in and the money to pay for them was in her pocket and in the basement.

But her nerves tingled and her skin felt tight. And her thoughts wouldn't stop their ceaseless chatter. To top it all off, her mind kept pushing forth an image of Charlie standing on the bank of the creek: angry, in charge, and stunningly naked. His eyes had spit fire, his body was firm and strong and lean. Arms akimbo, he told her he was in charge and dared her to challenge otherwise. He looked like one of the pictures she'd seen of a Greek statue, only he didn't have a grape leaf in a strategic place. That was fine. It probably wouldn't be big enough.

And it all made her heart beat so much faster she could barely keep herself from feeling dizzy.

The back door opened and Charlie stepped inside the kitchen, making it feel much smaller than it was. He stood by the door, staring at her and daring her to stare back.

She couldn't take her eyes off him if she wanted to. Everything in her thoughts was now in her heart.

"You know what's going to happen," he finally said, his voice so low she felt the words more than heard them.

"No."

"Sooner or later, we're making love."

Her breath got caught again. How could he say it aloud and expect her not to react? How could he be so blatant about his wants without asking her what she wanted? Oh, she wasn't crazy; she wanted him, too. *That* was this feeling of restlessness that had built up inside. She might be a virgin, but she knew everything she needed to know about men. Her aunt, bless her heart, had not left her without knowledge of more than how to make a carrot cake.

"What makes you think I would do that?" she asked quietly.

"You tell me."

Kathleen dropped the dipper in the water.

Charlie couldn't stand the silence. "You want me. It's plain as the nose on my face. And I want you."

"Am I supposed to be sweet and kind and demure and say something like, 'How can you say that, Mr. Macon? You're so forward!' Or am I just to strip down to my undergarments and let you have your way with me?"

Charlie's eyes never left hers. He gave a shrug. "It's your choice. But the third choice would be to participate and enjoy the moment as much as I will."

"No, thank you, Brother John. I'm going to bed.

Alone." She turned, her heels clicking against the linoleum floor.

"Wait," he ordered.

She stopped, looking over her shoulder. She wasn't sure what he was going to ask, but she knew she wanted to find out.

Excitement sizzled through her.

Charlie came so close to her she stopped breathing. His belt buckle was just a breath away from her abdomen. He placed his hands on her waist firmly, turning her around to face him. "You forgot something."

She looked up but refused to ask.

Grim determination etched his face. His hands tightened on her waist. "You forgot to kiss me good night."

"I don't thi—" she began, but it was too late.

Charlie's lips covered hers in a kiss that demanded participation. She pretended she had no choice. She remained acquiescent for all of a few seconds before her fingers crept up his chest to curl around his neck. *One kiss,* she thought, *just one kiss . . .*

Then Charlie deepened the kiss and she was lost. He tightened his embrace; otherwise she might have fallen. With her eyes closed, she felt as if the room were spinning around like a child's top. All she could do was hold on for dear life until he chose to end the ride.

Capable, careful, and trustworthy Kathleen O'Day was swooning in Charlie's arms like a naive, pampered maid in some eastern publisher's dime novel.

Amazing.

Then she stopped thinking and gave completely in to feeling. She wasn't sure how long she could remain standing. Her legs shook with the wonder of Charlie. Her control was gone, and she didn't care a whit.

His arms smoothed her skin as if she were made

of precious gold. Intense, melting heat touched her
wherever his palms drifted, and she loved it. Her own
hands were busy feeling the strength of his chest
muscles bunched to hold on to her and not let her
fall. She was secure and being cared for just as she
had dreamed on many a lonely night.

She wanted to cry with the pure joy of being with
him. All her life she'd wondered what the feeling of
being with a man was like. Now that the time had
come, she was stunned. No one, not the animals she
took care of, nor the sister-in-law who tittered like a
chattering squirrel, nor even her Aunt Hattie, had
ever mentioned this wondrous feeling of completeness that came with being in the arms of a man who
treasured her.

Her fingers rested on his chest again, and the heavy
beat of his heart thudded against her palms. The vein
in his neck beat with the same pulsing rhythm. Her
own heartbeat matched his, fluttering like a trapped
bird in a cage. His warm breath touched her skin
and she heated to it, becoming more pliant with every
passing moment. Every move he made tantalized her
with the promise of more wonder, more sweetness,
more love . . . .

"Let me, Kathleen," he murmured, pulling back
enough to sip at her neck, touching the very spot
with his lips that she was feeling on his neck. "Let
me," he said again, and just the thought of more of
Charlie was an aphrodisiac.

"I . . . " She pulled him back and kissed him with
a fervor she didn't expect to feel, let alone act upon.
This time she captured his mouth, her hands holding
his head, her body molding to his body. It was so
much; it was too much. It would never be enough.
Her fingers slackened; her lead faltered.

When Charlie pulled away, her eyes were glazed.

She saw him through a haze of dark and light. But the heat of his body told her he was still holding her.

"That wasn't so bad, was it?" he asked, his voice soft and dark as velvet against her skin.

"No," she said, forming the word slowly but not remembering why she was saying it. "Are we done?"

His laughter was shaky. "We haven't even begun," he said, his voice as rough as gritty sandpaper. "Come on, then, my sweet Kathleen." He dropped his hands from her waist and linked his fingers with hers, walking backward slowly, leading her through the parlor and into his bedroom. Once there, he kissed the tip of her nose. "Scared?"

"No. Yes. No," she said, her voice a mere whisper.

"Me, too," he said, a smile tilting his mouth for just a second. "My God, you're so beautiful," he said, his gaze drifting over her. "I want to feel you. Most of all, I want to see you wearing nothing but moonlight."

She felt a blush begin in her toes and go all the way to the top of her head. "I . . . "

"It's easy," he said. "Just turn around and let me unbutton your dress." His words were said as he let go of her hands and turned her around. She did so obediently. Her mind had long ceased to work in any organized way. She felt the cool breeze on her heated skin, and the touch of Charlie's knuckles on her back was as erotic as his words.

Her dress fell in a puddle at her feet and she stood in her chemise top and a single, light slip. He reached for the tie and gave a gentle tug. It unlaced and fell, following the dress. Now there was only the chemise. Charlie's breath was the only sound in the room. Kathleen had long since ceased breathing.

Very slowly, Kathleen turned to face Charlie. It was his turn to stop breathing.

With hands that shook, she pushed off each strap

and let it drop, the white material against her skin skimming down her body.

"Dear, sweet angel," he finally managed in a voice that sounded remote and far away. "Don't stop now."

She didn't. What had seemed impossible just moments after walking into the house was now a reality. Kathleen stood, stark naked as the day she was born, in front of Charlie and waited for him to do the same thing.

When he didn't move, she prompted him. "Am I here by myself?" she asked.

Suddenly he went into action, taking off his shirt, ripping the last button off in his hurry. Boots and pants were gone in less time. And then she was in his arms, feeling the hardness of his body as he pulled her back in his arms and buried his head in the curve of her neck.

He breathed deeply and let it out in a moan. "I'm gonna try to be gentle, sweet. Please let me know if I do something wrong."

"How will I know?" she questioned softly, her eyes as big and round as an innocent emerald moon.

"Damn," he muttered, emotions welling inside him he didn't know lived in him anymore. "That answers it."

With hands that shook, he gently pushed her out of his hands and led her to the bed. "Here, sweet. I'm gonna do this right if it kills me." He gave a laugh. "And it might."

As gently as he could, Charlie laid her down and came down next to her, his hands drifting over every part of her as if to reassure himself that she was really there. His touch was soft, his callused fingers gentle with her as he found the curve of her waist, the flare of her hip, the roundness of her belly . . . and then the fullness of her breasts.

His thumb flicked at her nipple just seconds before he captured it in his wet, warm mouth.

She moaned with the feeling of wonder as his tongue laved it in sensuous detail. A shaft of passion blazed through her like an arrow finding its true mark. She never wanted his hands and mouth to leave her body. One callus-roughened hand reached to hold her hip closer to his, but it lost its way and strayed to stroke her rounded bottom, exploring, sensing, teasing.

Everything he did fueled the growing pleasure inside her. Moans that sounded like a purring kitten echoed through the room, and she knew it was coming from her—and didn't care. With hands that knew exactly what she wanted, she held his head to her breast and luxuriated in the feelings he evoked. He evoked so many emotions she couldn't even put a name to them. All she could do was enjoy them.

Her senses were alive as never before. Until tonight she never quite knew what she was supposed to feel like. Now she didn't care if this was supposed to be it. It felt so very perfect she wanted to cry from the happiness of it.

Charlie angled kisses down her breast, brushing the underside, then going farther down, blazing a warm, damp trail to her navel. His fingers searched the folds of her, wetting her before carefully seeking the inside, as if she were a precious gem. She felt his hand shake as he touched her, and she was so grateful he knew what he was doing. She didn't, and she didn't care as long as the tense buildup he was creating was relieved.

"Dear, sweet heaven." His voice rasped against her skin. "I can't wait much longer."

"Then don't," she whispered. But he heard her, clear as a bell. His body claimed hers, his mouth clamping onto hers as he found his way inside her. "I'm sorry," he said, stopping all motion as he felt her stiffen with the sharp pain of losing her virginity. "So sorry." His hand pushed back her hair as he kissed her face. Distracting her, he kissed her brows, her cheeks, her nose and mouth, then wound his way down to her breast.

Her breath came back slowly. The feelings he'd originally aroused had fled in the face of pain, but just as quickly as the pain had come, it left. She wanted back the feelings Charlie had generated earlier.

He started the rhythm slowly at first. But as her body accommodated him, so did the pace grow. He pressed his head next to hers as they reached for the feeling of fulfillment Charlie knew was ahead of them.

Then, suddenly, she was there. "Charlie!" She cried his name and he reveled in the power he felt as he brought her to that special place and pushed both of them to the mind-numbing edge.

Then it was time for both of them to fall over the brink of the cliff and feel the wonder of their union.

After softly spoken words were murmured between them, confirming the wonder of their actions, sleep came quickly.

In the middle of the night, Kathleen curled to Charlie's form, her mouth touching the back of his neck and shoulder. He turned, enveloping her in his arms, and they made love again, this time slowly, sweetly, and with sighs of contentment flowing between them.

Kathleen's last thought before sleep claimed her once more was that Charlie had found the perfect way to introduce her to the fine art of lovemaking.

She smiled. Definitely the perfect way . . .

Fourteen

When Kathleen awoke, sun was streaming across her bed, proclaiming it way past time to start her chores. Today she had to buy her seed and get it in the ground.

Instead she moved slowly, stretching her arms contentedly above her head and pointing her toes toward the wall that separated her room from Charlie's.

Then, very slowly, she felt the unexpected tug of muscles not used before. The ones across and under her breasts, the insides of her thighs, the arch of her leg just under her bottom.

Of course.

Her face blazed red and she held tightly to the white sheet that covered her. Underneath it, she was stark naked. Nothing. Not one scrap of fabric separated her from the thin bedding linen. Why, just thinking of lying there with nothing on was decadent! It was probably just what hussies did! Every night!

She listened to the house noises: a creak here, a

snap of wood there as the house warmed under the summer Texas sun. No sound of Charlie.

Just the thought of seeing him made her blush again. After all, she'd behaved with wild abandon, doing and saying all sorts of new and different things she'd never done or said before last night. Heat washed through her limbs, settling in the pit of her stomach. She gasped with the provocative images of her and Charlie that sprang to mind.

One thing stood out in her mind: Charlie, naked, beautiful, and gentle as he smiled at her just before entering her. He'd been kind and caring and so loving, ensuring her maidenhead was gone with as little pain as possible.

He succeeded. It was.

Kathleen couldn't help her blush any more than she could the smile that tugged at her heart. After making love, Charlie had curled her into his warm, hard body, spoon fashion, given a hearty sigh, and promptly begun snoring gently in her ear. She listened to every note, too nervous to do the same. Besides, she was fluctuating between abandon and shyness.

It took forever for her to fall asleep. Her mind wouldn't stop spinning with thoughts and seesawing emotions. But the one topic her mind refused to cope with was marriage.

Never. No. Never. There wasn't a hint of indecision in her mind about that subject.

It was not up for discussion; there was no other way than for her to remain single until folks called her the old maid on Bliss Creek.

The back screen door squeaked open; then Charlie's boots echoed as they clomped across the kitchen and parlor floors.

With the fourth step, she pulled the sheet up over

her head to block out the sight of the man who had done all sorts of strange and wonderful things with her body and mind last night.

Despite her quickly mumbled prayers, his footsteps continued toward the bed. Her heart raced in triple time to his steps.

The bedsprings protested as he slowly sat on the edge. "Kathleen?" he said, then was silent.

She held her breath, still praying he would leave so she wouldn't have to look him in the eye.

"Kathleen," he said. "I brought you a glass of fresh milk from Hilde. She said to say hello and thanked me for delivering her from such a full feeling."

She grinned under the sheet. Darned if he wasn't endearing. But her hands still held the sheet tightly over her head.

"And the chickens said good morning, too. They were thankful that someone brought them seed this morning. They didn't see you anywhere. They even came and clucked under your window, but you didn't answer."

"I was tired," she finally answered, her voice muffled through the cover.

"And rightfully so." Was there a hint of devilment in his voice? "After all, you played hide-and-seek all night, and gave a new and wonderful meaning to the game."

Her grin turned to soft laughter. She'd been so used to battling the railroad for the town's fight that she'd lost her sense of humor lately. But Charlie, who was the least likely candidate to make her laugh, was doing just exactly that. "So did you."

"Of course," he said easily. "I was the one seeking. Well, sometimes. The rest of the time you were all over my body, making me do all kinds of things I never would have thought of if you hadn't started it all.''

The sheet came down to her breasts so she could show him just how much that hurt. "That's not true!" He was grinning from ear to ear. His hand covered hers so she couldn't move the sheet back up.

"Yes, it is. You wanted me and you wanted to know what it was like to make love. You weren't going to stop pestering me until I did just that.''

"You're lying!''

"Nope," he stated calmly. "I only tell the truth." But his grin belied the words. He bent forward and placed a quick, soft kiss on her pouting mouth. "Good morning, you lovely woman.''

"Good morning," she stated warily. What was his next move going to be? "And now you call me a woman?''

"That's right. Boys become men when they've bedded a woman; why not the other way around?''

"Don't be so crass," she stated, relaxing her indignation. Not that it had been strong anyway.

"Crass? Me?" He looked so innocent, so sweet. And the twinkle in his eyes attested to his mischievousness. "I'm not crass, just truthful. As you should be.''

"If that's the case, Mr. Macon, then please leave my room so I may get dressed to receive company. *Your* company.''

His eyes widened. "Why, Miss O'Day, how shocking. I have just spent the whole night kissing you on every part of your body, and now you pretend to be a modest miss? I don't think so," he said.

Kathleen blushed from the tips of her toes to the top of her red hair. It must have been just as obvious to Charlie, for he watched her cheeks with interest. "It is not nice to bring up such things to a lady.''

Her tone was imperious, hopefully putting him in his place.

"Why? Do ladies not have feelings, too? Do they not feel the hand of a man in intimate places? Do they not lounge in bed with the man they love? Do they not feel the joy of spouse and family?"

The last words hit home, draining the blush from Kathleen's cheeks. It must have done the same for Charlie, for from the way he looked at her, he could have been seeing a stranger doing strange things.

Family. Children.

"Damn," he whispered.

For the first time in her life, she stated the same word. "Double damn."

"Don't worry," he said quietly, all the joy of the moment gone. "I'll marry you."

"No, you won't," she said, finding her voice. "I don't want marriage. I can handle myself."

"You cannot handle being ostracized from your friends. No woman should have to," he said. "Besides, the baby will be mine, too."

"There isn't any baby," she stated in a no-nonsense voice, letting the sheet drop as she slipped from the mattress and reached for her dress, which was still crumpled on the floor beside her bed. She didn't want to admit just how scary the thought of carrying a baby was. How could she not have thought of that? She was so good at carrying the banner of independence, yet she never gave a thought to the chances of becoming an unwed mother . . . until now.

Heat filled her for a moment before turning to ice in her veins.

"You're so beautiful." Charlie's voice was low and sensuous. So very loving. But the thought of being with child outweighed any other thought, including that of being made love to by Charlie.

"Thank you," she said, quickly slipping her wrinkled dress over her head and shoving the buttons inside the buttonholes.

"And cold."

"Not cold," she said, snapping the hem of her dress in line before heading for the door. "Just sensible."

"If you were sensible, you'd come back to bed and make love to me all day because I deserve it."

"You are sick, dear brother. Very sick," she stated haughtily as she swept from the room with all the dignity she could muster.

Charlie grinned. He knew better.

When he woke up this morning, he could barely contain his happiness. He was thrilled to be with the most beautiful woman in the world, with her making him feel as if he'd won all the wars and she was his prize for doing good.

He either had to make love to her again or get the hell out of the bed so he wouldn't touch her. Knowing this was her first time and she would be sore for a while, he chose the latter. Besides, he heard chickens scratching under the windows and was reminded that chores waited for him.

There was a certain rightness about chores. The same routine always gave him a feeling of completeness, of satisfaction at a job done. He fed the chickens, gathered eggs, then milked Hilde and took care of the milk. Hell, he'd even walked down to the river and caught a fresh bass for breakfast. He just didn't cook well, so he put it in the tub in the kitchen to see what Kathleen wanted to do with it.

Meanwhile, his every thought had been on the woman he'd made love to last night.

But the thought of making her pregnant was

enough to chill the desire out of him. He had one
child and couldn't take care of her. Every time he
thought about Becca, he felt so damn guilty. What
would he do with another?

After his wife had died, he promised himself that
he'd never get close to a woman again. Life was too
uncertain, and the pain of losing someone he loved
went too deep. He didn't want to lose someone close
to him again. He couldn't take it. His wife's death
had ripped his guts out; what would it be like to go
through that again? What were the chances it could
happen again?

Too good.

Suddenly birds weren't singing any sweeter than
yesterday. The sun wasn't any brighter. The breeze
wasn't any cooler. It was just another day, and he'd
pray like hell that he hadn't messed up by taking
Kathleen to bed.

He stood and tucked his shirt back into his pants,
then left the room. He didn't look back at the bed
in which he'd made love to Kathleen last night. He
didn't need to. All he had to do was shut his eyes,
and every move she made, every touch she gave, was
clear as sight.

It had better be. It was all he was ever going to
have to relive this time. He wouldn't take the chance
of making her pregnant. It wasn't worth it.

Damn. How could he go from such a wonderful
feeling to being a big brother to feeling like a snail
in such a short time? It wasn't easy.

Kathleen stared into the tub she washed dishes in
and wrinkled her nose. Did the man have no sense
of decency? First he made love to her all night long,
not bothering to ask about her participation after the

first time. Now he took the liberty of placing a fishy bass in her dishtub. The very place she cleaned things!

It was still alive. Charlie had added water, but it barely had enough room to flop.

She raised her voice without turning around. "Brother John, please come fillet this fish."

His voice seemed to come from the front porch. "I caught it; you clean it."

She tossed down her kitchen towel, wishing he were standing in front of her so she could stab him with a look. "When I catch it, I clean it. When you catch it, you clean it."

"Like hell," he muttered.

"Like hell," she repeated angrily. Then Kathleen smiled. She was pleasantly surprised at how good it felt to say those awful words—especially in the same tone that Charlie had. It felt good. Decadent. Wicked. "Like hell." She said it again, letting it roll off her tongue slowly, giving her a taste of the freedom of saying anything she wanted.

"Don't swear," Charlie said from right behind her. "It's not right coming from a lady."

She turned to face him, her expression still angry. He always made her blush, and this time was no different. But she wasn't about to back down. She stuck out her chin. "Like hell."

He came forward, meeting her toe-to-toe. His eyes blazed into her, heating her as if she were in front of an overstoked oven. "Say it again," he said, his voice low and urgent.

"Like hell."

Before she could finish her last drawled syllable, Charlie's mouth had captured her sound and kept it in his own. He gave it back as a moan, low and growling in his throat, and it vibrated against her own tongue.

His arms came around her, and as forceful as his kiss was, his grasp was gentle.

Kathleen pulled him closer. She made his kiss last longer. She lovingly stroked his neck and shoulders, feeling the muscles tighten beneath her touch. Kathleen gave a small moan of protest as he finally pulled away.

And then she turned around and walked out the back door. "Clean the fish," she said over her shoulder as she walked toward the barn.

Charlie never answered.

With a pace that was as lightning-quick as her heartbeat, she entered the dim coolness of the barn. The sun was high, it was lunchtime, and it was going to get hotter before the day was over. Her skin already felt like it was a hundred degrees.

Closing her eyes, Kathleen paused, then leaned against the interior wall of the barn. What was wrong with her? She wanted to be in Charlie's arms; then she wanted to yell at him and tell him to go away and never return. Leave her to be alone. But the moment she thought of it, she wanted him back again.

Wasn't that the way crazy people felt? Years ago, she remembered, when she was just a child, old Mrs. Hadgett lived about a quarter mile down the road. She would rant and rave at the children if they passed by or cut across her land, swearing worse than Kathleen's daddy ever dreamed of. Once or twice she came toward them swinging a scythe, threatening to cut off their heads. But the very moment after she did that, she would smile and say to come back and she'd give them a cookie.

Her mama used to tell her Mrs. Hadgett was lonely, and lonely people went batty sometimes. Her brother used to tell her that Mrs. Hadgett wanted her to go back so she could chop off her head. She had hundreds of heads in the spring cellar of her shack, John said. Hundreds! It made Kathleen shiver just to think of those days, although now she was much wiser than when she was six.

Now she knew that they had been walking across the old lady's potato bed. She grew everything she had and couldn't afford for kids to ruin it. And Kathleen's mother was right. She was lonely. Kathleen learned all about loneliness the next year, when her mother died and left her to care for a selfish brother and an even more selfish father. She'd never known such heartrending, head-splitting loneliness and depression in all her years since.

But to be fair, it wasn't all the menfolk's fault they were the way they were. Her mother had spoiled them unendingly. They expected no less from the other female in the family.

She'd sworn to herself that if she ever found a man she wanted to have children with, she'd teach him from the beginning just how they were to live. Then as she grew older, she realized she never wanted to be in a position to answer to anyone. Ever.

Going to bed with Charlie had been putting the cart in front of the horse. She didn't need babies. Not unless she was properly married. And since she wasn't marrying, she needed to rethink her options.

With a heavy sigh, she walked over to the hay bales and sat down on the loosest one, ignoring the mice in the corner that were working hard at making a home in the straw. She leaned against the wall and waited for her heart to stop pounding so loudly that she couldn't hear herself think.

Very slowly, she calmed down enough that her thoughts weren't racing in a hundred different directions. Only in one . . . a very big one.

What would she do if she was with child? A chill swept through her.

Being a pariah was not her idea of a life. Being married to a man who didn't want her for more than a toss in the hay wasn't her idea of a good life, either. Charlie had already made it clear that this town was not for him. He wanted to go back to Oklahoma and his ranch. He'd already given up one daughter, so it was plain he didn't want another. Probably didn't want a son, either. Charlie didn't want any children or he would have kept the one he had.

That made it plain that she couldn't rely on him for support. She had to handle her mistakes herself.

All she could do was wait until her next bleeding. That should be in two weeks. Once that happened, she'd breathe a sigh of relief and promise herself never to get in this predicament again.

And if she was pregnant, she'd send Charlie away immediately, ride to the next town, and return with a wedding ring. Just before the baby was born, she'd announce that her new husband was killed in a gunfight while hunting down a master criminal. He'd be a hero, she'd be a widow, and the baby would be a wonder in her life.

There. That felt better. She had a plan. A plan meant there was action to be taken, and that meant that she was in control.

Not all was lost.

"Kathleen?" She kept her eyes closed. If she didn't see him, he wasn't there.

"Kathleen." She opened her eyes, compelled by his quiet voice.

Charlie stood in front of her, his outline dark and hazed against the barn entrance. His broad shoulders were emphasized by the shadows, his hat tilted high on his forehead, from the angle of the brim. He looked sexy. Frustrated. And she wanted to be in his arms again.

"Yes?" she said politely, resisting that urge.

"Are you all right?"

"I'm fine," she said sweetly. "Thank you for asking."

"Then what are you doing sitting in the barn?"

She wished he wouldn't ask such questions. "Thinking."

"About having a baby?"

"No," she said sharply. "That isn't a worry. Not yet, anyway. Besides, there are lots of things to think about besides you and your childish antics."

"Making love is a childish antic?" he asked, incredulous that she could say such a thing.

"Yes. There are other things in life, Charlie Macon. One of them is your finding a killer and then getting him out of here. That is, if he's here at all."

His stance stiffened as if he'd added starch to his spine. "There's one here, all right. But you're on target when you say I should be finding him instead of sniffing around you like a hound dog smelling out scraps. I don't need scraps, Miss O'Day. I can find a feast all by myself!"

Before she could tell him how outrageous that thought was, he'd turned, dug in his heels, and left the barn. Whatever had made him angry, it couldn't be half as bad as her own feelings about herself. She could drop into his arms in a minute, with no regrets until it was over. That was bad. Very bad.

Within minutes, Charlie was in the barn again, buckling on his holster as he aimed for the stall he kept his horse in. "I'm leaving for a few days. Have a nice time without me."

"I thought you were supposed to be my visiting brother!"

"I am. And now I'm visiting the next town for a while."

"Charlie," she began, not really sure what she was going to say to keep him here. Or if she really wanted him to stay.

He swung the saddle onto his horse, then cinched it tight before readjusting it. "My name's John for now, and I'll be discreet. Don't worry, dear sister; your reputation is safe with me." He led the horse out of the stall.

"You couldn't ruin my reputation," she answered swiftly. "No one would believe you."

His brows rose daringly. "Why? Because you're such a model citizen?"

"Yes," she said haughtily. "And you're obviously not, or you wouldn't be discussing something like that with anyone."

Charlie barked a laugh. "You haven't been in a saloon or a bunkhouse, have you? Men say anything. And everything. When it comes to discussing women, they're like gossiping old maids."

Heat seared through her body. Would he really do that? No, he couldn't. No, he wouldn't. She put her fears into words. "Tell me you wouldn't do that."

"I wouldn't do that," he said obediently, but there was a taunting quality to his tone.

"Promise me."

"Promise me," he repeated dutifully, this time there was a definite glint in his eyes. "But when I get back, we're discussing what happens now. You'd better think about it."

Anger swept through her body, acting like a hot-air balloon filling the insides of her, and she rose with the heat of it. "Charlie, promise me," she said, her hands unconsciously turning into fists at her sides.

She took a step toward him. Then another. "Promise me now!"

"Don't threaten me, Kathleen." His voice was as soft as hers had been shrill, and it was laden with just as much demand. "My reputation is just as important to me as yours is to you, Miss O'Day, and I resent that you'd think otherwise." He stepped up to her, staring down with dark brown eyes that blazed with fire. "I'm acting as a sworn deputy right now, and it wouldn't be good for me if I took advantage of the situation just for the hell of it. So keep your shoes buttoned and rest your mind. I'm not asking for anything I wouldn't want for myself. Respect. Mutual and even." He readjusted his hat, his eyes never leaving her face. "So take care of yourself and remember that your brother is out checking the next town. And that I'll be back, Kathleen. One way or another, even if it's just to say good-bye, I'll be back."

Holding the reins, Charlie leaped up on his horse and slowly walked him out of the barn, not even giving her the courtesy of a backward glance. "You have a nice day, now."

The even clip-clop of horse hooves against the dry, packed dirt faded away as Charlie rode out of the barn and into the bright sunshine.

Kathleen stared at the spot she'd last seen him long after he left her farm. As anxious as she'd been to rid herself of him earlier, she now felt a loneliness she didn't know was possible. Being alone had never bothered her before. She'd always loved her privacy. But now . . .

Now she needed to think through what had happened in the past two days and find her balance again. She felt giddy, slightly disoriented, and scared.

And all of it was due to Charlie—or to Charlie's leaving; she wasn't sure which.

Apparently she had a few days to figure it all out. She hoped she found her footing by that time.

"Be careful," she said softly to the place where he had stood before.

Fifteen

Kathleen was filled with boundless energy and had to use it all up before Charlie came back. She tore the kitchen apart, wiping down shelves with lye soap and hot water. Then she dusted the parlor from ceiling to floor, scrubbing, then beeswaxing the floor to a sheen.

By the time she began cleaning her own room, she was wondering why she was doing this. With a heavy sigh, she retied the head scarf tied at the nape of her neck and started stripping the room. Laundry was piled in the center of the kitchen floor. Quilts and her rag rugs were hung over the clothesline to air in the summer sun. Dresses were shaken. Mattresses were dragged to the front porch steps for a good whipping. Windows were cleaned with vinegar, newsprint, and elbow grease.

By the time the sun began its spectacular setting, Kathleen was winding down. She had done everything but the laundry and baking. Not bad for half a day's work in the heat of summer.

Her legs ached from bending and stooping all day. But it felt satisfying to look around her home and see it sparkling.

Finally, with a giant sigh of satisfaction, she sat on the porch rocker and drank cool milk from a jug; ate cold roast, cheese, and butter on dark, crusty bread; and stared at the setting sun as if lazily wishing on the stars that would visit next.

Tomorrow she would tear apart Charlie's room. It was her house and her furniture. And if, in cleaning, she found something about him while she checked, then all the better. After all, he was only a guest in her home, not the owner. Come to think of it, he wasn't even a guest. A guest was usually invited into the home, but Charlie had definitely invited himself. With a gun, no less.

It took the rest of the evening to lug her mattress back inside and make her bed. Then, once finished, she got out the old copper tub and filled it with heated water. She unwrapped her aunt's expensive Parisian soap, now kept in the bottom of her clothes chest wrapped in a cloth that held the same scent of ancient tea roses.

Her favorite.

Piling thick, copper-colored hair on top of her head and fastening it with two combs, she stripped down and stepped in. Luxuriating in the heat immediately, she relaxed and let her muscles feel the lack of tension and ease of doing nothing. After last night, she felt a tightness in muscles she didn't know she had. She ached.

Although the heat was higher than usual this day, the setting sun had allowed the westerly breeze to cool the land quickly. It felt wonderful to be encased in the warmth of the water while the outside was cooling down.

Within half an hour, Kathleen's eyes were drooping. Her body was completely relaxed. It took effort to lift herself out of the tub and dry herself off, slip into her modest nightgown of pink and white cotton gauze, and empty the tub out the back door.

Everything could be put away tomorrow. With her soap resting on the windowsill to dry, she blew out the lantern and went to bed in the dark.

She had lived in this house for four years. For two years she'd lived alone. This night reminded her of those years. She was alone once more.

And she would not bother to relive last night. It was only one night in all her life. She refused to bear it without dignity.

Moonlight sprayed over her bed, lighting the room as if several candles were glowing. With a contented sigh, she climbed between the crisp, clean sheets and stretched her weary legs. Bringing up the sheet, she carefully tucked it under her chin and closed her eyes.

It was time to go to sleep.

The rest of the night was spent trying to fall asleep . . . to no avail.

Damn Charlie Macon!

Charlie leaned against his saddle on the ground and stared at the small fire he'd built to heat coffee. Beans from the can were cold and that was fine with him, but a hot cup of coffee at night with the stars above was one of the things he enjoyed most. It reminded him of the cattle days, when he and one or two other cowhands were on the range for one or two weeks at a time, rounding up, branding, and checking for disease.

He tossed the dregs of the cup on the coals. The sizzling sound was short and loud, dimming part of the fire. Reaching for his blanket, Charlie slid down to the ground, facing the fire, and used the saddle as a pillow for his head. He gave the blanket a tug over his long-sleeved shirt and tried to cover up enough to keep out the north Texas chill. Then, for the millionth time—and more than anything—he wished he were at Kathleen's.

If his ego hadn't gotten in the way, he'd be curled up next to her, holding her, feeling the softness of her skin, the firmness of her breasts in the palm of his hand. He'd know the wonder as the sweet length of her legs opened to wrap around his body and hold on.

He was getting hard just thinking about it.

Charlie turned his back on the fire and readjusted his body and blanket again.

It wasn't that he was hard up for women. Well, yes, it was, but that wasn't the point. He'd seen lots of women he didn't get excited about. Well, maybe not a lot. But some. The point was that he had never taken one of them up on it. He'd never followed through any invitation. Not from the nice ones, anyway. The ones who weren't so nice, he'd visit quickly and then get on with his life. It was for relief, not because they were beautiful and loving and caring and he was lonely or tired or needing the feel of human company and caring.

Now, suddenly, those were only a few of the reasons for his wanting to be with Kathleen. The list could go on forever.

Charlie gave a grunt, elbowed a stone away from his side, and determinedly closed his eyes again.

This whole damn trip was to capture Vic. That was it. It wasn't to see Kathleen, visit tea socials, eat carrot cake, or make love all night. And he certainly didn't make this god-awful trip in order to milk Hilde morning and night.

It was time to get on with it. Find Vic. Get back to his ranch. Work hard. Live alone.

Images popped into his head. One image of Kathleen sleeping, her enticingly tangled sunset-red hair spread out on the cream-colored pillow, her face the picture of an angel.

Another when she sat on him, gloriously naked, her hands on either side of his face as she stared down at him with a brilliant, wondrous smile tilting her full mouth into the most tantalizing look he'd ever seen. That image would stay with him forever and a day.

Or Kathleen sitting on a bale of hay, her back lazily pressed against the barn wall as her wide green eyes trailed his every move.

Kathleen when she told him she didn't want to marry. Somehow it made his generous proposal sound like nothing at all . . . .

A coyote gave a lonely howl to the moon, mimicking Charlie's own feelings. He was less than five miles or so away from the bed he wanted to be in, the food he wanted to eat, and the woman he wanted to make love to. If he had any common sense, he'd ride hell-for-leather back to her and do just that.

But he had his pride.

Damn Kathleen O'Day!

As the moon arched over the house, the lightness that shone into her room had slowly disappeared, shining on the roof instead.

Kathleen dozed off and on, never deeply enough to find rest in sleep, just enough to know it was tantalizingly close and teasingly outside her reach.

Even before the sound registered, her muscles tensed in reaction to the soft sound of a horse's hooves making their way to her barn.

She leaned on one elbow, straining to hear something—anything else that would give her an explanation. Several minutes later she heard the back door open, then close.

Kathleen rested her head back on the pillow and waited. Her hand drifted down to the side of the bed, feeling the small gun she kept tucked in the mattress there. But she wasn't ready to use it. Instead, her heart pounding so loudly that she could barely hear the footsteps, Kathleen waited.

The shadow that filled the doorway was as familiar as her dreams. Charlie stood, not moving. Finally he reached for his shirt buttons and began unbuttoning them one at a time. Once finished, he shrugged off the shirt, reached for his belt, and undid the buttons on his jeans. Then, stealthily, he walked to the wooden bootjack, slipped his boot in the holder, gave a push, and slipped them off, one at a time.

Kathleen held her breath, watching through her lashes as he walked to the side of her bed.

He stared down at her for a very long time. "I just want to hold you," he said softly, but his low, gravelly voice sounded like the sexiest of whispers.

"Yes, please," she answered simply. She took the quilt and held it aside for him to slip underneath.

And when he did as she bade, Charlie's arms came around her waist, pulling her toward him, warming himself with her own warmth and softening his own body against hers.

He gave a heavy sigh in her ear, stroked her breast,

placed a kiss on her neck, and fell asleep almost instantly.

Surprisingly, so did Kathleen.

As dawn crept slowly into the room, it gave just enough light to see what made the shadows. Charlie woke from his sound sleep slowly. As he took a deep breath, his nostrils filled with the scent of Kathleen. Kathleen. He was still curled into her body, feeling the warmth and softness of her.

Without thought, Charlie cupped her breast in his palm once more and softly flicked her nipple with the pad of his thumb. She moved, giving him more accommodation. He kissed the back of her head, his mouth moving toward her neck until he touched flesh.

She moaned, a soft, kittenish sound that touched him somewhere far inside him, where he didn't even know he had feeling.

Gently turning her on her back, he kissed her all over her face—except on her mouth. His lips sipped at every part of her, trailing down her face and throat to the tops of her breasts. Finally, with just a slight hesitation, Charlie took one breast in his mouth and gently suckled. Her hands came up, holding his head with a touch that was more for reassurance than for restriction.

"Charlie?" she whispered in a sigh.

"Relax," he said softly. "Enjoy."

"But," she began, and he knew what her concern was.

"I'll be careful. Trust me," he said.

"Charlie," she said once more, but this time her voice told him she was giving permission.

Knowing she was probably a little sore, he entered

her as gently as possible and, once enclosed in her luscious body, felt the relief of coming home to the beautiful woman in his arms. She seemed to sense his care, and showed him she was happy with his being with her. Then other, more primitive urges encompassed him and he began the rocking rhythm that would bring them both relief.

Her arms wrapped around him, and her mouth sought his as she raised her hips toward his in welcome, finding his movements and matching them to her own. Her heart fluttered against his chest, hers a light thudding against his heavier beat. He forced himself to hold back, even when the pressure built to such a crescendo that he almost blacked out. Then Kathleen stiffened in his arms and held on as if she were falling off the edge of the earth, her moan turning into a faint keening sound that delved inside him, melding with his own emotions. He gave a satisfied moan. He'd done it. He'd made her feel the loving wonder of a man and woman being together.

Quickly pulling out, he suddenly fell over the edge and gave a heavy moan, spilling his seed on the bed.

Then they were both silent. Kathleen's quick breath echoed in his ear just as his did in hers. Lightly, he soothed the side of her body, his hand traveling from hip to breast and back again.

"Are you all right?" he finally asked.

"Yes," she said.

He raised his head and stared down into the greenest eyes he'd ever fallen into. "Kathleen," he began.

Her fingers crossed his mouth, pressing ever so lightly and filling his head with the scent of her. "Shhh," she said. "We're here now. That's all that's important."

"And later?" he couldn't help asking.

"We will worry about later, later," she promised with a smile.

Charlie rolled off her, unwilling to move any farther away than her side. "You're not supposed to be in bed with your brother."

She didn't smile. "When you walk through my bedroom door, you are Charlie Macon. But once outside the door, you become John, my brother."

"And you can keep those two identities separate?"

"Yes." It was stated emphatically. "Can you? Because if you can't, then you need to leave now."

His eyebrows rose. "Just like that?"

"Just like that." The look on her face was as obstinate as the words were direct.

"Lady, I accept your terms."

Her smile was more brilliant than the sunrise. "Thank you."

Her hair was a delightful riot of curls that circled her face like a brilliant halo. He brushed a curl away from her cheek. "I'm leaving this morning. I'll be back in a few days."

"I thought you left yesterday."

"I didn't want whatever was between us to grow And the way I left yesterday wasn't what I had planned."

"How far did you get?" she asked, her hand stroking the side of his jaw.

" 'Bout five miles." Damn, he hated to admit it. It made him sound like a sissy, not going any farther away than he had to before returning to Kathleen's bed.

Her green eyes widened and he almost fell in. "And you came all the way back?"

Suddenly he felt shy. He wasn't any good at talking about his feelings, like some other guys. Not unless he was speaking in anger. Anger was easy; he just shouted or looked mean. But soft and vulnerable, like Kathleen, that was hard. He gulped. "Yes."

"Because of me?"

"Yes."

"Oh, Charlie," she said, her tone saying a thousand more words than the one she chose. She was touched by his honesty and even more touched by his return.

"You're more special than you'll ever know," he said, and it was from his heart. It was the biggest admission he'd made to her, although he'd tried to show her his feelings when he made love. "I want you to know that if you ever decide to marry, ask me first."

"Oh, Charlie," she said, tears filming her beautiful green eyes and making them sparkle like the brightest emeralds. But this time she breathed the words into his mouth before pulling him toward her again.

And this time, Kathleen was in charge and Charlie was just along for the ride . . . .

An hour later, when Charlie rode out of the yard, Kathleen watched him leave with different tears in her eyes. She felt so much better. This time she worried about him finding Vic and getting hurt in the process, but she wasn't worried about not seeing him again. He would be back. She knew that and delighted in the sheer thought of it.

She had given herself to him, in trust and in—she refused to think of love—in commitment. And he had repaid her by taking precautions. If anything, it made her feel even more treasured and close to him. What a wonderful, elated feeling that was! He even allowed her to have her own opinion of marriage.

And she prayed for his return soon.

After he left, Kathleen walked back into the darker

coolness of the house and began the last stage of what she had started yesterday. She promised herself that she'd clean the house for the summer. It was time to tear apart Charlie's room—she was no longer able to think of it as the guest room.

The male scent that permeated the bedclothes was Charlie. The carpetbag and extra blanket were Charlie's. The furniture had been touched by him. The room had been permeated by him. They had made love on that bed.

The carpetbag was open, the shirt he'd worn yesterday flung over the top. Kathleen picked up the shirt and held it to her face, loving the feel of the soft fabric and the scent of him. She took a deep breath and closed her eyes and remembered his intimate, gentle touch as the morning sun crested the small hill beyond the creek.

Then her eye caught the papers on the inside of the open bag.

Slowly releasing the shirt to fall to the bed, she stared at the papers. Guilt assailed her for what she was even thinking of doing. But why? She had a man in her life she knew little about—truth to tell, this was a golden opportunity to find out more about him.

Kathleen sat on the bed next to the bag and tried to resist the temptation. Certainly she could control her curiosity.

Too late. Her will was gone. She reached out, then pulled back, then tentatively reached out again. She touched the sheaf of papers tied carefully with string. It was about two inches thick, and there seemed to be at least twenty or thirty letters in plain blue envelopes. With gentle hands, she pulled the packet out and carefully laid it on her gingham-clad lap, staring at the letters as if they had flown there by themselves. They looked old and worn, as if read several times before being tied together with the twisted bit of twine. In the center, a corner peeking out, was a photograph just a little larger than the envelopes that surrounded it. With little effort, Kathleen pulled the photograph out and stared down at a family. Charlie stood behind a straight-backed chair, one hand on a woman's shoulder. The woman held a toddler of three or so years. Both mother and child had light brown hair and the same heart-shaped face and eyes. Doe eyes, some would say. They were beautiful, both woman and girl. And she could tell from the set of a younger Charlie's shoulders how proud he was of them. Who wouldn't be? The woman possessed high cheekbones and such a feminine, heart-shaped face that even Kathleen knew what the daughter looked like today just by looking at the mother. Her sweet gentleness shone in her gaze. This was Charlie's family, torn apart in death.

He obviously carried this packet everywhere with him—even on an estimated two-week trip to chase down a vicious shooter. It must mean more to him than Kathleen could ever imagine. Instead of untying the string, she slipped the last letter out of the packet and looked at it. It was addressed to Charlie in Oklahoma from Marie Macon. His wife. She opened it and read.

My dear husband,

　Christmas is coming, snow is on the ground, and my thoughts keep turning back to our first Christmas together in that little house you now use as a line shack. Remember? Such a wonderful time we had! You and me and our baby on the way.

　Now our baby is eight years old. Becca misses you so very much, but not one-tenth as much as I do. Every night I dream of you and our life together. I wish I could have stayed with you on the ranch. But I realize, my husband, that would have been impossible. That does not mean that I do not miss your presence in my everyday life. It means that the pain has gotten worse and I am happy to be near a doctor who can help alleviate it. Nothing can take it away, just ease the intensity. It is my barometer. I know from the measure of pain that it will not be long before I have the opportunity—I tell myself on bright days—to meet my maker. I pray to him that the end will be swift and easy. I can only hope.

My parents are doing well with both Becca and me. However this illness that I thought was only mine is also hard on them. I see it in their eyes and their turned backs when I am in pain and want no one near me. Those times I want only to pluck out the offending illness and toss it away so I may get on with life and love: raising our darling child and loving you. I crave holding another baby—our baby. And raising the rest of the bright and sweet children we never had a chance to have.

I imagine it is hard on you, too. Living alone, though married, and trying to do the ranch chores and housework must be taxing.

I try to keep my most pain-free time for Becca, who is so sweet and loving and sits with me and asks of stories about when we were growing up, or on the ranch, or before she was born. And then, sometimes, she needs the stories of when we were a family, together and happy. I try to tell her all the ones I can, but sometimes the medicine gets in the way of some memories. I fear I must rely upon you to fill in the blanks for her. I know you will do so. It is so important for her to know we all had a happy life before this illness robbed her of her family times.

This illness has stolen so much from me, too, my

darling. I will not be robbed of my dignity when I pass from this world. I am lucky in that respect. I will forever be young in your eyes. And if God is kind, your memories of me will be sweet and kind and loving. Promise you will forget those times I was angry, frustrated, or just plain ugly. Share your good thoughts of me with our daughter. She deserves to know you cared for us both as much as she now realizes I do.

But I am not silly enough to want you to give your life for our memory of wedded bliss. Please. Do marry. Find the right woman and give yourself to her as you shared yourself with me. And make sure she's a good woman, Charlie. She must love your daughter. She must! Becca needs to have sisters and brothers, and grow up laughing and with friends both in and out of the family. She needs to be strong, and you are part of her strength. Without you, she will never achieve what you and I have shared. Please, Charlie. Whatever you do, find a woman who will raise our child with her best interests at heart.

Do you believe in angels, Charlie? I hope I am one to you and ours, my darling. You can believe I will ask God for that assignment.

Please remember and know that I will love you forever and ever. My kisses are sent on the wind, surrounding you, wishing you well now and forever.

> *Your beloved wife and friend,*
> *Marie*

Kathleen dropped the open letter to her lap and closed her eyes. Tears flowed freely down her cheeks and chin to dampen the yoke of her gingham dress. She gave a swipe to her chin, but the tears paid no never mind. As if having a life of their own, they continued to flow.

His wife. Nothing made his marriage, his love, his

daughter—his life—more real than this letter. He was an honorable man who had suffered more than most. The loss of a wife was very bad, but the loss of a beloved wife was a life-altering devastation.

She cried for all the women who loved and died. And for all the children who knew a hard life without a mother to buffer the way. She knew how Becca's double loss must feel, losing her mother to illness and then her father to grief.

And Kathleen realized that deep inside her was a yearning for that depth of love. Some people never experienced it.

Some only once.

Kathleen wanted to be one who did. She wanted it more than her heart could say. She had to face it. She was jealous of the kind of love a dead woman had experienced.

And Charlie must be worth it for this woman to still love him while dying.

For the first time since Charlie entered her life, Kathleen bent her head and cried. She cried great, gulping sobs that wrenched her shoulders and hurt her head and throat.

Poor Charlie. He'd lost everything he'd held dear. But he wasn't alone.

Kathleen recognized what Charlie's wife had lost, and what young Becca had lost. She had lost her own mother at that age.

But she cried most because Kathleen knew that what they had all lost, she had never had . . . .

Sixteen

A very angry E. Z. stood hunched over in the middle of her plowed field. He stomped around like a misshapen elf having a terrible tantrum. The angrier he was, the more bent he became. "It ain't right, I tell ya! I ourta be the sheriff for a change! I had dibbs on it long afore Zeke did! *Long* afore!"

"I don't even know if we need a sheriff for the next play, E. Z.," Kathleen said calmly, but on the inside her nerves were tensed. "Why don't we see what happens at the meeting tomorrow evening?"

" 'Cause Mabel's already got a story she wants to do. It's gonna be the last one, three days after the board meetin' next week, and she says she's written a doozy!" His face got red again just thinking of his missed opportunity. He took a couple of steps back and forth over her newly dug mounds of dark brown earth as if wanting to squash them but knowing better. "An', dagnabit, I wanna be the sheriff!"

"E. Z.—" she began.

But he wasn't about to listen to reason. "Now listen to me, girl." Every line in his face was emphasized. His expression was as somber as an undertaker's. "You always promised you'd let me be sheriff some-day. You said it more'n once, an' I been patient, Kathleen, you know I have. But it's time for what you promised over two years ago!"

Now wasn't the time to tell him she'd lied to keep the wizened old man off her back. No one could be a more unlikely sheriff than E. Z. and she'd only lied so as not to hurt his feelings. She thought something would save her from actually saying the word *no.*

She leaned on her hoe and gave a sigh. "Let me look at the story and I'll see about it," Kathleen said, placating him while she thought of an excuse to say no later. She frowned. "Why did Mabel tell you about her story? No one else has even seen it yet, let alone read it!"

" 'Cause I seen her in town and we started talkin' and all, an' she was so happy to have such a wonderful story to tell that she said I ourta be playin' the sheriff cause it's jes right fer me!"

"Well, I'll certainly look into it," Kathleen said, but she felt more determined to wring Mabel's neck than she'd ever felt before. Was the woman insane? E. Z. wasn't even as large as the smallest woman in Blissful!

Suddenly E. Z.'s anger was gone. He stared at her through wise, narrowed eyes that made him look as if he held the wisdom of the ages. "You promise?" he asked solemnly.

"I promise," she said, equally solemn. "Now, will you either help me plant this crop of carrots or get out of my way?"

A wide grin lit up his entire body. "I'm goin to the general store. Did you already git your seed?"

"Yes, thanks. And I'm going to plant it if you get out of here and let me be."

"All right, then," E. Z. said, finally settled down to his usual brusque self. "We'll talk later."

"Wonderful." Kathleen picked up the hoe and began covering the seed in the shallow trough. "I'll see you later, E. Z."

"You kin count on it, little lady!" he said as he walked quickly across the field toward his horse, which was tethered at the back door.

Kathleen gave a glance his way several times as he rode away, wondering what in the world had gotten into Mabel. She had noticed that lately the woman was full of spit and vinegar. But this was a first. Mabel had never written a play before. If she and E. Z. were that excited about it, maybe it was good. One thing was sure: Kathleen would find out at tomorrow night's meeting. Maybe then she could find out why Mabel had chosen E. Z. for such a part.

She dropped the hoe and picked up the reins of her horse attached to the plow. "Heya!" she called, putting the horses and the plow back in motion. With Charlie gone, there was no reason to go inside and cook. She might as well make the most of her free time.

She'd known Charlie for two weeks, and now that he was gone for a few days, she was the loneliest she'd ever been. What was wrong with her?

Charlie took the same path he'd taken before, but this time he went much farther in two days than he had in the one day he'd traveled the last time. This time he wasn't going back to see Kathleen until he finished what he had to do. He had a lot to accomplish before that could happen.

Ever since he'd gotten to Blissful and to Kathleen's house, he had forgotten his purpose for being there. He was supposed to be finding Vic and killing him, like that scumbag killed his partner. And if for some damn reason he couldn't find the courage to kill Vic, he needed to capture him and get him to the next sheriff's office. Either way, the no-good was going to pay for what he did. And Charlie had to make sure that it happened before he could find any peace for himself.

He stopped by a stream he thought was an offshoot of Bliss Creek and filled his canteen while his horse drank deeply of the crystal-clear water running over limestone. The quiet sounds of gurgling water, birds chirping merrily in the branches, and the soft sigh of the breeze in the pines all made for the perfect spot to enjoy nature. Even the soft, mossy bank looked inviting enough for a nap in the late-afternoon heat.

Suddenly it was the perfect day, and he wished Kathleen were with him here to see what he was seeing, feel what he was feeling, and share the experience.

He was going to visit the sheriff in the next town, then start a spiraling circle out of Blissful until he caught on to something, anything that led him to Vic. The man had been there, and he was probably still doing something wrong somewhere. He wasn't bright enough to stay out of trouble.

In fact, from everything that Charlie had found out about him, Vic was both stupid and cruel, with just enough charm to get into spots that looked legitimate and just enough impatience not to be able to keep it up for long. He'd show his own wickedness soon enough to anyone he was around.

That alone told Charlie there ought to be a trail of tears behind this jackass.

He looked out at the trail he was about to travel and wondered how much farther he had to go to reach the town. One more look at the bed of moss convinced him that he wanted to stay here. He could catch a fish for dinner, relax, and hit the trail again in the early morning, when it wasn't so warm. The hardtack and cheese and ham could wait until tomorrow.

Without another thought, Charlie unhitched his saddle and dropped it to the ground. A twig snapped in the distance and he stopped still, his gaze searching the trees across the trail. He saw nothing.

With a shrug he told himself he was getting nervous at being on the road after spending time with Kathleen.

It was understandable . . . .

Kathleen gave Blissful's mayor, Fredrick Johnson, silent encouragement as he tried to keep a handle on the town's general meeting. But from the beginning it was too much for him. It showed in the blank look in his eyes, the edging of his booted toes aimed toward the door, and the frustration of his fists in his baggy pockets. He wanted out of the argument between E. Z. and Mabel on one side and the rest of the group who felt different. Only the good townspeople could afford to sit back and keep quiet, while poor Fredrick was the one who had to open his mouth and say the words that E. Z. didn't—really didn't—want to hear.

And Mabel's stubbornness astounded everyone. Looking like a banner, she wore a bright blue dress that was far too frilly for her plump form, and the color blue was too deep and brilliant for her complexion, which seemed to border on red most of the time lately. Kathleen had never seen her so vocally determined. Come to think of it, she'd been this high-spirited, as E. Z. called it, for the past few weeks or so. And now she had written a play that everyone agreed was a great way to—hopefully—end their years of plays. Everyone wanted to have a part in it. Including E. Z. And strangely enough, Mabel sorely wanted E. Z. to play the part of the sheriff, too. It was the rest of the town who thought it wasn't realistic.

"Please, please!" Mabel stood, clearly angry. Her face was so red Kathleen was worried for her. Her hands shook as she held them up to quiet the room. "I wrote this play and I ought to have a say in the casting. We all promised E. Z. a part someday, even Kathleen. . . ." Mabel looked daggers at her, a long, drawn-out note of suffering in her tone. "And now we need to go forth and do the right thing. I wrote this for E. Z., and I think he should have the part. And I don't *care* whether anyone thinks E. Z. isn't right for the part. It's my play, and I say he is!" She gasped the last word, her ample breast heaving with the effort. Mabel dared everyone she could match eyes with. Then, with a satisfied harrumph, sat down on a barrel top and waited for the town to agree.

It didn't take long.

Fredrick gave a heavy sigh and looked around the room for a very dramatic moment before speaking. His German accent, usually slight, was practically impossible to understand. His body language said it all. "E. Z., he is da sheriff. An' dats dat!"

The flow of voices rose and fell, but no one wanted to continue the argument. If they had wanted to, this was the time to stand up and say so, although Mabel was ready to pounce on the first one. That was enough to keep the men quiet, and the women were wise enough to choose the fights they could win. This wasn't one.

"Den da actors meet here da day before da railroad meeting next week."

As the meeting finally broke up, Mabel made her way to Kathleen. Her expression was victorious. "It certainly seems everyone likes my story, Kathleen."

"The play is well written, Mabel," she said softly. "Very well done."

The other woman's brows rose, her chin quivering slightly. "Thank you for admitting that."

"Why wouldn't I? You did a good job."

"You've been jealous of me before. I didn't know what your response would be now."

Kathleen's eyes widened. "I didn't know that," she stated dryly. It went over Mabel's head. "When was this, uh, jealousy?"

Mabel's eyes sparkled with satisfaction. "Don't pretend you don't remember. It was when I made more money selling my shawls than you did selling your carrot cake last year. My ten percent contribution to the city was larger than yours, despite all your ideas about how the town should earn or spend it."

Kathleen's mind whirled with this new view of herself. She hadn't even remembered Mabel's sale . . . or at least she didn't think she did. "And," she said thoughtfully, earnestly trying to remember, "did I say something that led you to believe I was jealous?"

Mabel's face became a deep red. "As if you don't remember!" she spat. "You said, 'How wonderful for you, Mabel. Perhaps we could travel up to Waco and buy ourselves some nice calico for dresses. Maybe even spend the night and splurge a little, since neither of us has someone to take care of,' " Mabel said in a singsong voice that wasn't anything like Kathleen's.

"I said that?" she asked in a surprised tone, vaguely remembering the incident now, and wondering what would have ever possessed her to give such an effort at friendship to a tense, occasionally mean-spirited woman like Mabel.

Mabel nodded emphatically. "You certainly did," she said. "I knew right away that you thought I wasn't capable of finding a man. But you were wrong."

Now Kathleen was really confused. "Capable of finding a man? How on earth did you jump to that conclusion from my considering a trip to buy material?"

"I know you, Kathleen. You're all sweet on the outside, but you're lonely and bitter on the inside. You just hide it well. You wish you had a man in your life." She looked like a puffed-up frog sitting on the bank of Bliss Creek. Kathleen thought she detected a little green around the gills. "Well, maybe someday, Kathleen. Everyone can't be lucky."

A slow-burning anger bubbled up in Kathleen's stomach. "Listen carefully, Mabel. I was *not* jealous of you. I invited you to Waco because I thought you might like it, and for no other reason. I do *not* feel bitter inside and I do *not* need a man in my life. If I did, I would have stayed home in North Carolina, where I had been asked for my hand in marriage!" She refused to mention how she hated the man. That wasn't the point.

Mabel stared at her in astonishment for a full minute before she knowingly smiled. "Don't worry, Kathleen. Your secret is safe with me. I certainly won't tell anyone."

Now she was really confused. "Tell them what?"

"That you're lonely and you lie."

Kathleen stared in stunned silence. Before one single thought could trip to Kathleen's tongue, Mabel turned and walked to the far side of the general store to the counter, where Jacob and several others were discussing the upcoming railroad board. Kathleen

couldn't take her eyes off her. Mabel smiled at the
men, said a few words, and then nodded her good
nights to them. Without another look around the
crowded room, she walked out the door and disappeared into the night.

"Did Mabel finally show her hand, Kathleen? Or
does that look of amazement come from something
else she tripped over on the way to putting her foot
in her mouth again?"

Kathleen forced her mouth closed as she turned
to look into the knowing eyes of her friend Mildred.
"She thinks I'm jealous of her."

Her friend laughed. "She always was too full of
herself," Mildred said, a grin still teasing her gentle
mouth. "But don't you know, she has a shock coming
when she finds out you don't care a whit about keeping up with her."

"Have I missed something? Did something happen
that I don't know about? She acts as if I should want
whatever she has, and she thinks she has so much.
Obviously including her talent for writing plays."

Mildred's dark eyes twinkled. "I know, and isn't it
a shame that this is our last play? Think of all the
contributions she could have made in the past two
years . . . and didn't."

"No. I gather she wanted me to fall on my face
first."

"Of course. Mabel hates you."

"She does?" Kathleen asked.

"Of course. And she'd stab you in the back if she
had the chance."

"Mabel?" Kathleen asked, confused now.

"My thoughts, too," Mildred said. Then she
frowned. "I would be worried if it were anyone else.
Lately, Mabel seems to be on some very shaky ground,
and no one knows why. But she's bought a couple of

horses from Waco, and ordered several new dresses. Amy said she heard that Mabel ordered half a dozen gowns that will be delivered from Mason in the next day or so."

"Mabel?" Kathleen asked again. Mabel was never a clothes horse. Never.

"Mabel," Mildred stated firmly.

Kathleen remembered the comment the other woman made about men in their lives. "Maybe she's decided to go husband hunting."

"Not here, certainly. Perhaps she's thinking of taking a trip. Going out of town, where her reputation as an aging snapdragon doesn't precede her?"

Mildred gave a low chuckle. "And bring him back here, hogtied and begging for mercy?"

It was a vivid image—one that made her smile. "Maybe," Kathleen said "She just informed me that she can find love when I can't find anyone willing to marry me. She told me so." An image of Charlie flashed in her head.

"And she's right," Mildred said. "Because she has no taste, so anyone will do. While you . . . well, you have too much taste to settle for the first cowboy to want to put his boots at the foot of your bed."

Charlie's boots at the foot of her bed . . . She felt her skin heat with the thought of it. That was where the boots had been the night they had made love, then held each other until dawn. It was the most wonderful night of her life, and she was making fun of a woman who wanted that unique and life-shattering experience as much as she did. How could she make fun of the woman for wanting the very thing Kathleen wanted? Craved? Needed?

"Mildred," Kathleen began.

But her friend would have no part of her sympathy-laced voice. "Kathleen," she threatened. "Don't you *dare* to defend the very woman who slapped Amy and called her indecent for saying Sven had a strong set of arms and carried lumber well. She is the same woman who shunned poor Mrs. Heine for having Zeke over for her homemade dumplings.'' She took a breath but cut Kathleen off from saying a word when she continued. ''And especially the same woman who has belittled every woman in this town who even *looked* content with her lot in life!''

''I know, but . . . '' Kathleen couldn't think of a thing to say. Mildred was right. Mabel had made, if not an enemy, at least a cautious neighbor out of everyone in Blissful. Her rudeness and unusual and selfish opinions had hurt almost everyone. Those she hadn't hurt with careless remarks or glances, she hadn't had a chance to be around. She searched her mind for a redeeming quality. ''But she did a good thing for E. Z. when she wrote the part for him to be a sheriff.''

Mildred made a face. ''You searched until you found one good thing about that woman. And it has just happened. You've been here four years and that's all you can say.''

''That's it,'' Kathleen confirmed sadly.

Mildred grinned impishly. ''I'm so glad. Because when I searched my memory, I couldn't find one. She's a self-serving woman, and there's got to be something she's going to get out of this play that we don't know.''

''Of course. She's got the praise of her neighbors,'' Kathleen stated reasonably. ''That's got to be heady.''

''This is Mabel we're discussing, remember? There's more to it than that. And since you happen to be her favorite person to snip at, I'd be careful if I were you.''

Kathleen gave her friend a hug. ''Thank you for

worrying, but I'm fine. She's all excited about this play and has something else to focus upon."

"All I know is that I'm happy your brother is visiting."

Kathleen hoped her lie wouldn't show in her eyes "He's in Mason for a while, visiting friends."

It was Mildred's turn to look surprised. "He has friends in Mason?"

"Yes, but John hasn't seen them for a while, so he decided to see if he could look them up." She wished Charlie were here right now, although she didn't know how she would explain all the activity that went on before a show. It would look to Charlie as if she were in a sewing frenzy. It was just as well.

"He doesn't know about the town, does he?"

"No. And I don't think I'll tell him. He would only worry, and you know how older brothers are."

"I haven't got a clue," Mildred said breezily. "I come from a family of six girls, and at some time each of us wanted an older brother. No luck. Mother said she would have no more after my baby sister, Amelia, was born. I guess she meant it, because Amelia was the last. Dad now sleeps in the barn. We hear him call his cow all sorts of sweet names."

Kathleen had to laugh. Mildred was one of the wonderful people in her life who gave her such a wonderful sense of the ordinary in everyday life. She always brought Kathleen back to the present and showed her that it was an integral part of life that it handed you problems.

"Lucky you. Brothers can be a real problem." If Charlie were her real brother, she'd be entirely accurate. As it was, she counted the hours until he returned. The ache in her heart was directly proportionate to the hole Charlie's absence left in her life.

"Will he be joining you at the Fort Worth railroad meeting in two days?"

"No." Kathleen shook her head, emphasizing the point to herself more than to Mildred. "He won't be back until a day or two after our play."

"He must like his old friends very much to spend all that time with them."

"I believe so, although he probably won't be seeing them again once he heads for home and his wife delivers his first child. I doubt I shall see him again unless I go to North Carolina and visit."

"And what is the likelihood of that?" Mildred asked, her sharp eyes seeing far more than Kathleen wished her to see. Kathleen purposely kept her expression bland. "About the same likelihood of Mabel's finding a husband. Nil."

They both laughed.

Later that evening as Kathleen walked back home with a group of the townspeople going the same way, she realized how integral a part of her life they had become.

Conversations were carried on in small groups, the men walking behind the women. Anything from crops, cattle, sewing, recipes, and babies was being discussed.

"Good night!" Daniel Ruben and Florence Klee called as the group reached their street and they parted from the crowd and walked, hand in hand, to their own homes.

Kathleen listened to several of the women as they spoke about their children, and was torn between enjoying the conversation and wishing she had a child to love. Regret for not marrying when she had had the chance was a feeling she periodically felt. But she wished it could have been with someone she loved, and never as much as now, when she heard her friends discussing child rearing.

"Good night," Amy and Troy called as Amy gave Kathleen's shoulders a light hug and left the group.

Two others peeled off, then another, and another. Finally it was just Kathleen and Mrs. Hanrahan, the sweet lady who lived across the street from her.

The older lady's bright yellow shawl hung low on her back, a beacon against her dark dress. Every year saw her dowager's hump grow a little, her stoop become more pronounced, her hair continue turning from gray to white. But the attentive, alert look in her faded blue eyes never dimmed. From the very first time they met, she and Kathleen became fast friends, but each allowed the other plenty of space and solitude, ready to be a friend only when it was needed.

Kathleen noticed that Mrs. Hanrahan leaned a little heavier on her walking stick this evening. She couldn't ask the proud woman about her obvious pain. She chose another conversation instead.

"How is Jimmy, Mrs. Hanrahan?"

Her teeth gleamed in the moonlight as she smiled. "Oh, dear, he's doing so well on Long Island in New York. He loves it there and thinks he might well be the owner of the biggest dry-goods store on all the island."

She took the older woman's elbow and slowed her own steps to match. "How proud you must be."

"I am. Many times I have wished that he had stayed here in Blissful, but now I know I made the right choice when I told him to go with my blessing and seek his own fortune. He's worked his way up to owning his own store. What a wonderful opportunity."

"That's wonderful."

"That's fate, my dear. I knew he was meant for something bigger than what our little village has to offer." Her eyes danced merrily as she glanced up at Kathleen. "However, that was before we had a visitor who changed our little town into a thriving money-maker."

"The town was ready for a change. I didn't change it; I just gave an idea or two."

Mrs. Hanrahan patted her hand. "You believe what you believe, and I'll stick to the truth, my dear." She chuckled. "Just like the story of your brother."

A lightninglike heat sped down her spine. "My brother?"

"Isn't that what you call him?"

"Johnny? Of course."

"For the first week I think he was called Charlie, wasn't he?"

Now the heat fused through her legs. "No. Of course not."

"Oh, I see. Well, I just wondered. I saw him calling to you a time or two, and then there were the times you told him off."

They reached Mrs. Hanrahan's porch. "You *heard* me?"

"My dear, on windy days, I can hear shouts. And laughter. And other sounds."

"Oh, my goodness."

"Just don't hurt yourself, my dear. You deserve a husband and family. The best thing that ever happened to me is my Jimmy. Even though he's in another state now, I know he thinks of the young me who raised him, and he has wonderful thoughts. I can tell by his letters that I have done well with him. It's worth all the tea in China, my dear. It's a mother's badge. Don't let yourself lose the chance to have that experience."

"I can't guarantee that," she said softly, wondering if the rest of her life was going to be as lonely as she felt right now, without Charlie. What would a lifetime of being without him be like? Someday would she be the spinster some young woman would walk home?

"It's fate, dear," Mrs. Hanrahan said softly. She walked up the front steps of her home and turned around, staring as if she could see the rich prairie beyond their road. She finally stared down at Kathleen. Her form, dressed in dark colors, blended against the screen door—except for the shawl. "Never turn your back on fate."

"I'm not even sure I know what fate is," Kathleen said, her thoughts caught up in the older woman's words.

"It's when you've been handed an opportunity to take a different path, and your life changes for having chosen it."

Neither woman said anything for a long time.

"Good night, Mrs. Hanrahan."

"Good night, Kathleen. Don't forget to follow your heart and have a wonderful life."

She prayed that she would, but wasn't sure what the word *wonderful* entailed.

All she knew was that Charlie wasn't with her, and even if he were, she had turned him down. It didn't matter, though. Although she was sure she had made the right decision, he had already made such a deep impact upon her heart . . . .

The following afternoon, Zeke found Mrs. Hanrahan in her bed. There was a smile on her lips, as she seemed to have died a peaceful death. Kathleen mourned her, knowing her neighbor was a wise and intelligent woman. Her loss was great.

Within a day, Timely had bought the place and registered it, pending the written permission of Mrs. Hanrahan's son back east.

It was a bittersweet loss, and Kathleen was glad she had walked home and talked to Mrs. Hanrahan the day before.

If only it were simple to have a wonderful life . . . .

Seventeen

Drizzle. Charlie hated drizzle. It wasn't cloudy or a downpour of rain and it wasn't sunshine or moonlight. It was just wet enough to be irritating and not coming down strong enough to get prepared.

"Damn," he muttered, tilting his hat enough to make sure that the water collected on the brim would drain off his shoulder and back. Two drops collected and dripped. *Drizzle. Damn.*

He was a hundred miles from Blissful, following a trail toward Galveston, just in case Vic continued to go this way. In fact, several days ago he'd talked to a rancher who thought Vic Masters had passed through and stolen a horse. The old man had given a general description of him, and his methods seemed to check out, too. Vic was good at switching horses; he'd done it often enough. But this time he was seen. He'd been tracking the animal ever since.

At one house a man swore someone spent the night

in the barn, then milked the cow, stole some eggs, and headed southwest.

Charlie was following. But it wasn't what he wanted to do. Not at all. Suddenly his quest for Vic Masters wasn't as important as other things, and if it weren't for the burning hole in his life that his dead partner made, he might have abandoned the search after making sure the law was notified all the way through Texas.

Instead here he was, traveling in the drizzle and wishing he were in Blissful.

What he really wanted was Kathleen's soft, sweet-scented body close to him, her contented puffs and sighs blended with his and filling the room with the only sound available until dawn. Then he would snuggle in and listen to the birds starting their own cacophony and the cat scratching and rubbing against the screen door until she was let back in so she could recuperate from chasing birds and newly awakened field mice.

Until then he could lie next to her, his hand on Kathleen's waist, and dream of how lucky he was to be exactly here exactly then.

Instead here he was, in the plains part of Texas, where marsh and river blended together to form bogs and long stretches of hard-to-ride land. Because of the stolen horse he was following, he was sure that Vic was ahead of him. It was just a matter of time before he caught the scum-sucker. Then, once Vic Masters was behind bars, he would return to Kathleen and tell her what he felt.

He was a man of few words, even fewer when it came to love. He found it hard to speak what was in his heart. But as he got older, he also realized it was more important to say it aloud to the person who needed to hear it as much as he needed to say it.

But somehow he had to smooth-talk Kathleen into coming back to Oklahoma with him. He realized Kathleen thought they were through with each other. But she was wrong. He didn't know where this was leading, but he was smart enough to know it wasn't over.

He wanted children; he wanted his ranch to succeed. He wanted a family who would surround him until his dying days. He didn't know if it was Kathleen that he would spend his life with, but right now he wanted Kathleen most of all. Without her it didn't matter how many children he had; his life would be lonely—lonelier than he had ever imagined possible.

He had loved his wife. He had loved her with all the fervor of youth, and had God granted them the opportunity, he would have loved her forever. But loving Kathleen was a full-grown man's love. It was different, special, and wondrous. And fun! Damn it, the woman was everything rolled into one package. And he wanted the whole package.

And if he could convince Kathleen to be with him, perhaps he could talk her into helping him raise Becca. That would be the best of all possible dreams.

His heart beat out the rhythm of her name. *Kathleen. Kathleen. Kathleen.*

It would be another week or two before he'd be back in Blissful. It was going to be the longest fourteen days he'd ever spent.

The sun peeped out from behind the lazy gray clouds, then decided against sticking around to dry up the drizzle.

He hoped that Kathleen missed him half as much as he missed her. It was only fair. He pictured her sitting in the kitchen, working on the smaller pieces of fabric to be made into another quilt. The kitchen would smell like carrot cake and creamed frosting.

The light would be dim and she'd be leaning toward the lamp, her green-eyed gaze narrowing on the piecework. In a little while, she would put the cat out, lock the back door, and turn down the light. Then she'd climb into her bed, tug the blanket and sheet up to her chin, curl into a ball on her side, and close those beautiful eyes. Within minutes she'd be contented, calm, happy, and asleep.

But he wouldn't be. He was riding in the rain, following some damn tracks that might or might not lead him to Vic. He turned his collar up and stared through the mist.

He had half a canteen of sulfur-tainted water, two hard-boiled eggs, and some jerky to chew on. Instead of being here, he should be curled up and safe with Kathleen, having a contented life.

"Damn."

Kathleen, Zeke, and Jacob stepped off the train and walked to the Stockyard Hotel in the heart of downtown Fort Worth. It was the largest cattle town in Texas and held the key to all the railroads in the state . . . or so the rumors went. From this town the railroad ran down to Houston and Galveston, the big port city, and to San Antonio and the hill country, where both horse and cattle were profitably raised to send to San Francisco and the Pacific, and also north to Chicago.

But it didn't matter right now. They had come from Blissful, Texas, just three hours down the road. They were on a mission to save the town—the last mission they would participate in, no matter what the outcome of this meeting.

Beneath her white gloves that clutched her reticule, Kathleen's hands were chilled and clammy. Her heart raced erratically, pounding against her ribs like an amateur drummer in a neighborhood parade.

This was the opportunity she'd waited for. She'd plotted and prayed for this meeting, all the while taking steps and making plans to make her dream the town's dream—and the town's dream a reality.

And now that the opportunity she'd worked toward for the past two years was here, she felt as if her ears couldn't hear more than a dull roar, and her tongue was twice the size it usually was. Nobody would understand a word she had to say—if she could think of the words she had to say!

She glanced at Zeke. His face seemed forged in a concrete scowl.

However, Jacob had his perpetual smile in place. It looked as fake as a mask. He caught Kathleen's gaze. "Nice town."

The smell of the cattle yard filled her nostrils. She wrinkled her nose. "Difficult smell."

"Well, yes, but the streets are . . . " He looked down just in time to circumvent horse dung on the cobblestone.

"Difficult." Zeke's tone held a disparaging note.

Kathleen's nose was still wrinkled. "And the walkway isn't easy, either," she said, feeling each rounded stone through her soft leather shoes. She should have worn her boots.

As if knowing what direction her mind was heading in, Jacob said, "Your dress is sure pretty, Kathleen."

She gave a grateful smile. "Thank you." Amy had worked hard making the gathered, forest green cotton dress before Kathleen attached Mrs. Hanrahan's exquisite handmade lace to decorate the collar, bodice, and cuffs. Her new outfit was the main reason she'd worn the thin slippers. Vanity. She was a slave to fashion, she thought with a laugh, and it made her forget—just for the moment—what she was doing. She was wearing her first new dress in over a year, and wished she hadn't so she could go barefoot or wear her comfortable boots.

Jacob took her elbow and helped her up the steps to the large wood-and-brick structure. The railroad's board of directors had set aside a private dining area for them to meet. She just hoped she could remember all her arguments.

The lady at the front desk directed them down the hall to a small desk area where an older woman sat, separating several sheets of paper into piles in front of her.

Jacob spoke up. "We have a meeting with the railroad commission this morning."

The secretary looked up through wire-rimmed glasses, focusing on each one of them for a long moment. So did the rest of the men and women milling in the hallway. Suddenly there was silence. "And your names are?" she asked, her imperious tone rising at the end in question.

"Miss Kathleen O'Day, Mr. Jacob Thinn, and Mr. Zeke Hershel," Jacob stated, his eyes staring the woman down. Kathleen was surprised; she'd never seen him this way.

The secretary looked down at her book, then up again, a tight smile pursing her lips into a grimace. "Please have a seat. Your turn will come in an hour or so."

"We were told to be here at eight-thirty this morning," Kathleen stated firmly. She glanced at her watch, which was pinned to the breast of her new dress. "I believe it is that time now."

"Your belief is correct, Miss O'Day. However, the meeting before yours is still going on. Until it is completed, no one will be allowed to disturb the board."

She gave a tight smile again. Kathleen was sure this woman went home and privately sucked on lemons.

There was no sense in making her any angrier. The woman seemed to be the only guard at the gate. A glance at her ring finger told Kathleen that she was a spinster. This was her place of importance. Kathleen knew that feeling. She smiled sweetly and, swallowing the words that wanted to work their way up to her mouth, said only, "Thank you." She motioned to the side bench. "We'll just wait over here."

"Suit yourself," the woman said with a shrug. Once more she busied herself with stacking the papers, this time in different stacks.

Zeke plopped down, his angry expression wrinkling his forehead. "That woman deserves to be whipped," he muttered.

" 'Course she does," Jacob stated as if it were a foregone conclusion.

"Nobody deserves to be beaten," Kathleen stated automatically. These were the usual responses of men, and these men were without women in their lives to remind them of civilities. She wasn't about to hear any more without saying something. But secretly, she wouldn't have minded letting Miss Secretary overhear the comments. After all, they had come a long way for this appointment and were nervous enough already. They were on time; why couldn't the commission follow the same rules of courtesy? Besides, after the long train ride and the walk to the hotel, they didn't need the help of a spinster who didn't have an understanding of others' feelings.

Spinster. A jolting thought. Someday, probably soon, someone would look at Kathleen and whisper that word. That thought hurt. She would be labeled, just as she had labeled someone else, and she would have to live with those thoughts made aloud by others.

As her aunt used to say, what goes around comes around.

She closed her eyes and took a deep breath, forcing her face and shoulders to relax so she wouldn't look like the pinched-faced spinster she was fast becoming.

Suddenly, washing over her without warning or thought, the overwhelming need to have Charlie with her brought tears to her eyes. She kept her eyes closed and tried to change her thoughts, but it didn't work. Charlie's face danced in front of her closed eyelids, smiling down at her as if she held emeralds in her eyes and pearls in her teeth.

When he laughed at something she said, it was the deep baritone sound that made her feel as if she'd won the Kentucky Derby or single-handedly fought the Mexican government for the Alamo. Although he wasn't close to her right now and she didn't see that smile anywhere but in her mind, that same wonderful feeling permeated every muscle in her body, washing her with the warmth of winning the great fight.

"Kathleen? Are you all right?" Jacob asked. He placed his hand on her arm, bringing her back to the long hallway in front of the prune-faced woman who acted as a secretary.

"I'm fine, thank you," she said in a whisper, not willing to lose the feeling that Charlie was with her.

"Then why is she smiling?" Zeke asked. "Why are you smiling?" he asked directly.

"Shhh," Jacob silenced. "She's happy, and that's all that matters right now. She's getting ready to face hell, so whatever she does to prepare for that, it's worth it."

Kathleen's eyes popped open. So much for wonderful feelings of winning the good fight. Instead she looked straight into the eyes of the secretary. The woman stood in front of the large double doors of the conference room, her back as straight and rigid as her gray dress was drab and starched.

It certainly wasn't like looking into a mirror. The only thing the woman had in common with her was that neither of them wore a wedding band. Kathleen suddenly hoped that she would change that. Someday.

It was doubtful that this woman could, even if she began hunting today, this moment.

"Miss O'Day?" she said, clipping each syllable. "The board will review your petition now."

Her heart suddenly skipped a beat, then pounded like a hammer. "Thank you." She looked at Jacob and Zeke and then stood, her knuckles white against the deep green of her reticule. "Shall we?" she asked no one in particular.

"After you." Jacob sounded strangled by his tie.

His apparent nervousness did nothing to alleviate Kathleen's jitters. She had counted on Jacob's ability to fill in whatever facts and stories she forgot.

"Relax," she said as she took a step forward. "This will work. Honest."

They walked in. Like compass needles pointing north, all eyes turned toward Kathleen. The room held a long mahogany table filled on three sides by nine older men with muttonchop sideburns, vests, and dark-colored suits expensively tailored. Four wore glasses, but they all stared. As if on silent command, they all opened the file in front of them and studied the papers inside. Then, in unison, they looked up at the small group and sized them up.

From Kathleen's viewpoint, they were either found lacking or a supreme disappointment.

These were the same nine men they had met before. At that time they were told to continue with the shows and the board would continue to monitor. No wonder. The board made money from their shows without putting out any effort. Money just fell into their laps, thanks to Blissful's reputation. The only time the train was filled to capacity was when it was stopping quickly in Blissful.

When neither Zeke nor Jacob said anything, Kathleen decided it was time to break the silence. "Good morning, gentlemen," Kathleen stated, her voice louder than she meant it to be. She cleared her throat. "It's a pleasure to see you again."

"Good morning," the solemn board said in unison.

She gave a quick look toward her two partners in this crime. Their eyes were huge, and she was sure Jacob's throat had closed completely.

"Sirs," Kathleen began, noticing that, although she was the one talking, they looked at Jacob, "thank you for your time."

The president nodded. "You are most gracious."

She took a deep breath and began. "Blissful is a growing and prosperous community, made more so by the plays we've put on in the past two years. Thanks to those, we have made money by selling our wares as your trains stop, and you have sold more tickets on this route than any other in Texas, other than the route between Fort Worth and Amarillo."

"How do you know that?" the president asked, continuing to stare at Jacob.

Jacob tried to answer but it came out as a croak instead.

Kathleen picked up the slack of silence. "Because several of the train conductors are our friends, and they have let it be known."

"But they're not certain, are they? It's unsubstantiated," the man stated rather than asked. "They don't have the numbers or the records?" He continued to talk to Jacob.

In the silence, Kathleen's gaze dared lock with each and every member of the board, finally finding a sympathetic gaze. The man looked too much like a scared rabbit to buck one of the board members, but he was more attentive to her than anyone else. And he looked back. "It seems to be common knowledge among all train workers. They were kind enough to share it. I'm sure your records are far more accurate, sirs. And I'm also sure you know exactly how many passengers are on each run and each line, and how many more travel through Blissful when you have a stop in our community."

There. That should help them understand just how much they knew.

"I see," the head man said, and they all looked down at the charts in the folders.

"As I understand, you have all ridden the railroad yourself sometime in the past two years and know what shows we put on and that the passenger cars are always packed."

The head man snapped his folder closed and looked at a man on his right, who was slightly younger and far more blunt. For the first time since she'd entered the room, she was looked at directly when questions were asked. "And why should we want to stop for a full hour in Blissful, taking on cattle that you now ship through Mason, and lose the show's draw? That doesn't seem like good business for the railroad."

Kathleen's look was just as direct and just as challenging. "You're right. It's not good business, sirs." She looked at each one of them before continuing. "And if I were you, I wouldn't be too thrilled about losing the extra business, either."

The second in command leaned back in his chair. He was cocky, but at least he looked directly at her. "So what is the point of this meeting?"

Kathleen raised her brows. "Why, I thought you knew. We cannot keep the plays going anymore. We're ending them as of next week. Thursday will be our last play."

All the men seemed to sit a little straighter at that announcement. *Good.* It was about time she had their full attention.

"Why?" It was barked out by the president. For the first time he looked straight at her. It couldn't have been put more bluntly. It was also the one question she hadn't bothered to put an answer to until Charlie came on the scene. Thank God for Charlie.

"It is too dangerous to continue." Kathleen looked around the room again, and this time everyone looked back. "Right now, thanks to the shows, we have made much money and invested it wisely while we waited for your decision to make our town a major stop. But in six months, if you don't make us a regular stop, we'll be back to where we were two years ago. It will cost us too much money to take our cattle to Mason, to have no one stop and buy our goods. Because of our reputation, no one will use our town as a tourist place along the way. Then we will slowly go downhill again, with many of our young people leaving to work in larger cities with more things going on. All in all, you will kill Blissful. And there is nothing we can do anymore. The secret is attracting too many of the wrong people. Criminals will finally come to realize we are helpless and enter our little community, and we will lose all we have gained. Then we will never attract any major industry to keep us going."

"All this because we don't designate a stop in your

fair town? Or is it because you don't want to bother putting on the plays anymore?''

Obviously he was not listening to what she had to say. She stared at him a moment, not willing to back down from the truth to save his feelings. Too much was at stake for this board to pass over their explanations without understanding the situation. ''Both. It's too risky.''

''What's so risky about putting on plays that give a feel of the Wild West and that people enjoy enough to take a long ride on the railroad to see?''

''And pay good money for the tickets,'' she reminded him, unwilling to allow them to pretend the railroad wasn't prospering from little effort except for the town's hard work.

A cold light sparked the president's gaze, but instead of saying something he might regret, he nodded reluctantly.

''Well, it seems that our reputation has grown so well, outlaws from other areas have heard and believe the stories we tell. They now think Blissful is a good place to come, stay a while, and be safe. We've heard rumors that there are a few of them on their way to our safe haven now.'' She let that piece of information, a little inflated but nonetheless true, to sink in. ''And that will be Blissful's death. As you gentlemen know, we haven't even had a sheriff in over two years.''

''Why not, Miss O'Day? That doesn't seem prudent for a town your size. Especially one that wants a weekly stop.''

''In the beginning, when you pulled our stop away, we lost much money. Many good neighbors and friends moved on to more flourishing communities. We didn't have the money to pay a sheriff. The town was dying. Then, when we began the shows, gentlemen, the outlaws stayed away because we were such a wicked town. But now, the most wicked of the wicked is willing to come because it's open season on stupid innocents who have glamorized death in the Old West, which is exactly what we do. That's us.

"It's very simple, gentlemen. We either get the stop, or we die. The choice is up to you. We have the business to support your stop, as well as seven smaller communities around us willing to help with that support. We are logically and strategically stationed for a stop. And we are now a growing community, thanks to you and to our town working together these past two years." She sat back. "The rest is up to you."

The chairman looked at the man on either side of Kathleen. "What say you, gentlemen?"

Zeke gave a sharp giggle. "Could'nta said it better meself," he said.

Jacob cleared his throat and tugged at his collar, as if that were the only problem he had that kept him from speaking. After giving one or two more test squeaks, he gave up. "What she said," he managed in a high-pitched tone.

Kathleen looked straight at the board, but her hand patted Jacob's arm to reassure him that he had done fine.

"I'll tell you what, Miss O'Day and gentlemen. As I understand it, your next show is next Thursday, is that correct?"

"Our *last* show is on Thursday, yes," Kathleen said softly but firmly.

"What if we decide not to stop? Will that extend your plays?"

She sat rigidly straight. Her eyes followed the path in front of her directly to the pompous man at the end of the table. Her fingers clutched her small purse for courage. When she spoke, it was with a quiet but forceful voice. "Our town has voted that no matter what your decision, our last show is next Thursday."

The room rang with silence. Finally a small sigh echoed as the chairman stood. "I understand. Thank you for your patience in this matter. We will discuss this and see what we come up with. Meanwhile, if you don't mind, some of the board might just watch the last show from the comfort of our passenger cars on Thursday. Will that be all right with your town?"

It was Kathleen's turn to breathe again. "That would be lovely. Especially if you brought enough change to partake of my wonderful carrot cake, sold only on the stop in Blissful, Texas."

Now that the tension was released, the entire board laughed—just a little too heartily, but it was good just the same.

"You can be sure we'll look for you, Miss O'Day."

"Please buy from whomever offers to sell it," Kathleen said. "I'm afraid I will be working on the play, so one of my neighbors is selling my carrot cake for me."

"Very well, Miss O'Day, and . . . " He looked down at his notes but found no record of the men's names. Instead he smiled expansively and said, "Gentlemen."

"I have had some of my famous carrot cake delivered to the hotel from your train, gentlemen. I hope you enjoy it with your luncheon."

Finally. Although not one of the men looked as if he'd missed dessert in the past several years, they perked up and smiled. "Thank you."

No one shook hands. No one escorted them out. They turned invisible. The spinster secretary didn't even look up as they walked out the door and down the hall toward the exit into the main room of the hotel. Sheer nerve carried her legs down that long wooden floor.

They reached the street and walked along the boardwalk in continued silence. Kathleen sighed, too tense to bother stating the obvious—they didn't know any more now than they did when they stepped inside the conference room. She made her way toward the hotel they stayed in while visiting Fort Worth. Neither man spoke, which told her that they were as tense about what happened as she was.

When Kathleen stopped in front of the hotel they were staying at, she turned to both of them. "Gentlemen, if you don't mind, I would like to take a look at some of the dry-goods stores, then eat early, say around six this evening."

"What time does the stage leave in the morning?" Zeke asked. His eyes reached inside the building to check out the customers inside.

"The stage doesn't leave until six in the morning. If we get rest, we'll be more than ready by then. It is up to you to be ready and in front at five-thirty in the morning. The stage won't wait. Until then, we are on our own until dinner, and then again afterward."

Zeke tipped his hat, a wicked grin on his face. "Yes, ma'am. If'n you don't mind, ma'am, I'll skip dinner tonight. I have a few things that need tendin' to, and I won't make it back here on time."

"But you will be at the stagecoach in the morning? Amy and Troy will be waiting for us in Mason and driving us home in their wagon."

"Yes, ma'am. I'll be there at five-thirty in the morning. Promise."

"Jacob," she said, turning toward him. "What about you?"

"I, uh, have a few things to do also, Kathleen. I will see you in the morning." His look was one of anticipation mixed with fear that he wasn't going to be allowed to do whatever it was that he wanted to do.

She didn't want to know either man's plans. She smiled. "Then I'll see you both in the morning!"

It didn't take ten minutes to be directed to her room, check to ensure her luggage was brought in from the train station, and to leave again. It was almost noon and she had all day to shop in the big city!

There was no time to waste . . . .

Eighteen

Charlie felt lower than a snake's belly lying in the cracks of cobblestone. He'd reached a dead end.

By the time he had tracked down the horse that was supposed to lead him to Vic Masters, he found out he'd been part of a wishful-thinking goose chase. He hadn't been chasing Vic. Instead it was someone named Stan, who gambled and drank his way across the southeastern plains of Texas. Stan, it turned out, was holding on to what little money he had had when he hit the barn he'd stolen the horse from. A damned goose chase was all he'd been on.

When he finally found the man, he walked up and called his name. "Stan?"

Stan turned around, his fingers still wrapped around a glass of whiskey he'd just ordered. "Yeah?"

It didn't take but a single punch to knock him out. Charlie hit him square in the jaw. His eyes rolled back in his head and he tilted forward, right over Charlie's shoulder like a good friend. Charlie walked

straight into the jail with him, told the sheriff what
had happened, and dropped him off like a package
at Christmas.

But Stan wasn't Vic, and so he hadn't accomplished
his goal.

Meanwhile, he smelled so bad from riding for a
week without a break that the good people of the
port town of Galveston politely edged around him as
they walked past. He needed a rest, a hot bath, a
good bottle of whiskey, and to head back to the area
of Blissful. Once the rest was accomplished, he'd send
a telegram to Kathleen and let her know his success—
or lack of it.

If he was lucky, he'd find Vic's trail again. If he
wasn't, he either had to pick it up again or make the
decision to hightail it back to his ranch. Whether he
liked it or not, he had no reason to hang around
Kathleen like some mangy dog in heat. She deserved
better—someone from her town who would stay
there. Some gentleman who didn't have a million
problems of his own and would take care of her in
the style to which she should become accustomed.

There. All the pent-up emotions he had ended on
that one point. She was too good for the likes of him
and needed to be set free.

Then, if she decided he was her man, she could
let him know and they'd go from there. One thing
he was certain of: Kathleen O'Day would let him know
exactly where he stood.

With that he walked into the hotel and ordered a
bath.

One hour later, clean-shaven, sweet-smelling, and
dressed in newly pressed black and gray, Charlie
walked into the telegraph office next to the train
station. Grabbing a pencil and a piece of paper, he
carefully wrote out his message and signed it, *your*

loving brother, John Macon. From what she'd said, Kathleen would know it was from him. Her brother would never sign a message that way.

"Can you send this telegram right away?" he asked the young man behind the cage.

"Sure, for two bits extra."

Charlie fished in his pocket and found the money, then slid the paper with it. "I'll wait."

The young man shrugged, engrossed in reading and ciphering out the message before beginning the process of finding the town code and sending it. The *rat-tat-tat-tat-tat* of the clicker was comforting. He knew that the message would reach Kathleen's door in less than an hour. It was to let her know he hadn't found his friend and would be returning to her place in three or four days. Jacob would probably ride it out to the house; after all, he was anxious enough to walk her home from the quilting bee. A shaft of jealousy stabbed him in the chest. He changed his thoughts, knowing full well he had no leg to stand on.

Right about now, Kathleen would probably be busy, filling the air with all the homey scents of baking: warm yeast, melted sugar and butter, the fresh fragrances of cinnamon and vanilla wafting through the air. His mouth watered at the memories.

When the tapping stopped, the young boy carefully wrote in a large log book what the message was and how much was paid to send it. He turned the book around. "Mark here," he said, pointing to a line.

Charlie carefully wrote his name. He wasn't called upon to do it very often, so his handwriting was rusty.

Just as he finished, the tap-tapping of an incoming message began. Charlie turned away. His business was done.

"Sir? Just a moment, sir." The young man's head

was bent as he scribbled the coding coming across. "This is for you."

Charlie halted, hand on the doorknob as he waited for a further explanation. There was none. A woman with a child came to the door and he opened it for her, tipping his hat as she strode past him to the train ticket counter. She reminded him of a small sloop making a wake. And in her wake was a young boy who looked up at him with rounded brown eyes and a large red-and-white swirled sucker stuck in his cherub mouth.

Dressed all in black and wearing a frown, Charlie must have looked more fierce than he thought. He impatiently waited for the young man to tell him he could go. He tried to soften his expression. The child removed the sucker and stuck out his tongue before ducking back into the folds of his mama's skirts.

"Sir," the telegraph boy said, catching his attention. "The message reads: 'Kathleen in Fort Worth for railroad meeting. Stop. Will return on Wednesday in time for last scheduled play Thursday at train time. Stop. Will give message then. Stop. Timely.' "

Charlie's mind was a blank. What the hell was he talking about? She had mentioned the railroad meeting, but the rest was gibberish. What play? There weren't plays during those stops; there were killings and hangings and gunfights . . . .

Colors flashed in front of his eyes. A wash of dread filled him as everything suddenly fell into place.

Helltown was just an illusion. It was a contrived place. That was why there were so many decent folk there. So many quilting bees. Dinners. Camaraderie. Even when the town's reputation was the worst in the West. That was why Kathleen was so surprised when he told her Vic was in town. Hell, that was why she was hanging her clothes up in a slip! No decent outlaw would dare enter that town, unless they were plumb loco. The town was closed tighter than a bar on a Sunday morning.

Plays. Dramas. They weren't real. All those damned awful things that happened to the sheriffs—and ladies of the evening and outlaws—were plays put on by the townsfolk week after week. That was why she was going to the town meetings—and why Zeke and E. Z. were always delivering messages.

And he'd been too stupid and gullible to think of it as a sham. All this had been going on under his nose and he hadn't sniffed out one wrong thing.

No wonder Kathleen tried to drug him to sleep that first week. She couldn't take the chance that he'd follow her to a "town meeting" and see what was *really* going on! And he'd been dumb enough to think that she was safe when she was with the townspeople, so he never bothered to go there. His thinking had stopped at Vic Masters—who certainly wouldn't have shown up at one of those get-togethers!

He wished he could kick himself. He'd been so smug he honestly thought they'd all gone to that meeting to see if they could rid themselves of the outlaw element, and he wasn't interested in their problems. He wanted to know where the outlaws *were*—and didn't care about where they *weren't*.

What a damn fool.

Charlie looked down at the little boy, who still stood with his mother, who was completing a transaction. Charlie gave him one of his sternest looks. The child slipped the sucker out of his mouth long enough to give the most angelic smile he'd ever seen outside of his own daughter's. Charlie couldn't help his response, and grinned back as if they were best of friends.

"Hi, mithter," the little guy said.

"Hi."

The mother looked over her shoulder and smiled. She was a sweet-looking woman whose face showed a little tiredness. "Francis is a good little boy," she said, speaking more to the child than to the man. Her hand gently ruffled the boy's sun-bleached hair.

"I bet he is," Charlie answered, wishing they would conclude their business so he could receive the information he needed and get on with it. But the truth was, in the back of his mind he saw Kathleen and her son standing in a train station. She wouldn't be that tired but twice as protective of her son.

"You're nith," Francis said.

"Thank you. So are you," Charlie answered.

Just then the clerk handed over the tickets to the woman, along with instructions, and she turned, taking her son's hand. "Say good-bye, Francis."

" 'Bye," he said sweetly as he was pulled toward the door, once more in the wake of his mother's skirt. The impish light returned to Francis's dark eyes. Just as he walked past Charlie, he held out his arm holding the sucker and deliberately swiped it against Charlie's pant leg, giving it a good coating of sugary stickiness.

"Aw, hell!" Charlie said in a slow, easy voice.

The young mother turned around and covered her son's ears. "Sir!" she reprimanded.

Charlie looked at her, then down at the boy, whose body quickly moved into a childish, cowed behavior, scooting behind his mother's skirt. But his face was a huge wreath of a smile.

It wouldn't do any good to explain what happened. The mother would believe he had brushed against the child. Besides, the damned stickiness wouldn't go away just because he complained. "Sorry."

With a stiff rustle of skirt she took her son's hand

and exited the station. Charlie was left with a pair of
pants that would have to be changed immediately.

"I need a ticket to Blissful, Texas," he finally managed to get out to the ticket master.

"Blissful, hmmm," the elderly clerk said, looking
in a huge book on a podium on his desk. "That will
be for a week from Monday. You'll have a stopover
in Houston, then another one in Spring, arriving in
Blissful next Thursday afternoon at two o'clock."

"I need to get there by *this* Thursday. Two days
from now."

"We don't have one on Thursday unless you're
leaving from Fort Worth." The man was a pillar of
patience—and twice as thick. "The next one leaving
from here arrives next week Thursday."

Charlie tamped his panic down. He could do what
he needed to do. It was just a matter of finding the
fastest way. "Is there any other way? Can I take a ship
to another port and catch another train?" He was
grabbing at straws. But that was the time of the play,
and whatever instinct was driving him to be there,
he was damn well going to listen. He'd been wrong
before, but not often.

"Well," the clerk said thoughtfully, "you could ride
to Houston and catch the nine o'clock morning train.
That goes directly up the road past Blissful to Buffalo.
Then catch the twelve-thirty from Fort Worth to Blissful. That will get you in on the Thursday two P.M.
train."

"How far is Houston from here?"

The older man scrunched up his face as he
gummed the places in his mouth that had no teeth.
There were a lot. " 'Bout a two-day ride if you stop
at the inn for the night." He must have seen Charlie's
pained look. "But if you ride straight through with

only a couple of rest stops along the way, you should hit the train station around six in the morning.''

Charlie grinned. He knew there was a solution. "Thanks," he said, slapping his thigh. But his hand didn't come away. It stuck to the sucker stain. "Damn," he muttered. It would take the afternoon to clean his pants and dry them for the journey. Either that or he could buy a new pair of pants and get on the road.

Charlie bought the pants at the nearest general store in the Strand Street area, where shops and warehouses lined a half-mile area, ending at the docks where ships came and went.

In two hours he was on his way to Houston. He was a tense ball of frustration at the thought of Vic Masters. He should have been able to find the man and stay on his trail. That made this whole trip a waste of time. Vic Masters could still be around Blissful or gone to South America by now. For all Charlie knew Vic could have killed another ten people and was still wandering around looking for his next victim. Or he might have stopped in some town, fallen in love, and begun a family by now. Who knew . . . ?

Meanwhile, instead of going off on wild-goose chases, Charlie could have been curled up, spoon fashion, with Kathleen in his arms for the last week. To add insult to injury, he was even forced to spend three dollars of his precious money on a useless pair of pants that didn't seem half as sturdy as his sticky ones.

"Damn."

Kathleen stood very still as she allowed one of the seamstresses to measure and pin the hem of her new leaf green light cotton dress. She was having a dress made. Professionally made! And it was all being done on a contraption called a sewing machine. Kathleen had heard of them, but had never seen one in action. Nor had she ever heard one before. They were loud.

Three women sat at three machines, their feet moving the wide, metal pedals back and forth as the needle whirred in and out of the fabric. Another three women sat in wide chairs with even wider arms. Their fingers worked quickly and efficiently on their handiwork. When she had asked about it, the woman who owned the shop called it a production line. She said it was a term they used in the wool industry.

All Kathleen knew was that she would have a new dress by this afternoon to take with her on the train tomorrow morning, and three new dresses would be sent by rail at the end of the week.

It was the first time she had had new dresses in the two years since her aunt died. But the best part was that she had just ordered a new pair of dress shoes and a new pair of boots. And not one thing was out of the catalog! They were made for her—only her!

"Hold still, madam," the seamstress ordered around a mouth full of small straight pins.

"I'm sorry," she stated obediently. "I'm just so excited. I haven't had new clothing in a long time."

"And you will be able to find a new husband quickly with this color against your lovely skin and hair," one of the women smiled and said.

Kathleen blushed. With her fair skin, the red tinge was obvious to everyone. "No, I . . ." She cleared her mind of the picture of Charlie, naked as the first spring morning except for his boots. Her blush deepened. "I don't want a husband. I have more than enough trouble already."

One of the seamstresses gave her a knowing look.

"Me, I don' know, but I think you already know the man you wish to have as an *esposo*."

A husband. Her face flamed. "Goodness, no!"

"Stop teasing her, Meagan," the head seamstress chided around the pins in her mouth. "That is not fair."

Kathleen looked around blankly. "Meagan?" she asked. The woman's raven's wing black hair was streaked with brilliant white and tied into a neat bun at the nape of her neck, much as was the hair of the others working in the room. Her skin was the color of deep, rich mahogany; the nails of her dark hands and the bright flash of white when she grinned were the only light colors on her.

"*Sí,*" the woman said proudly, her head tilted up. "Me *abuelo* came over here as an Irish mercenary against Maximilian and Carlotta. When the war was done, he settled with my grandmama outside Refugio, where he built a ranch. He was a man as proud of his heritage as I am of mine. He named me after his sister, who died on Irish soil."

"I see," Kathleen said, glad the focus was off her and on someone else.

"All done," the seamstress announced as she leaned on the nearby stool to rise. "We will send by train in the next week, señorita. They will all be fitted like this one. You will love them." It was more a pronouncement than a hope.

"I know I will," Kathleen said as she let the material fall off her shoulders and stepped out of the puddle of fabric.

"And maybe you'll let us sew your wedding dress when the time comes."

"You'll have to wait a very long time for that," she said, reaching for her own dress and quickly putting it on over her chemise and single slip. It was hot inside the small shop, with no open windows or doors to let a breeze in for fear of some man barging in accidentally. Perspiration trickled between her breasts.

She couldn't wait for Charlie to see her in her new finery. But she didn't want to think of wedding dresses. It sounded too much like the wishes built on the seamstresses' way of thinking. That wouldn't do. That wouldn't do at all.

She ignored the pain in her heart.

Later that evening Kathleen ate alone. The men had given their apologies, knowing she would be safe alone in the hotel restaurant. She busied herself by watching the guests coming and going through the lobby and dining area.

There were very few other women by themselves. One woman had two children she was trying to manage, but neither child seemed to be worried about her threats of telling their father about their behavior.

Three men sat together at a table, drinking brandy and waiting for their dinner to be delivered. Their voices as well as the smoke from their cigars drifted to Kathleen in waves. One man seated on the side with his profile toward her reminded her of Charlie.

Her dear, sweet Charlie.

If there was a wish that she could make come true, it would be that Charlie loved Blissful as much as she did and decided to stay with her forever. That was more than a wish; that was a dream. And then he'd give her children and help her raise the whole passel of them. It would be heaven on earth . . . .

"Poppycock," she muttered, attacking her cooked tomatoes as if they were the very idea of subservient marriage itself. What a stupid idea.

But deep down inside, she knew what she needed. She really needed no less than his complete love, and that was an impossibility. Charlie loved only his land and his daughter. Nothing else was ever mentioned, let alone promised—except for his dead wife, who, according to Charlie, hung the stars and the moon, resembled Cleopatra, and had the patience of Job. If there was anything else, other than Kathleen's cooking, that he loved, she didn't know about it. Charlie kept them a secret—probably from himself as well.

Thinking of Charlie made her acutely aware of just how lonely and isolated she was. Funny, but she hadn't felt like that since her aunt had died. For the first two months or so after that, Kathleen knew the meaning of loneliness. Her aunt was the only person who had loved her without reservation. She had never felt so cared for and safe and content. And she had to come to terms with the fact that she probably never would again.

For just a little while these past few weeks Charlie had reminded her of that feeling of connected security. If anything, being with Charlie intensified it all and added a few emotions she was just delving into— emotions that dealt with love and commitment and need. And kisses that made her dizzy with the thought of . . . *No.*

She didn't need a thing.

Kathleen reached for her reticule and found the money for her meal. Placing her white cotton napkin on the side of her plate, she stood. It was time to go to her room and read herself to sleep. She'd just gotten a couple of the new dime novels, and couldn't wait to open them.

And reading those novels would be certain to divert her thoughts into a more profitable direction. Kathleen had secretly sent three stories to publishers in

Chicago and New York. After all, she'd written enough plays in the past two years; what was the difference?

So far there had been no answer, but she had her fingers crossed. If the railroad made Blissful a regular stop, she would still sell her cakes in the depot, but not at the rate she currently did. Although the town's coffers would increase, her personal income would likely decrease. She had to be ready for that.

"Miss O'Day?" the clerk behind the desk said in a strong voice.

She turned and looked over at him. His eyes were appreciative. She smiled. "Yes?"

"You have a telegram." He held it out but didn't step around the rich, dark desk in front of him.

Kathleen came down the steps slowly and walked to the front, taking the piece of paper he held out. She frowned, wondering who would send her a telegram.

But when she opened it, her frown disappeared.

Will you be back in time for play? Stop. Please try. Stop. Mabel. End.

Mabel was so obsessed with showing off her writing talent that she had sent an expensive telegram to Kathleen in order to prove how wonderful she was and how much better her stories were compared to Kathleen's.

All the way up to her room, Kathleen worried about Mabel's sanity.

Once in her nightgown, she sat next to the oil lamp and began reading.

But in the back of her mind was the image of

Charlie. She wondered where he was and if he was
all right . . . .

Charlie stared up at the night sky and wished he
were already in Houston. According to the stage master at the crossing a couple of miles back, he was
close enough to make it by dawn. He wished he were
close enough to be there now.

Between the disappointment at losing Vic Masters's
trail and the disappointment of sleeping without
Kathleen, he wasn't doing too well. He wanted her
encased in his arms, where she knew she was cared
for and loved and cherished . . . and where he could
shake the hell out of her for keeping the town secret
from him. Him! He was a deputy sheriff, for Pete's
sake! What the hell did she think he'd do? Take over?
Make her stop?

Well, maybe. But he deserved a chance to show
what he'd do!

The sky turned a burning orange as the sun began
peeping over the horizon. Very slowly, Charlie rode
up the small knoll and stopped. The bayou running
next to him flowed wide and big right here, but
looked as if it narrowed the closer to the mouth he
got. And where it narrowed was a large, close-knit
group of buildings that rose two and three stories
high. One or two were even higher.

Houston.

If he was lucky, he'd be there in an hour. Once he
made it to the station, he'd telegraph the sheriff in
Mason and ask about Vic Masters. Surely the man
couldn't keep undercover for this long without someone spotting him or his doing something that would
get him in trouble. Cattle rustling was his favorite
thing, but he was one hell of a petty thief, and there

were plenty of opportunities in the small towns to take advantage of the citizens' feeling of security.

Even Kathleen never locked her door.

By two o'clock tomorrow, he'd be getting off the train in Blissful and hunting down Kathleen so he could confront her about the town secret and how dangerous it was to have kept it from him.

But not until he made mad, passionate, skirts-flying-in-the-air, boots-slung-across-the-room love to her. And he'd do it every day until it was time to head back to Oklahoma and leave her alone so she'd find some man who was worthy of her love. Hell, at least he'd have a memory to last him the rest of his born days.

"Giddyap," he said. But he had a smile on his face at the thought of how long he could drag out the first step.

Nineteen

Charlie stared at the answering telegraph in his hand. There had to be a mistake. He'd wired the sheriff of Mason and asked him about Vic Masters, never really expecting to find a lead, let alone this answer.

Taking off his hat and rubbing his brow, Charlie looked at the young man who handed the paper to him. "Son, are you sure this is the right message?" he finally asked. "You didn't mess up a beep with a burp, did you?"

The telegraph man behind the counter stood straight and tall, showing all five feet three inches of himself. His gaze however, was deadly. "I am Mr. Haas and I graduated from the New York School of Morse Coding three years ago. I am fully aware of the beep and burp sounds and have translated them correctly."

Charlie had to admire the way the little guy reacted.

He'd do the same thing if someone tried to intimidate him.

"Those beeps and burps are dots and dashes and they say the same thing the sounds made. The sheriff gave you the answer you requested. Anything else I can do for you?"

"Nah," Charlie said, putting on his best Western drawl. "You done your best, boy. That's all I was askin'." Before he got any more lip from the young man, he walked out of the office and stepped down off the boardwalk, finally leaning against a post and reading the message again.

Texas Ranger Tom Trudioux says Vic Masters was spotted outside Blissful. Stop. Promised backup by tomorrow. Stop. VM killed two ranchers outside Mason. Stop.

"I'll be damned," he muttered, the message finally sinking in. Charlie doubted Vic had been in Mason all this time. That town had too many people coming and going and a granary that farmers around the countryside used. It was a more open town than Blissful, and someone would have noticed the mean son of a bitch and questioned the sheriff about him. Hell, when Charlie had gone into the sheriff's office there, he'd had to explain where he was from before the sheriff would even answer a question or two about the surrounding area.

In most small towns, the sheriff and the bartender were the two people who knew everything going on. It wasn't any different in Mason. And if Blissful had a sheriff or a bartender, it wouldn't be any different there, either. But they didn't.

That town was so small and closed that it had a

secret that didn't get out . . . but for how long? Charlie
would have guessed at least two years. That was when
all the rumors of gunfights and killings began. Shortly
after that, Blissful changed the township signs to Helltown.

Charlie stepped outside the train station and
walked to one of the Mexican vendor carts. Within
minutes he had a fluffy tortilla filled with fresh fried
eggs and Mexican pepper salsa. He took two bites
and tasted heaven.

His mind began jumping, churning on what was
ahead. He was getting on a train in less than an hour
and heading toward Blissful . . . and Kathleen. And
Vic. *Don't forget Vic,* he told himself. That damn animal
was the reason he'd traveled all over hell and back.

Suddenly he was scared. He needed to be there,
protecting Kathleen from that bastard. But all he
could do was cool his heels in Houston and wait for
the train to pull out.

Could Vic Masters have been in Blissful all this
time? Could he have seen Kathleen as she swam in
Bliss Creek, naked and glistening in the early evening?
His breath caught in his throat, and anger twisted
into a tight knot in his chest. Vic had known enough
to hide his horse in Kathleen's barn. How much else
had he done?

Just the thought of Vic being near Kathleen was
enough to set his stomach on fire. And that animal
could do worse—much worse.

He'd killed that young Mexican woman along the
Texas-Oklahoma border slowly and with much pleasure. He beat and raped her time and time again as
he held her hands over her head and into the fire
until she screamed so hard and long that her neighbors' dogs heard her and barked relentlessly. When
the neighbors got there, she was dead and he was

gone. Her hands were charred to stumps and still smoking in the fire like barbecued meat.

Charlie tossed the rest of his breakfast away. Suddenly he didn't have an appetite anymore. He felt a thick, heavy blanket of dread cover his soul. Charlie dug in his heels and strode back to the station. He had to get to Kathleen. Pronto.

Kathleen wasn't talking to her committee companions. If Zeke hadn't gotten "lost" yesterday morning, they would have been home by now. And Jacob was too timid to go to the nearest bar and pull their friend out! He decided they could all wait for Zeke.

"No one leaves a friend in need," Jacob had said in a rebuking tone.

"A true friend would not put us in this position," Kathleen had retorted, but it didn't seem to matter to Jacob. If anything, it made him more rigid. Then she realized why. Jacob must have been at the same place the other night! Jacob? With a lady of the evening? Impossible. Gentle, stooped, almost-elderly Jacob?

She stared at him in wonder. It never occurred to her that Jacob might need the comfort and companionship of that kind of woman. But why not? He'd spent yesterday morning and early afternoon renting a horse and riding across the prairie to visit his daughter, who lived on the outskirts of Dallas. He'd returned in time for dinner last night and said he'd enjoyed every moment of it. But when he met her for breakfast in the hotel restaurant, he came through the outside doors, not from the direction of the lobby.

He had staunchly defended Zeke when the small man had finally shown up on the platform yesterday morning, an hour after the train had pulled out.

Despite Zeke's apology and Jacob's defense, Kathleen was angrier than she could say. This was their final play, and they would not be there before the train pulled into the station. All the work was left to others.

The rest of the unexpected day in Fort Worth was not a loss, however. She spent it shopping for goods she couldn't get at Jacob's store, and she enjoyed every minute of it. Finally, even though she was still miffed, she lost some of her anger and relaxed.

But this morning, both Zeke and Jacob were at the railway station an hour earlier than necessary. They were doing penance for their behavior—most of which Kathleen had no idea about.

Now, as they chugged along the track and headed toward the outskirts of Fort Worth, Kathleen realized that her temper, although slow, was potent, and might have gotten the best of her. These were friends she had known a long time, and she needed to be more forgiving of others. After all, she had a few things to hide also.

"Jacob?" she asked, gaining his attention as they made themselves comfortable in the railroad car.

Jacob sat directly across from her. He held his pipe in one hand and tamped tobacco into it with his thumb. He looked up absently. "Yes?"

"Sorry I was so short with you earlier," she said, unsure how to open the conversation.

"I understand," he said, clamping his pipe in his mouth and lighting it.

"What did she do?" Zeke asked his new best friend. Since Kathleen wasn't talking to him, he had no choice but to speak to Jacob instead.

"She didn't do anything," Jacob stated, staring out the window he'd cracked open a bit before sitting.

Zeke looked at her, his defensive gaze proving to her that he knew he was guilty of holding them up for a day and allowing them to come in just in time for the play. Instead they'd wired ahead just as they stepped on the train and let everyone know that they would be on the train instead of being there for the train. Zeke had to pay the price for it.

"Have you seen any of the railroad officials or the board members?" Kathleen asked.

"I checked every open door between here and the next car, but I didn't see no one," Zeke volunteered.

"Well, they're supposed to be somewhere around here. Maybe they have their own car," Kathleen said to no one in particular, reaching for her knitting to keep her busy. She'd also gotten several new skeins of yarn while in the big city.

Zeke stood, shifting from foot to foot, as usual. "Think I'll look around, maybe talk to a conductor or two." He hopped toward the door and closed it behind him with a snap.

"He's sorry, you know," Jacob finally said quietly.

"He cost our friends more work."

"That doesn't mean he isn't sorry."

Kathleen gave a sigh. "I know. It's just so exasperating. This is the last play and I wanted everything to be perfect. Instead we won't even get there until it begins."

"Zeke is a lonely man, Kathleen. I know you don't think about it, but just because he's older doesn't mean he doesn't have a need to be with a companion."

Jacob wasn't talking about Zeke as much as he was about himself. And who was Kathleen to judge him? She was dying to be with Charlie again. She was hoping and praying he was at home when she returned, even though she knew it wasn't good for either one of them to become more involved. More in love . . .

"I know. I'll try to be more understanding," she

said. But how could she compare her relationship with Charlie to what Zeke did?

He had spent the night with God knew who, while Kathleen was in love.

Change your thoughts, Kathleen, or you'll be upset again, she told herself.

She had her new dress on and another two new dresses in her carpetbag, thanks to the seamstresses who had made and sent them over when she informed them she was staying another day. At least some good had come from her stay.

If Charlie managed to be back by the time she returned, then he would see a more cosmopolitan her than he'd seen slopping around in her uncle's old boots and her aunt's old dresses . . . or worse yet, in nothing.

She wanted to sock him right between the eyes with her beauty and sophistication before he walked out of her life. She was going to be the one who got away, and she wanted to make sure he knew it. If he didn't notice she was worth loving dressed in her newest and finest, then he wasn't the man she thought he was.

She already knew he was special. So special that she was crying inside every time she thought of his leaving. Yet, as sure as she knew her own name, she also knew he would soon leave her and return to Oklahoma and his ranch.

And she would remain in Blissful. Her roots were here. Apparently she was meant to be alone, for she had fallen in love with a man who would never be happy anywhere but his own place.

Kathleen blinked twice, making sure the tears that begged to form didn't have a chance. She was old enough to know the way the world worked, and young enough to dream silly dreams. She would continue to do so until it was time for Charlie to leave. Once that time came, she'd be ready to face that reality. But she was going to enjoy every minute of him while she could.

She prayed she had more time than she thought.

The train chugged along and she dropped her knitting in her lap and leaned her head to rest on the side wall of the car. Closing her eyes, she let the sway of the car lull her to sleep and sweeter dreams than the reality she and Charlie faced.

With each stop, and there were many, she awoke and looked around. Zeke hadn't returned yet, so it was just her and Jacob, who was reading several of the papers he'd picked up in the lobby. The *New York Times* and the San Francisco *Examiner* were among several others.

Kathleen knew that when they returned, he would have them memorized by heart and would stand behind the counter of his store, letting tidbit after tidbit drop into the conversation. People would stay in the store just to hear the conversations he would begin with the information.

After several hours, Zeke finally returned, slamming the door. Kathleen grabbed her hat and sat upright. "What? What happened?"

He took off his hat and slapped his leg for emphasis. "Well, missy, you'll never guess who's on board."

Jacob looked up from his newspapers, his gaze alight with interest. "The president?"

"Almost as good as that," Zeke said, loving the complete attention he held. "Maybe even better."

"Who?" Kathleen asked, cutting to the chase.

Zeke looked from Jacob to Kathleen then back again, drawing out the moment for as long as he could. When he saw their impatience, he finally decided to answer. He leaned forward as if imparting a secret. "We have got the entire board of directors of the railroad, right here'n this train," he whispered importantly. "They gots their own car in the front of this here train, and they're bein' served by three waiters dressed in gray and one woman who is surely the most wonderful salve for the eyes."

"You saw them?"

"No . . ." he drawled. "But I talked to the conductor an' he introduced me to th' waiter and *he* tol' me about the rest." He puffed his chest out like a peacock impressing the only peahen in the countryside. "Then, as I was standing there chewing the fat, uh, talking to the man, this here woman walks out looking like a goddess from the clouds," he said, breathless with the telling and plainly in awe of the woman's beauty.

"And what did she say?" Jacob asked. "Anything about Blissful?"

"Naw. She said they were warned about some no-good sidewinder somewhere near Mason and that the train needed to beef up security."

"Near Mason?" Kathleen asked. "Did they say his name?"

"Nope. Didn't ask. Didn't care. Ain't got nothing to do with us."

"Honest, Zeke. I wonder about you," Kathleen stated in frustration. "It has to do with our friends in Mason. Was there anything they thought they could do?"

"Nope," he said, looking completely unrepentant despite the guilt she tried to heap upon his head. "Nary a thing."

"What about the board? Are they here to see Blissful?" Jacob asked.

Kathleen thought she heard that same frustration in his voice that she felt.

"They're on their way to Houston. They gots some meetings with the cattle association there. Something about a new line heading toward the valley, down in South Texas," Zeke said. Then he smiled triumphantly. "But yeah. They're gonna be seeing the play. They tol' the waiters to wait and see what they see and tell them what they think about it."

Kathleen felt a surge of excitement. They were here and they were going to see how prosperous the town had become, how nicely painted the town was, how great the people were.

"Did you hear anyone in the rest of the cars talk about Blissful?" she asked.

"Why, missy, half the train's talkin' 'bout Blissful and how dangerous it is!" Zeke looked prouder, if that were possible. "Why, there's a party of about twenty dandies in the dinin' car, and everybody's gonna be drinking champagne while they see the killin'!"

She ventured a guess that most of the people on the train were riding the rail to see the next tragedy unfold in Blissful. They could feel the danger and excitement of the Old West and yet be safe. And they could go home and tell of the exploits of being a traveler in Texas.

Kathleen felt a sad tug at her heart as she realized this day was probably the end of a time she would remember fondly for the rest of her life. She had learned so much from her friends and neighbors in Blissful. And from her aunt, who taught her not only about money, but about making it and keeping it and how to earn a living. Thanks to all that, she now had money in the bank, and a livelihood no matter how old she was. In fact, with Josetta's continued help, she could make more carrot cake than usual and send them to other restaurants. The Fort Worth restaurant owner had tasted her cake and liked it so much, he ordered as many as she could make to be sent on next week's train north.

As Jacob and Zeke continued talking about the people in the other cars, Kathleen leaned her head back against the side of the car and closed her eyes again. But she wasn't listening to them any more than she was sleeping. She was remembering how lucky she was. Counting her blessings might just be the way to step out of the doldrums the thought of Charlie's leaving brought.

Right now, her life was falling into place so well, she could eventually be an even bigger entrepreneur than she was already.

Her inner smile slowly drooped. But no matter what she did, she would never be as happy as she'd been these past weeks with Charlie. Who would have known that the man who broke into her home, ransacked her barn, and held her hostage would also steal her heart? *Goodness!* Until he had held her in his arms, she didn't even know what love felt like!

Yet here she was, in love with a man who was more in love with his wife's ghost and his own land than he could ever love her and Blissful.

Around noon, Kathleen brought out the picnic basket and they ate thick-sliced beef and fried-egg sandwiches the hotel had provided. It was thrilling to watch the scenery change from golden flat plains to softly rolling hills. It meant they were close to home. Close to Charlie.

Zeke and Jacob talked on and off, but Kathleen listened with only half an ear, nodding occasionally.

When the train conductor strode through the hall outside calling, "Next stop, Blissful! Blissful!" She looked at her travel mates, her heartbeat growing faster with just the word. Home. They were almost home.

"Well," Jacob said as he placed his hands on his bony knees and pushed himself up. "We'll be working the minute we get off the train, I reckon."

"Now, don't you go blamin' me again!" Zeke protested.

But Kathleen wasn't in the mood to listen to his protests. "Zeke, please be quiet and help me with my bags and the basket of food. We *do* have to get off the train quickly and we *do* have to get to work the moment we get off the train. You cannot argue the facts."

"Yes, ma'am," he said, but it was with a surly disposition that he began the task of rounding up the luggage and taking it to the departure aisle of the train.

"And when we get off, Zeke, we'll just put it on the station platform until the show is over. We can pick it up then," Jacob said.

"Good idea," Kathleen stated as she straightened her bonnet. No one would get off the train to steal their things. In fact, all eyes would be on the town, and someone would surely notice anyone who attempted to steal their belongings.

The train slowed down and Kathleen looked at both men. It was in their eyes, too. It was time for a show, and the blood was pumping through their bodies as they focused on what needed to be done as quickly as possible. This was the most important show of their lives. The town depended upon them, and certainly, whether they admitted it to each other or not, they needed to impress the board of directors of the Texas Railroad Commission. This was their only chance.

Kathleen grinned. "Ready?"

Zeke's Adam's apple bobbed. "Yup."

Jacob grinned back. "I'd say so."

The sound of high-pitched screeches as train brakes were applied made her grit her teeth, but it was welcome nonetheless.

After one more quick look around, they made their way out of the compartment and toward the end steps of the car. The scenery flew past, and it took a minute for Kathleen to focus on the outskirts of town.

A water tower, the stable corral, then the stable. Finally the sides of Jacob's general store, the building that bookended one side of Main Street.

When the train came to a quick halt Jacob held her so she wouldn't fall. Wiry Zeke was down the steps and piling the luggage near the steps quickly and not quite efficiently.

The conductor's whistle burst shrilly into the air. The play had begun at the signal.

Once Jacob was down, he helped Kathleen manage the steep stairs; then they both turned and quickly headed toward their assigned places.

From the first corner, Mabel was walking toward the train platform, a small valise in her hand.

E. Z. walked down the street with a bowlegged swagger, pretending he had nothing else to do, when one of the older children ran toward him. "Sheriff! Sheriff! Quick! Bad Bart is robbing the bank!" he screamed loudly enough to let the audience know what was going to be staged.

"Bad Bart?" E. Z. shouted back. "Where is he now?"

Kathleen almost laughed. Apparently a little rewriting had been done in their absence. She continued on her way to the back side of the bank, where she was to direct the children to take large hoops into the street until E. Z. had the shoot-out with the robber.

She spied Jacob, one hand holding his hat as he ran toward the bar. He was just about to begin the loud piano music that would accompany the shoot-out.

Once she reached the side of the bank, Kathleen leaned against the rough wood and tried to catch her breath. Five young boys stared at her, waiting for her to revive. She closed her eyes for a moment, but when she opened them, they were still staring at her, their eyes bright and wide and terribly scared.

"What is the matter?" she teased. "You never saw your mothers out of breath?"

"Yes, ma'am," they said almost in unison.

"Good," she said, taking one and turning him around to face the street. "Now, get going. You first, Joey; then Harold goes after you. Remember, you all meet in the middle of the street and stare at the bar as if you're curious until you hear the gunfire from the bank."

"Miss O'Day?" Clarence said, his voice as timid as the rest of the boys looked.

"What?" she asked, trying not to show her impatience. The music was starting.

"That man is robbing the bank."

"He's supposed to, Clarence."

"No, ma'am," Clarence stated firmly. "He's supposed to pretend to. Instead, he's really robbing the bank."

"I don't think so," Kathleen said. "Troy's just a very good actor."

"It ain't Troy, ma'am."

"It isn't?"

"It sure isn't," the twins said, nodding their heads emphatically.

Kathleen glanced at the watch pinned to her breast. Two minutes before, all five boys had been due to be in the middle of Main Street. "I'll go check, but you make sure you do your parts. Okay, boys?"

They all looked so relieved, she felt it. "Yes, ma'am," they said, all turning to watch her walk to the side door of the bank.

She twisted the knob. It was unlocked. She gave one more quick warning to the boys. "Don't forget. Do your part!" and she slipped inside. Her soft kid shoes barely made a sound on the wooden floor as she quickly walked past the bank president's office and headed toward the lobby.

As she reached the larger open area, her steps hesitated. The lobby had none of the business that was usually related to one of their bank-holdup plays. No voices. No people lining up ready to ooh and aah over the goings-on in the street shortly. No one cuing the players at the door.

She felt slightly confused, but some instinct told her not to speak up. Her eyes darted around the room. Evelyn, the head of the sewing circle, and Amy stood in the corner, both softly crying. Silas stood with them, his mouth moving either from fear or prayer, she wasn't sure which. They stared straight ahead, and Kathleen followed their gaze.

Two men were behind the cage, both stuffing saddlebags with packs of money banded by strips of paper from the large, walk-in safe.

A man stood in front of the cage, tall and ugly in a handsome kind of way. His profile was as jagged as the scar running from the back of his head to the side of his neck. He casually held a gun stuck inside a little girl's mouth.

Evelyn's daughter, little Trudi, was pushed against the wood paneling below the cage. He didn't bother hanging on to her. He knew she wouldn't move. Her eyes were squished shut. Tears ran down her cheeks, making silent tracks to plop in rhythm on her pale pink bodice, turning it a darker hue. Her little hands were clenched at her sides.

Kathleen's breath stopped. Her throat closed.

As if sensing another presence, the man turned, looking straight at her. His gaze was as cold as gray skies before the winter snows. His thin lips curled into the semblance of a smile. "Well, well, well. The carrot cake lady," he said in a growl. "I was hoping you'd get here quick. Come join the party."

Twenty

At exactly ten-thirty in the morning, Charlie stepped off the baggage train in Mason with his horse. Once on firm land, he rode to the sheriff's office.

The sheriff of Mason sat in a straight-backed chair on the boardwalk, the chair tilted against the side of his office. He stared at Charlie as he rode up.

"Howdy," Charlie said, stepping off his horse. "I'm Charlie Macon, and you sent me a telegram in Galveston about Vic Masters."

The sheriff nodded. "Yup. That's what I did, all right."

"You said that the Texas Rangers were waiting for reinforcements. Have they arrived?"

"Not yet."

"When?"

"Whenever they get here."

Charlie muttered an expletive.

The sheriff finally looked interested. "You know somethin' I don't know?"

"I think Vic Masters has been living in Blissful or somewhere right around there. In fact, I'm sure. And I think he knows this afternoon is the last play the town is putting on. I think he's gonna act."

"Act how?"

"I don't know," Charlie stated, aggravated. "I'm sure he was in town because I located his horse, and it's a nice piece of horseflesh. He's not leaving it behind—if he hasn't taken it already."

"Where is it?"

"In Kathleen O'Day's barn."

It was the sheriff's turn to curse. "I been here all along, so why didn't you say something about this earlier?"

"I didn't put two and two together until I thought I was trackin' him to Galveston. Then everything kinda fell in place."

"And I'm supposed to believe you?"

"Yes."

The sheriff stared at Charlie a long time. Charlie let him. One man needed to size another up before deciding if he was going to trust him.

"How do you know Kathleen O'Day?"

Hadn't he given the sheriff enough time to size up himself and the situation? Couldn't the damn man make up his mind? "I'm her brother," he gritted.

"You don't look like her," he said, staring at Charlie's dark hair.

"We had a different father. What the hell does this have to do with Vic Masters?"

"Don't have no idea," the sheriff said. "But then, I don't know if you're in cahoots with the bastard and just decided to turn him in so you could do what you wanted to—whatever that is."

Charlie felt as if he'd hit a blank wall. "To hell with you. I'll do it alone," he stated, turning away.

"Do what?"

"Save the town and win the girl," Charlie answered as he walked back to his horse. "You can sit here and look like an idiot in front of both towns, for all I give a damn." Charlie climbed on his horse's back. "I've got to get to Blissful before the train."

The sheriff stood. "You'll never make it."

"Watch me," Charlie stated grimly. "And while you're at it, telegraph the Texas Rangers and let them know what's going on and where Vic Masters is."

"But you don't know for sure."

"Yes, I do. You'll have to trust me on that."

"In that case, soon as I finish, I'll be right behind you."

"Good idea," Charlie called, never looking back as he angled out of town. He had a little more than an hour to go twenty miles on a tired horse. He didn't look like the Pony Express, but he was going to pretend he was one of its riders.

Kathleen gathered her strength about her, but her knees and teeth were quaking so much she hardly heard his voice above the noise in her head.

"What?"

His laughter wasn't deep, like his voice. It was a high titter that raked her nerves. The laughter ended abruptly, as did his smile. "Git over here."

Her legs moved like trembling twigs as she walked. But slowly the shock of seeing a real, live robbery that could hurt a child was replaced by pure, undiluted anger.

She reached his side and stared up, her gaze unblinking. "Mr. Masters, I presume?"

His gray-eyed gaze narrowed. "How'd you know?"

"You're infamous," she stated disgustedly.

"Infamous," he said, repeating the word as if he were tasting it on the tip of his tongue. "I like it."

"It wasn't meant as a compliment." She watched in fascination as his hand rubbed against his chin, as if watching a snake slither across the floor toward a rabbit.

"I like that better." He shot her a quick grin that never met his eyes. "Help the men with the bags." He waited a second or two. "Now!"

As if she had no will of her own, she began to move in the direction of the back counter. Both men, Troy and David, carefully adjusted one bag on each shoulder.

"Are you all right?" Troy asked softly.

She nodded. *Be ready,* she mouthed.

"Kathleen—" Troy began.

Vic interrupted. "Get over here! All of you."

The men followed Kathleen around the back side of the cage area.

"That's right, men. Know that you hate me. 'Cause it won't hurt me at all to kill you right on the spot. Or better yet, kill this little one."

Both men stood, hands in fists as they waited for the next move. "Get in the safe. All of you."

"It's on a time lock," David said.

"I don't give a damn. Get in there!" He motioned to the women. "You, too."

"We'll die!" Amy stated angrily.

"Do you really think I give a damn?" He laughed. "Maybe your friends and neighbors can get you out in time. Isn't that what they're for? To help out in time of need? That's what I was told, even while you were snubbing one of your own."

"Who?" Kathleen asked, and his attention was drawn back to her.

"None of your damn business, sweetie. Now shut

up and help them in, then shut the door. I've still got my hand on the trigger and I intend to keep it there until she's dead or I am. It's up to you."

Icy cold fear flowed down her spine and froze her muscles. She moved jerkily to do as he said, praying she wouldn't fall flat on her face or faint dead away before she could get Trudi out of danger. She didn't know how she was going to do it, but she'd do it.

She did as she was asked, quietly closing the door and hoping he wouldn't notice she hadn't locked the big handle. She prayed that someone on the outside would realize that there was something wrong and come in to investigate. That might distract Vic, and if Vic could be distracted long enough, together they might overpower the man.

"Lock it."

With a heavy heart, she shifted the lever that locked it.

Her gaze darted around the room again, landing quickly on the person in the room beside Vic. For the first time the little girl's eyes were open, wide and scared half to death. Kathleen gave her a reassuring smile.

"Don't give her hope, Kathleen," Vic warned softly. "There is none right now. Not until I'm on that train and out of here."

"You wouldn't kill an innocent child," she admonished.

He reached out and stroked her hair. "Poor dear," he said, almost in a whisper now—a very deadly whisper. The room was so silent, his voice seemed to echo off the walls. "Yes, I would."

Her mouth formed the word even though it was never said aloud. *No.*

He nodded, a small smile tilting his thin upper lip. "Oh, yes."

A sniffle came from Trudi, and Kathleen looked down at the child. Her eyes were now scrunched shut and her little baby mouth wobbled.

Kathleen reached out to stroke the small girl's shoulder in comfort.

"Don't touch," Vic warned, but she didn't listen. Instead she gave a light squeeze, then released the child's shoulder. "Don't do a damn thing," he stated.

"Don't worry, Trudi. This will all be over in a few minutes," she said, defying Vic's order.

He gave her a hard look but ignored her disobedience. He took one of the saddlebags from her shoulder and arranged it on his own. She hadn't realized just how heavy they were until he took one off and she felt light enough to fly. He then relieved her of the other and did the same, using them as a shield over his chest. "Now, my Irish Kathleen, it's time we got on the train."

"We?"

"As in you and me. And Princess, here." He motioned to Trudi.

"Let her go and just take me," she bargained. Her heart raced with the thought of going outside with him, but she knew she had to do it alone.

"Not a chance." He motioned to the front door. "Let's go. And remember, this is part of the show. Play along and you'll do fine. Don't and I kill whoever I can, this sweet little girl first, then you, and then anyone I can." He stared down at her with a cold gleam in his eye that told her he'd rather fight than walk away. There was a deathlike quality to his soul. She could sense it, feel it.

They walked to the door and Kathleen stood in front of it, awaiting instructions.

"Open it and step outside. Go slow so little cutie

here can walk without stumbling and me accidentally shooting her.''

Kathleen opened the door and did as he said, taking two steps out to the boardwalk.

It felt as if she'd lived a year in the space of time she'd been inside, but it had been only seven minutes, according to the watch on her breast. Three more minutes and the train would leave the station. Could she stall long enough?

E. Z., playing sheriff, was lined up with his "deputy," another townswoman dressed as a man. Their grins of relief quickly turned to confusion as Kathleen stood alone, no Amy in sight. Amy was supposed to come out as the hostage, crying and screaming at Troy, who was supposed to be holding her as well as holding up the bank.

Nothing was as it was supposed to be.

"What the . . . ?" E. Z. said. Then he acted as if he were whispering, which he wasn't. "Whatcha doin', Kathleen? You're supposed to be by the side, helping the boys!"

"Sheriff, this man is holding up the bank!" she shouted.

"Shut up," Vic said, directly behind her. "He'll catch on when he takes a good look at cutie."

Trudi, her mouth still around the barrel of the gun, made a noise. She whimpered in a high, keening voice; whoever heard it knew what stark fear sounded like. It went straight to the heart.

Kathleen turned toward Vic. "Please," she began pleading, her own defenses crumbling under the strain.

"Come here," Vic ordered.

She walked the two steps back to him. When he withdrew his other gun, she forced herself to stand silently, waiting to see what he would do next. Somewhere, deep inside, she was calm. Every part of her being was tuned to Vic Masters. She knew what she would do; she just didn't know how she would do it . . . yet.

She would get Trudi out of this and then she would kill Vic Masters.

It was as simple as that.

There was no great revelation, no wonder or shock. She'd already gone through all those reactions the moment she realized what was going on in the bank.

Instead she would wait for her chance to kill him. Hopefully he wouldn't kill her first.

"Help guide the cutie here, so she doesn't stumble and I accidental-like pull the trigger."

"Nothing you do would be an accident." But just in case, Kathleen stepped beside Trudi, holding her shoulders in a comforting grip.

"Step behind me, sweet Kathleen. You're supposed to be covering my back. 'Cause if I get hit from the back or the front, either way my finger jerks and this baby goes."

E. Z.'s eyes widened in shock. Then fear—pure and honest—clouded his face. He'd always wanted to be the sheriff; had begged, pleaded, cursed, and bargained for the position. Now that he had finally gotten the role he wanted—and they had given him the badge and a gun filled with blanks—E. Z. was in the position to be the real sheriff and could do nothing.

His gaze darted to Kathleen and back to Trudi, then began the foray all over again. It was clear this was not where he wanted to be.

Jacob stepped out on the boardwalk in front of the saloon, hands on his hips, and stared in shock. How could this have happened in less than seven minutes from the time he took his place in the play? He looked at E. Z. as if there were something the small man could do.

Zeke brought the buckboard up, then stared in wonder. "What the . . . !" he said before he was struck dumb. For the first time since Kathleen had known him, Zeke didn't move a muscle. He just stared.

Mabel, dressed in her finest purple silk dress with a matching bonnet, stepped from the train station, a small carpetbag in her hand. Her cheeks were as crimson as beets, her brows a black slash against the whiteness of her skin. She stood motionless, watching the proceedings.

Kathleen figured it would take another hundred yards to get to the platform and to the train before it left . . . if it left. Even the conductors were watching in fascination. It was obvious the man was trying to make it to the station and use the train as his getaway. This wasn't what they had been led to expect.

"Remember, everybody's watching. Remember your parts—all of you!" Vic stated matter-of-factly as he took one step down at a time until he reached the dirt street. Both hands held guns; both sides were covered by females. He gave a sharp grin. "Come on, little one, be guided by your friend, there." Although the words sounded caring, the voice held no warmth, no inflection of human kindness.

Kathleen looked around the side of his broad shoulder at Trudi, walking in a sideways crab walk. Now her eyes were open, looking up so high at the man beside her that Kathleen saw only the whites. She touched the girl's shoulder. "You're doing fine," she said in a soothing voice, and caught Trudi's eye.

Jacob realized Kathleen couldn't do anything without having Vic distracted, and he began the words to the play. "Hold it, you dirty, rotten scoundrel! I'm the new sheriff here and I say you're under arrest!"

Vic continued to move slowly toward the train station. "I don't care what you say, old man. I'm leaving this here town with or without your blessings!" Those were the right lines, but they were coming from the wrong man. Troy should have been saying them, not this man.

Kathleen bent her head. "You're doing fine, Trudi. You'll be there before you know it." She looked at her carefully, making sure she had her attention for the next statement, hoping the little one would catch on. "I know this is hard on you, sweetie. But you're doing fine, Trudi. Just a bit longer, honey," she said softly, hoping Vic was distracted enough.

"Keep going," Vic said softly. It was an order. Trudi looked from Kathleen to the big man who held the gun, then back at Kathleen, finally understanding what she was supposed to do.

"We'll do whatever you say, Vic. Just don't hurt us. Please," Kathleen said, hoping he believed she was scared to death. She was, but she was also so angry she could barely keep her fury in check.

Jacob edged around the side of the bank. Behind him was Thomas, who bent and ran with his friend. Once behind them, Jacob slowly pulled out a small gun from his crisp white apron and edged down the boardwalk. Thomas pulled one from the back of his pants. Thomas, the bigger of the two, couldn't seem to crouch low enough.

Kathleen reached her hand back, forming it into a cup and hoping Jacob could get his gun to her. She wanted the pleasure of putting a bullet exactly where he had threatened Trudi all this time.

It was as if Vic had guessed her thoughts. "Don't let him get behind me, or Trudi's dead and I grab you for cover." It was a simple statement that halted everything.

Frightened of Vic's harming the child, Jacob kept his distance, following about ten yards behind the captives. Thomas took several steps to the right, letting his guard down as he tried to position himself behind a barrel.

Without a blink of an eye, Vic aimed his gun and casually shot Thomas, hitting him squarely between the eyes. He was dead before he met the ground.

Everyone stared, stopping in their tracks as if they were trying to absorb the death of one of theirs.

No one—not the conductors, the townspeople, or the passengers—was going anywhere or doing anything. If something was to be done, it was going to have to be done by Kathleen and Trudi.

Kathleen let her hand trail to Trudi's hair and gave a light jerk. Vic didn't seem to realize it as he took another step toward the platform. She gave another tug, and Trudi's head pulled back off the barrel a little. Her eyes grew ever wider and more fearful. Trudi wasn't doing what she was told, afraid of what the bad man would do. Thomas still lay dead in the street.

But something had to be done if Trudi was to be safe. Kathleen gave a shaky smile of encouragement. "It's okay, sweetie-pie. You're doing fine."

They were only thirty feet away from the steps to the platform of the train station. She pulled slightly harder on Trudi's hair, and this time the child responded. Rolling her eyes into her head, she dropped to the ground like a sack of potatoes. At the same time, Kathleen pushed into Vic and he stumbled over the little girl's legs and toward the stairs. The gun that had been in Trudi's mouth shot harmlessly into the air once.

Trudi screamed, but was unharmed.

Vic's reflexes were even faster than Kathleen's. He

swiveled as his body hit the first step up to the platform and grabbed her around the waist, still holding tight to both guns. Her heart stopped. A gun barrel was pressed against it. Her breath stopped. The other barrel was pressed against her throat.

Trudi stayed down, her lashes fluttering just enough for Kathleen to know she was pretending. Kathleen prayed she wouldn't move. Not yet. Vic could still kill her and the child in one smooth motion.

He pulled her bottom tight against him and leaned into her. ''Don't move a hair, or I'll shoot you so full of holes you'll be a sieve in your own neat little kitchen. That'll be a shame. I always wanted to take you to bed, Kathleen O'Day, and see if you were as hot as your hair.''

''Don't move, Masters, or it will be my extreme pleasure to blow you away.''

Kathleen recognized the voice before she saw the man. Charlie. Charlie was here. Her heart filled with relief first, then overwhelming love and hope.

Then fear and dread set in. Nothing could happen to Charlie. She loved him and couldn't think of being without him. She would have given her soul for him to have been a hundred miles away right now—and safe from Vic Masters, the man who probably knew he was trailing him for a bounty—and to kill for revenge, the worst kind of killing.

''There you are. I was wonderin' when you'd appear,'' Vic said in a conversational tone. ''An' you're probably here to rescue the pretty woman.'' He gave a grunt as he held her tightly, feeling the softness of her breast with his knuckles. ''I can't wait to try her myself.'' He gave a shrug. ''But if you want to follow that big guy back there and taste the dirt of Blissful, then be my guest.''

"You'll kill me first," she said angrily, afraid to move but not afraid enough to tell him what she thought of him.

She felt another shrug before he spoke. "Whatever you say, my darling. It's up to you. But if you're givin' it to him, you can give it to me, too."

A gasp came from Zeke and the small crowd formed around him.

She didn't care that the town was shocked that she'd been sleeping with her brother. Given time, she could explain that. And if they didn't believe her, she didn't care. It wasn't important.

Charlie's life was.

A chill permeated her body. Vic had been watching Charlie and her all this while. He could have killed them at any time.

And then she'd never have the marriage she craved to have with Charlie. She had so much to live for! She never had the children she wanted to birth and mother through their childhood and beyond. She'd never know the joy of loving in her middle years and beyond. There was so much she'd never know. So very much . . .

"Get up the stairs."

She looked up the three steps. Mabel, dressed in her best and clutching her small overnighter as if it were gold, stood just off to one side of the station building. Her eyes were as round as hard-boiled eggs, her usual persimmon mouth was in the shape of a fingernail, frowning even while her chin trembled.

"You promised, Victor." Mabel's voice cracked under some kind of strain. "You promised I would go with you. My bag is packed."

"Shut up," Vic stated, not even deeming her worthy of a glance. Instead he dragged Kathleen up the three steps to the top of the platform.

"Where the hell do you think you're going?" Charlie said in a growl, his voice echoing across the distance. For the first time Kathleen actually saw him. He was on his horse, his guns drawn and aimed at Vic—and at Kathleen, who barely stood in front of Mabel. "This is it, Masters. There's no place to run."

"The hell you say."

Every window of the passenger car was pulled up or down so that passengers pressed against the glass could see—and hear—the play, or what was supposed to be a play and wasn't.

"I'm taking your woman and leaving town." Vic's high-pitched laughter filled the air. It was a horrible sound. "It's the only way I can teach you a lesson. I need to pay you back, Macon. And I can't think of a better way."

"You really believe you're gettin' on this train?"

"Yup. Right up front, where the engineer is. He's taking us out of town. You can follow if you want, but my bet is you won't be keeping up."

"The train won't take you anywhere."

"Yes, it will, unless the engineer wants to be responsible for this lady's death."

"You promised," Mabel said again, but this time it sounded like a whimper.

"Shut up."

"But . . ." she said. Her frustration quickly turned to hate as she looked at Kathleen. "You knew about this, didn't you? This is why you didn't like our play."

Kathleen couldn't answer. Wouldn't answer. Every thought she had was aimed at not getting on the train, at the same time trying to figure out how to keep Charlie safe. Her brain was fuzzy with light-headedness.

Nothing came to mind.

"I hate you," Mabel said to Kathleen, all the venom

and frustration she'd ever felt welling into those three words.

"Is this a confession?" Kathleen asked, still trying to slow down the process of Vic's leading her to the train engine at the other end of the platform.

Out of the corner of her eye, she saw Trudi crawl away toward Jacob, who scooped her up, bent down, and ran toward the open doors of the bar. Her little legs scrabbled like a crab making its way to the ocean. She gave a sigh of relief. At the same time Kathleen slowed down to keep Vic occupied with her rather than with what was going on.

"I hate you so much," Mabel said, and this time Kathleen was able to see the woman's actions. She reached into her small reticule and pulled out a snub-nosed pistol just large enough for her hand. "You took him!"

"Drop it, Mabel," Charlie ordered, his horse coming closer.

"No!"

"Damn it, Mabel!" Vic yelled, finally realizing what the woman had in her hand. "I told you I'd come back for you."

"No, you won't. You'll come back for *her*, but you won't come back for me. Never." She aimed her gun at Kathleen. "Ever."

Without thinking, Kathleen did exactly what she'd coaxed Trudi to do: she went limp—so limp Vic couldn't hold her up in front of him while keeping his gun trained on Charlie or anyone else. His grip slackened. His gun barrel dropped toward the ground for just a few seconds before he let Kathleen go completely so he could aim his guns at the real danger—Charlie and E. Z.

"Damn," Vic muttered calmly, as if bothered by nothing more hazardous than a mosquito.

But not before he assessed the situation. His one true enemy was at his side. Mabel, tears streaming down her cheeks as she openly cried, shifted her aim to a point just ten feet away, true and sure at Vic's heart. She quickly squeezed the trigger, closing her eyes as she did so—and shot him straight through the heart. His eyes were glazed even before he fell in a dead heap toward the rough, wooden platform— right on top of Kathleen.

Kathleen tried to catch her breath, tried to keep her eyes open, but it wasn't possible. Instead her head hit the wooden deck and she spiraled into a dark abyss.

Twenty-One

Kathleen's head was muzzy. The side of her head hurt, as well as a bruise on her hip. She blinked her eyes, wanting to have everything come into focus. It didn't. She knew she was on her bed at home and the door was open. The voices must have come from the doorway, for they were loud and she didn't have any trouble figuring them out. Instead of calling attention to herself, she kept her eyes closed, listened, and waited.

"As far as I'm concerned, you can go to hell for what you've done here!" Jacob shouted.

"I haven't done a damn thing but help her! I just tried to save her life, for God's sake! So did Thomas! For all that stuffed shirt's ways, he took a bullet protecting Trudi. And that's a sight more than you two did!" Charlie sounded as angry and defensive as Jacob was irate. "You both just stood there and did nothing!"

"Agh, Mabel and Thomas saved Kathleen's life,

man. Not you! You just made a fallen woman out of
her in front of the whole town! Her reputation is
ruined and her friends will never be able to look her
in the eye.''

"Mabel killed her lover; she didn't save Kathleen!
We're lucky that son of a bitch was a hardened criminal or she'd be in jail waitin' for the swing of a rope!
And Thomas didn't have the sense to keep something
between him and a vicious killer. He acted as if he
were invincible. Kathleen was the only one hurt!''

"Well, you're still the one who damaged her reputation beyond repair!''

"Are you her friend?'' Charlie questioned belliger-
ently.

"Yes, I am. That gal is like a daughter to me!''

"Then you'll look her in the eye and not blame
her, won't you?''

"Of course, but—''

"No buts!'' Charlie interrupted. "If you can do it,
so can the rest of this damn town!''

"We can only hope,'' Jacob said sadly.

"Kathleen has kept this town alive for over two
years! You and this place owe her a debt of gratitude
that no one can replace. She put food on the table
and money in the bank for each and every one of
you. And if you desert her now because you think
she did something wrong, you're either very stupid
or sadly mistaken!''

"Yes, but—''

"And when she marries me, we'll have to move
away because we can't afford to raise our children in
a place that is so biased against the sweetest, kindest
woman God ever made.''

Was Charlie stating that? Charlie, who never said
those things? Even if it wasn't possible, it was nice to

hear. Wonderful to hear! And he was saying it to another man? Kathleen kept her eyes closed.

"What makes you think she'll marry you? Because you've shamed her into it?"

"Of course not! You can't shame that woman into anything—least of all marriage! You and I both know that! I love her. It's as simple as that."

There was a long silence. *"Gottleib,"* Jacob finally said.

"Yeah, *gottleib.*"

"She won't marry you."

"She will once she knows that I'm right for her. '

"And how will she know that?"

"I'll just have to convince her."

"You won't."

"I'm not leaving until I do."

Kathleen's heart lightened considerably. She was just handed the way to make Charlie stay—just say no.

Zeke came stomping in. Kathleen could tell by his steps. "They got that Vic feller on a door and they're takin' him to Boot Hill now. Second one we've put in there in two years."

"Let's hope it's the last one for a while. A long while." Jacob's voice sounded as if he were plopping into a chair.

"Too late. Sarah Hornsby's husband, that Thomas? He died, too. Said something to the doc, then closed his eyes and drifted away, kinda quiet-like."

"Damn," Charlie said.

Kathleen felt her heart go out to the shy woman. She was so scared, and Thomas had always protected her from her own shadow. The last time she'd seen him alive, he was standing next to the general store, and Trudi had curled around his leg for protection.

"Is that where the rest of the town is? Helping to bury Thomas?"

"No, they're lookin' at Vic's death and burial."

"That son of a bitch?" Charlie's voice was belligerent. "They ought to be here—all of them! They ought to be in the front yard, praying to God that Kathleen is going to be fine, instead of following a dead man not worth the salt it would take to kill a snail!"

"He's in love with Kathleen and wants to marry her and make her honest," Jacob said with a sigh, obviously telling Zeke.

"Oh," Zeke said. "That might work."

"Not might, Zeke. It will work!" Charlie stated forcefully.

"That's what you think!"

"And why not?"

"Because Kathleen says she won't marry, that's why!"

"Why not?"

"Because she won't be beholden to any man, that's why!" Zeke shouted equally as loud.

Kathleen had obviously done a good job at explaining her views on marriage and husbands. At least two men believed her.

"She loves me."

"Did she say so?" Jacob asked, his tone a little incredulous.

"No, but she will."

"You're dreamin', cowboy. You might as well get used to the idea that Kathleen O'Day is gonna stay that way. She ain't gonna marry you. If she married anyone, she'd have married that guy who visited Evelyn last year. He courted her good and proper, too. No lying about bein' her brother an' all. He just straight-out asked her to marry him."

Charlie choked. Someone patted him on the back.

When he finally spoke, it was with conviction that had a slight dent in it. "She didn't love him."

"Maybe not."

"But we're not lettin' her love you, either. She's ours. You're not takin' her away from us, soiled dove or not."

"She's *not* a soiled dove!" Charlie exclaimed angrily. "She's the mother of my child, and that's all I'm gonna say about that!"

"She's in a family way?" Jacob said, his voice raised incredulously.

"Holy Mother o' mine," Zeke whispered.

Kathleen knew it would be all over town in an hour. She wanted to slap Charlie silly for saying such a thing. He needed to be told off good and proper, and then kicked out the door and ordered to go on his way. But to do that, she'd have to wake up. She'd wait another minute or two . . . .

"I don't know," Charlie said slowly. "I haven't got any idea."

"So you're *turning* her into a soiled dove!" Zeke's tone was triumphant. "You should be shot! Taking advantage of our sweet girlie like that and then trying to skip town!"

"I'm not skipping anywhere! I'm taking her to my ranch in Oklahoma."

"The hell you are!" Jacob stated.

"The hell I'm not!" Charlie stated, equally as stubborn.

Kathleen wasn't going anywhere. What made him think she would? Had she ever said anything? Done anything? Promised anything? Not once. It was all in his mind. As soon as she was ready, she'd tell him so.

"You'll work her to death out on some desolate ranch!"

"What the hell do you think you all are doing here?

She gardens, bakes, fishes, creates and runs plays, defends you against the big bad railroad, and then acts as friend and confidant and counselor to half the county! She's kept this whole damn town employed and put money in the coffers, I'd bet. You just want to keep her to yourselves because she works so hard.''

It was nice to be appreciated. In fact, she felt downright treasured. Kathleen gave a soft moan.

"Darlin'?" Charlie said, by her side in a flash. "Are you all right, darling Kathleen?" He brushed back her hair and touched her cheek gently, his finger stroking her as if she were rare porcelain.

She fluttered her lashes, finally looking up into his eyes and seeing the love he'd spoken of earlier. There was no more fuzziness. His concern and caring shone like a magnetic beacon. She smiled slowly, turning her cheek into his hand.

"You love me."

She'd had all kinds of things she was going to say and do, but the truth was, she didn't want to. "Yes."

His smile lit up the room. "Then tell these yokels that you're marrying me and we're going north."

"No." She looked straight into his eyes.

"What?" He looked stunned. "But you love me!"

"Yes, but I'm not leaving Blissful."

"But why?"

"This is my home. I didn't fight for it only to move away. The town will just have to be big enough for both of us." Her voice was soft but firm.

"I can't move here. I have a ranch!" Charlie stated. "Besides, you're a woman; you're supposed to move."

"Bullfrogs," Kathleen stated, sitting up with definite deference to her hip. Jacob and Zeke stood in the doorway, neither one positive who was going to win this argument but both unwilling to leave in case they missed a thing. "My business is here, and here is where I'm staying."

Charlie stood up, his anger just as apparent as on the first day they had met. "Damn it, Kathleen! You're a woman, and everybody knows a woman is supposed to follow her man. I'm leaving for Oklahoma in a week and you're going with me!"

"I am in business here and I plan on staying here. The railroad is giving us a stop and I'm going to ship my cake into restaurants in Fort Worth and Houston. Why, I may even go into other kinds of cakes! Who knows? You can have your other partner take care of our ranch, then send for your daughter and have her come here to live with us. Then you can buy Mabel's ranch and set up a second business here."

"Sounds good," Jacob said thoughtfully.

"This is a much better place to raise a young girl than a ranch out in the middle of nowhere," Zeke added as he left the doorway.

"Zeke is right. We have a good school, nice neighbors, and lots of children," she said. Her gaze went to the doorway. "Zeke! Don't you dare use"—they heard the ping of brass and her shoulders sank— "that spittoon," she ended lamely, knowing there was no use fighting the problem. "He and E. Z. will never learn."

"Whose is it?" Charlie asked, his eyes narrowing. He remembered the first time he had heard her yelling about that spittoon. It sat in the corner of the kitchen, and he'd never asked her about it before.

"My Aunt Hattie's," Kathleen said. "I keep it as a memento, but I refuse to clean it out."

"Then he will," Charlie said in a very loud voice "*Now,* if he knows what's good for him!" His voice was raised enough to echo through the house to where Zeke was. It must have held enough authority in it to scare Zeke, for the pump began pumping and water sloshing, and the ping of brass on tin echoed through the rooms.

Charlie turned back and took both Kathleen's hands and pulled her to a standing position. "Are you feeling all right?" he asked gently.

"Yes, thank you."

"And you'll marry me if I move here?"

"Yes," she answered. "In a heartbeat."

"And you'll love me and be mother to our children?" he asked, folding her into his arms and holding her softness close to his own body.

Her hand came up and stroked his jaw lovingly. "Yes."

"Ask iffen he'll be sheriff," Zeke said.

"Yes," he answered, never taking his eyes off Kathleen. "But the pay had better be good."

"It will," Jacob said. "No one wants to do it for real. Just for play."

"No more plays," Charlie said in a growl just before his mouth covered and took control of hers, showing her just how much he loved her. Her head swam as she lost herself in his arms. This—for the rest of her life. What a wondrous thought.

Charlie pulled away. "Say good-bye, Jacob."

Jacob's soft laughter filled the room. "Good-bye."

"And Zeke? Milk Hilde for us, would you?"

"This time, all right, but next time, well, I'm not sure," Zeke said.

"Just do it on your way out," Charlie stated, breaking into the old man's objections.

Before Zeke or Jacob could say any more, Charlie kicked the bedroom door shut.

"Now, future Mrs. Macon," he said softly as their friends left the house, "I believe it's time to show you just how much I love you."

"Why, Mr. Macon, I believe it is," she said, smiling softly. "But this time it's your turn to get naked first."

"Are you always going to ask tit for tat?" he groused as he watched her fingers move nimbly on his shirt buttons.

"Always."

"You're too strong-willed for your own good."

The shirt hung loose and she slipped her hands under the shirt and over his shoulders, pushing it off. "Maybe, but then, so are you."

"Yes, dear," he said, but the smug smile of delight on his face was her answer. She could get away with anything as long as she did it in his arms.

It seemed like a fair deal for the rest of their lives . . . .

Epilogue

Charlie watched the Herefords milling around the pen and ambling through the open gate to the pasture beyond. A little over six hundred acres of good grazing spread beyond the pasture. It was more than enough fodder for the six-hundred-plus head of cattle.

Sarah Hornsby, Thomas's widow, sat next to him on the wagon seat. She was saying good-bye to all that was familiar to her and beginning again somewhere else. It was Charlie's job, Kathleen informed him this morning, to insure she had a safe sendoff.

Kathleen would normally have accompanied him, but she hadn't been feeling well this morning. The baby was due in a week, and to Charlie it looked as if it were doing cartwheels inside of his beloved. He felt pain just watching her stomach move.

"It looks like a painting, doesn't it?" the widow Sarah said quietly, her gaze searching the land as if there were answers hidden in the high grass. There weren't. Her husband had died by Vic Masters's gun and she was alone. There was no changing those facts.

"Very, Sarah," Charlie said gently. "And I'm sorry you're leaving it behind."

She gave a quick smile. "I'm not. I never liked cattle, despite how pretty as a picture they look when they're far away from my nose." She gave her pert nose a wrinkle, as if she could smell them from the wagon seat. "They were Thomas's dream, Charlie. Not mine. He spent every moment with them, wrote about them, worked with them. I'm more than happy to place the herd in your capable hands."

"You're sure you want to do this, Sarah? You could sell them for a small fortune."

"It's too early to sell. Thomas told me so just two nights before he died. He wanted to maintain the herd for one more year so they were well established I want to honor that wish. It's the one thing I can do for him."

"But you're giving me every new calf."

"It's fair payment for all the work you're going to do. And I'll give you first rights when I sell this land next year. Besides, this will give you time to see if you like this English breed or not. I did give you all of Thomas's notes, didn't I?"

There had been three books full of notes on every calf and cow and bull in the herd. "Yes, and I thank you."

For the first time, Sarah Hornsby smiled the sweetest smile short of his own Kathleen's. Her unusual, gray-brown eyes lit up, and her lips were pure perfection . . . not counting Kathleen's mouth, of course. Nevertheless, he felt himself blush.

"Ready, Mrs. Hornsby?"

She gave a sigh that said good-bye to it all. "Ready, Sheriff Macon."

Charlie took hold of the reins and clucked the horses back into heading toward the railroad station. The wagon bed was filled with luggage and boxes. Sarah Hornsby was moving to Clear Creek, Texas, a small but prosperous cotton town northwest of Houston.

Once he loaded the luggage onto the train, and Sarah was seated nice and proper in the window that allowed her to see the town one last time, Charlie stood by the wagon and patiently waited for the train to leave the station. It was the least he could do. He shuffled his feet and nodded reassuringly at the figure perched daintily by the window, peering out as if she were about to bolt.

"Papa! Papa!"

He turned instantly, alert to that voice. His heart-beat quickened. His daughter, Becca, was on old Fred as she ambled toward the station. It was the first time since she arrived that she'd called him papa. Until now, her somber look and quiet voice had disguised the stubbornness that refused to allow that name to pass her lips. Instead she didn't address him at all. It was a bone of contention that Kathleen warned him to leave alone. Becca would come around in her own time. Forgiving him for sending her back east would take time. Forgiving him for pulling her west at thirteen would take even longer.

His gaze widened. He couldn't believe what he was seeing. Becca, who hated riding and had not gotten on a horse since the day after she arrived three months ago, was riding now. Her long, sandy brown hair bounced in her wake, her face wearing an expression as fierce as that of any warrior. She was doing what she had to do.

But why?

The look on Becca's face arrowed fear straight into his heart.

She pulled tightly on the reins as she got to him, and poor Fred shook his head in protest.

"Easy, easy," Charlie said as he pulled the leather to give the bridle some slack. "What's wrong, baby?"

"Kathleen," she said, hardly finding enough breath to say the word. "She's having the baby. Now."

"What?" More fear. He was supposed to be called immediately when she went into labor. "Why didn't you come get me?"

Becca's chin quivered, her golden brown eyes sparkling with anger. "Well, why didn't you stay in one place? I've been to Mrs. Hornsby's house, then to the water well on her cattle spread, then over to the jail, where E. Z. was sleeping. He's now out looking for you, too. And now here. I've been looking for you for over three hours, but you didn't leave a trail of crumbs for me to follow."

He hid his fleeting grin at her accusation. She was far feistier than her mother, and almost as feisty as her stepmother. A handful. "Don't go getting smartmouthed on me now, Becca. Where's the doctor?" he muttered, trying to keep everything in perspective. But he couldn't—his heart was beating so quickly it was ready to work its way up his throat and jump out of his mouth.

"He's at the house. Timely found *him* right away." She pulled the reins out of Charlie's hand and tried to turn the horse around, finally succeeding. "Come on! Kathleen needs us!"

Charlie jumped on the wagon seat and backed the horse away from the steps. He aimed straight down Main Street, heading toward what had quickly become his home. *Home.* For Charlie, that was the sweetest word in the whole world.

It took fifteen minutes to get to the front of the house. Charlie tied the reins around the brake pull and jumped down. He took the front porch stairs two at a time, swung open the screen door, and rushed in. Becca was right behind him.

The first sound that assailed his ears was the lusty wail of a baby. By the time he hit the bedroom door, the sound was twice as loud.

The tableau would forever be indelibly printed in his brain, and as important to him as the original in the manger was to that father.

Kathleen was propped up in bed, her red hair forming a glorious halo against the cream of the sheets and bed pillows. At her breast and still screaming was the tiniest, reddest, angriest baby Charlie had ever met.

The doctor stood over on the side of the bed, watching the process as if he had orchestrated the entire thing all by himself. "Well, Sheriff, it's about time you got here, although our beautiful Kathleen handled this all by herself just like the capable woman she is."

Becca walked over and sat on the bed next to Kathleen, allowing the baby to wrap its finger around hers. The look on her face was one of awe and happiness. It matched Kathleen's, who stared at her child in wonder even as she stroked Becca's hair.

Charlie started to speak, cleared his voice, and tried again. "What is it?"

"A girl," the doctor said proudly. "A beautiful baby girl."

The baby moved her head, greedily rooting for food, then found it and immediately silenced.

"Hattie Macon," Kathleen said, her voice low and

tired, but the sparkle in her eyes told him she was still her old self. "Come say hello to your daughter, Charlie. She won't bite . . . yet."

A baby girl. A daughter. He asked the second question that needed an answer. "Is she okay?"

"She's wonderful," Becca said softly. "Look, Papa, she's holding on to my finger as if she's the strongest person in the whole world!"

The doctor gave a laugh. "Right now I think she is, little one. If her lungs are any indication, this is an energetic baby growing into the formidable woman her mama is."

"Can I help with her, Kathleen? Please?" Becca asked.

"Of course you can. In fact, I'm counting on it. After all, you're her big sister. Your help and guidance for Hattie is as necessary as mine to help her grow to be as wonderful as you are."

Becca blushed, but she didn't stir from Kathleen's side.

Charlie walked around to the other side of the bed and gave Kathleen a gentle kiss on the forehead. "Thank you, darling. Thank you." He couldn't tell her what was in his heart at that moment. It was too overwhelming. But he felt every bit of whatever it was.

Her big green eyes, tired from the ordeal but triumphant from the outcome, gazed up at him. "Thank you, husband," she said softly.

They stared at each other, each conveying the depth of the moment.

The doctor cleared his throat, gathering their attention. He rolled down his sleeves and took his black bag in hand. "It's time I got back to helping people who need me," he said. "If there are any problems, just send Becca. She can ride that horse anywhere."

Becca beamed. "I was scared but I did it anyway."

"Yes, you did, little one," the doctor said as he stepped from the room. "Remember that."

Becca smiled at Charlie—just the way she used to when she was little and thought he had hung the moon. Well, he hadn't hung the moon this time, but Kathleen acted as if he had.

"I'm so proud and thankful you rode old Fred," Charlie said. For the first time in his life, Charlie wasn't ashamed of the tears that gathered in his eyes as he stared at the three most significant people in his life. "I might have missed this most important moment in my life if you hadn't found me, Becca."

"You're welcome," she said, looking comfortable and delighted with the role of heroine. "I just did what I had to do to get the job done, just like you said."

The baby gave a dainty burp, a little shudder, then fell into a deep sleep. Charlie was amazed at the tiny creature's being so perfect. Hattie's little tip-tilted nose gave a slight wiggle.

"Ours."

"Ours," Kathleen repeated.

"Thank you so much, wife, for all you've given me."

"Why, Charlie, I didn't know you liked babies so much," Kathleen teased. "I guess I'll have to give you one a year just to keep you happy."

"Darlin', you just have to be with me and I'll be happy." He smiled with all the love his heart felt. It must have shown, because Kathleen smiled back, warming the whole room with her sunshine. "I love you so much," he said softly, his voice a gravelly whisper.

"And I love you," she said, taking his hand and holding it against her cheek. Her eyelids drifted closed. The baby nestled against her.

Becca moved from Kathleen's side very carefully, leaving the room on tiptoe.

Charlie stood watching the woman who had made such a wonderful difference in his life. He thanked his lucky stars for bringing him to Blissful and helping him find the one person who could give him happiness and bring him the joy of completeness.

Gently he lowered her hand. Just as gently he took the baby and placed her next to her mama, making sure both were safe.

When he walked out on the porch, Becca sat in the swing, rocking back and forth.

"Both the girls are sleeping. It was a full day's work," he teased, "so I guess a nap's in order."

"Isn't the baby beautiful, Papa?" Becca asked shyly, as if suddenly realizing their relationship had bridged the gap of years, and much of her anger had disappeared in the birth of a sibling.

"She is, honey. She's almost as beautiful as you were."

"Really?"

"Really. You were so beautiful, so perfect and tiny, that I was scared to death of you." He gave a rueful chuckle. "I thought if I held you, I'd break you. So I stood back and let your mama handle you. It's one of my few regrets. I should have held you more."

"You really think that?" There was so much hope in her voice. So much vulnerability.

He held his hands toward her and she jumped from the swing and wrapped her arms around his waist, her head resting against his chest. She was growing so fast, but the little girl in her was still there, still waiting for her daddy's opinion. He had a second chance to make a difference with her. He damn well wasn't going to mess it up again.

"I think you're the sweetest, smartest, most wonderful girl in the whole wide world. And I think Kathleen thinks so, too, 'cause she told me so. And Hattie will, too, as soon as she's old enough." He brushed her hair down her back and gave a sigh. "I must be the luckiest man in the world."

"I think so too, Papa. I surely do," she said, her voice muffled against his shirt. "An' that makes me lucky, too."

"It surely does, honey. And when you grow a little older, I have a packet of letters from your mama that Kathleen is keeping for you. We both want you to know how much you were loved."

"Can I see them now?"

"Not yet. When you get a little older, darlin'. I promise."

Becca gave a light squeeze. "Okay." It was said easily, as if she trusted him to know the right time. "I'm gonna make a quick dinner. When Kathleen wakes up, she'll be hungry." She was gone in a second.

Charlie patted his pocket, feeling first his badge, then the small pouch that held his tobacco. He didn't smoke often, but this was one of those times. After rolling a cigarette, he stared out at the land beyond.

As soon as the new doc got back to the office and spread the word, their neighbors would begin the parade of food and gifts and advice that came with every event in Blissful. He figured he had an hour or so of peace left to absorb the wonder of the afternoon.

Less than a year ago, he'd come to this town searching for a killer. He'd gotten more than he bargained for. He had a life filled with more love than he'd ever had before, and every day he learned from others just how lucky he was, and how to be a friend, a father and a lover—valuable lessons most men never knew.

Kathleen and his family and friends in Blissful were his whole life. That made him the luckiest man in Texas. Maybe in the world.

What more could a man ask for?

KATHLEEN'S CARROT CAKE

1¼ cups salad oil
2 tsp baking soda
2 cups sugar
1 tsp cinnamon
4 eggs
1 tsp salt
2 cups flour
3 cups grated carrots

Cream oil and sugar. Add 1 egg at a time and beat. Sift flour, soda, cinnamon, and salt together. Add to creamed mixture. Fold in carrots. Pour in 3 greased and floured pans. Bake at 325 degrees for approx. 40 minutes. (Check for doneness by inserting toothpick in cake.)

Frosting

½ cup oleo
1 8 oz package cream cheese

Beat until light. Gradually add while beating:

1 box powdered sugar
1 tsp vanilla
1 cup chopped pecans

Mix well. Spread on top of cake.